reviewed Cont. Soc
1987 16:4: 483-84

Capitalism and Confrontation in
Sumatra's Plantation Belt, 1870–1979

Capitalism and Confrontation in Sumatra's Plantation Belt, 1870–1979

Ann Laura Stoler

Yale University Press
New Haven and London

Designed by James J. Johnson
and set in Melior Roman.
Printed in the United States of America by
Bookcrafters, Inc., Chelsea, Michigan.

Library of Congress Cataloging in Publication Data

Stoler, Ann Laura.
    Capitalism and confrontation in Sumatra's plantation
belt, 1870–1979.

    Bibliography: p.
    Includes index.
    1. Agricultural laborers—Indonesia—Sumatra—
History.   2. Agricultural laborers—Indonesia—
Sumatra—Political   activity—History.   3. Planta-
tions—Indonesia—Sumatra—History.   4. Sumatra
(Indonesia)—Rural conditions.   5. Social conflict—
Indonesia—Sumatra—History.   6. Economic
anthropology—Indonesia—Sumatra.   I. Title.
HD1537.I56S76 1985   331.7′63′095981   84–17331
ISBN 0–300–03189–0 (alk. paper)

*The paper in this book meets the guidelines for
permanence and durability of the Committee on
Production Guidelines for Book Longevity of the
Council on Library Resources.*

10 9 8 7 6 5 4 3 2 1

Contents

Illustrations

Preface

Most scholarship, I suspect, starts out with a cluttered assortment of personal, empirical, and theoretical baggage, though these sorts of insights and inspirations are often not all that apparent in a work's final and public form. The following account of labor control and confrontation in Sumatra's plantation history is no exception, taking its theoretical and practical motivation from a number of sources. On the most immediate (and ethnographic) level the project's beginning long preceded my fieldwork among Javanese estate workers in North Sumatra in 1977.

Its starting point was in fact five years earlier in Central Java, where I first became familiar with things Javanese in general, and specifically with the survival strategies of the rural poor and the socioeconomic constraints upon them. My Java-based work was concerned more with investigating the material conditions of existence than with what people thought about them, with the quantification of poverty in a research environment in which the norms of sharing were espoused by villagers and ethnographers alike as conventional wisdom, and with the evidence of capitalist expansion and "objective" class structure within a local context.

In counterpoint, the Sumatran research both fishes different waters and casts a wider net. Most importantly it examines a relationship between capitalism and community that is distinct—in contrast to Java's experience of more than 300 years of foreign hegemony, the international "pioneering" of Sumatra has been for less than a century. The Javanese communities on Sumatra's plantation periphery were created out of whole cloth by and for the estate industry with their economic and social space designed to serve those same interests. Here the force of vii capitalism clearly cannot be measured in terms of wage labor arrangements and land appropriations alone. (While in Java it may have been sensible but inadequate to do so.) In this study of Sumatra's plantation belt, I have sought to look less at the impact of capitalism than at its development, at both the contemporary contours of class and gender domination but as importantly at their historical constitution and ethnic context, and at not only who controls whom but at the changing policies and politics by which those asymmetries were couched and differently perceived.

What I have set out to describe in this ethnographic history are both the relations of *power* and *production* that structured the course of plantation agriculture and the lives of those drawn into its field of force. Here I have asked how the most basic social realities and relationships were often redefined in accordance with, or in direct opposition to, the industry's concerns. An essential issue that has strongly directed the book's content and form has been a concern with the relationship between structure and human agency in the process of social change. Rather than contriving to use Sumatra as a test case for the analytic preferability of an account stressing either, I have argued that the dichotomy itself is a false one. Instead, I have assumed a perspective that could address how and why certain social hierarchies, economic inequalities, and political privileges were created, made to appear immutable, contested, and reproduced.

In this effort to reconcile how it is that people can be both the agents and objects of their own history, I have tried to avoid certain assumptions; namely, that the short-term events of history are subsumed by the *longue durée* of structure, or that human experience itself is always myopic, contingent, and therefore limited by the structures in which it is lived. For some readers the result will be less than satisfying, since I argue that it is neither the structural imperatives of capitalism nor the willful acts of perfect revolutionaries which alone determine how societies transform, classes define, or social relations change. Instead I have underscored the conflicts and coincidences between corporate strategy and workers' interests, as well as some of the recurrent issues over which the assertion of power and protest ambiguously converged.

My observation and analysis of the constraints of capitalism and their consequences focus on the strategies of labor control and the resistance they engendered. Exploring these domains demanded inquiry into a wider temporal and spatial universe than I might have otherwise ventured. In doing so, I have made an effort to remain attentive to the contrasting visions of Wallerstein and E. P. Thompson, of Braverman and Foucault. Coupled with a feminist vantage point, these divergent influences have combined to make me look to the power of discourse, the force of fear, and the threat of violence as critical elements of dominance, and as weapons in the contest for control. In keeping the women and men of Sumatra's plantation belt within a local context but global perspective, I have tried to provide both a description of their participation in a world economy outside their purview, and an ethnographic sense of what they challenged and to whom they conceded—that is, an experiential, close-up account of everyday life.

The specific questions posed on power and production reflect the priorities and strategies of an analysis of class, a feminist perspective, and anthropological practice. The people who live and labor on the plantation periphery today have kept me close to the ground and keenly tuned to those categories by which they distinguish "we" and "they" in local life. Thus, expressions of domination are explored here in a number of domains. I argue that attention to the manipulation of gender hierarchies and control over sexuality is crucial for understanding the labor process and social hierarchies at large. Ethnicity and gender provide the charged idioms in which class relations are embedded and expressed.

Capturing this sense of control and contest required a very different sort of ethnography from that usually suggested by the term. First of all, what follows covers a much longer period (from the late 1870s to 1979) and draws on field data and archival sources of greater scope. For several months I visited more than 35 estates in Java and Sumatra, and even though the major part of the research was spent living in one community of Javanese estate workers in Sumatra, I regularly visited and collected data in a number of others.

Although resident in a workers' village, I interviewed up and down the corporate hierarchy: from temporary and permanent laborers, foremen, labor contractors, estate hospital workers, office clerks, assistant managers, head administrators, regional inspectors to the executive heads of the major foreign and nationalized plantation firms. These interviews were supplemented by those with government officials, agricultural extension workers, midwives, traders, foreign estate consultants, journalists, lawyers, agronomists, and other individuals knowledgeable about the estate industry and/or closely involved with those who worked for it. In addition, I used a number of more quantitative techniques of village ethnography, including more than 250 household surveys, employment and pregnancy histories, intensive studies of time allocation, income and consumption schedules in 60 households, and records of ceremonial and labor exchange collected in a number of workers' compounds on the estates and in communities on their peripheries. Although only a fraction of the quantitative data actually appears in this report, many parts of the analysis are substantially guided by them.

Whereas chapter 6 and sections of the chapters preceding it are based on material collected during the two years (1977–79) of fieldwork in Indonesia, analysis of changes in the strategies of labor control depended heavily on written sources. For example, chapters 2 and 3 on the prewar contours of labor control and protest are based on the Dutch colonial archives, published books and pamphlets, articles, novels, newspapers, and unpublished documents written by government officials, planters, and their critics. Unlike the record of more recent periods, these accounts are not counterbalanced by the voices from below. Thus, I have made an effort to read these "upper class" sources both right side up and upside down. While they often were intended otherwise, they are vivid testimonies of social inequity and clear prescriptions for social practice.

Chapter 5, which deals with the postindependence estate labor movement, draws on research done in the Netherlands from 1979 to 1980 in the colonial Archives of the State, the Ministry of Interior, and the Ministry of Defense. In Medan, Indonesia, I collected materials from the Sumatran Planters' Association (former AVROS, now Badan Kerja Sama Perusahaan Perkebunan Sumatera, BKSPPS), which houses circulars, statistics, correspondence, and reports on estate-related labor and squatter issues.

Chapter 4, on the Japanese occupation and national revolution, was originally intended as a bridge between two distinct historical "moments," marking the apex of colonial control, on the one hand, and the height of labor militancy, on the other. In preparing this chapter I used an oral and written historical record based in part on archival work and on interviews with retired plantation workers in Sumatra and former Dutch estate managers now resident in Holland. Since the book's completion, my interest and research into the 1945–49 period have grown. From the record of these years we can document the social organization of protest, the active agency of locally organized popular militia merging in fact and fiction with peasant fronts, labor unions, and brigands. It is here that we can begin to learn something about the nature of popular politicization. Although I have only alluded to some of these issues in this study, they provide the core of my ongoing work.

Ortner (1984: 142), in a recent review of anthropological theory, rightly notes that many ethnographers of political economy produce accounts which are long on the economic and short on the political. In doing so, they display a distinct inattention to "the relations of power, domination, manipulation, control" that any account concerned with capitalist transformation would presumably want to convey. I hope this study will offer both a more balanced account and some redress to that bias.

Acknowledgments

The project has benefited from the indispensable assistance of many individuals and organizations in Indonesia. Among those I thank are: the Institut Pertanian Bogor for sponsoring my research in North Sumatra; the government and private plantation officials who provided me with information and statistics, especially those from the North Sumatran Plantation Association (BKSPPS) in Medan; local government and estate officials; the residents of the many villages I visited and where I interviewed; those individuals who assisted me in collecting oral histories and doing household surveys and who allowed me to translate "facts" into an understanding of village life and labor; and most importantly the people with whom I lived and who patiently, graciously, and openly allowed me to share the intimacies of their lives.

In the Netherlands I enjoyed the hospitality of a number of people: members of the Southeast Asian Vakgroep of the University of Amsterdam, particularly its director, Otto van den Muijzenberg; those individuals at various libraries and archival depots who guided me through their resources, especially those at the Algemeen Rijksarchief, the Ministerie van Defensie, the Ministerie van Binnenlandse Zaken, the Koninlijk Instituut voor de Tropen, and the AZOA library. I am also grateful to those current and ex-estate personnel who granted me long interviews; and to the many Indonesians in Europe who shared with me their own experiences as participants in the nationalist struggle and labor movement.

This study has been generously funded by a number of institutions: Social Science Research Council (predoctoral fellowship), Fulbright–Hays (predoctoral fellowship), National Institute of Mental Health (Training Fellowship #5 F31 MH07395-01/04), Ministère des relations extérieures, Republic of France (Allocation pour un séjour scientifique de longue durée) and the Graduate School of the University of Wisconsin, Madison (for the collection and preparation of photographs and maps).

Throughout various stages of planning, carrying out, and writing up this study I have been graced with the much needed advice and guidance of Willem Wertheim, who has encouraged my research in Indonesia for the last 10 years and has always given thoughtful and helpful criticism; Maurice Godelier, who welcomed me into a working group that provided a stimulating environment in which to think and write; Benedict Anderson, who offered sharp and provocative insights at a formative stage of the writing process; my sister, Barbara Stoler Miller, whose nonanthropological reading of my text always provided a welcome perspective; and James Scott and Jacques LeClerc, for their critical readings of various chapter drafts.

I have also received much needed support and encouragement from: Leonoor Broeder, Benjamin White, Lukman Halim and family, Mohammed Said, Joan Vincent, and most importantly my parents, Sara and Louis Stoler. Finally I thank Lawrence Hirschfeld, who has helped me to learn to think critically and carefully. Without his intellectual challenge and unqualified enthusiasm for this study it would never have been done. This book is dedicated to him and to those Javanese and their children who live and work on the plantation periphery today.

Source Abbreviations Used in the Text and the Notes

AR   Algemeen Rijksarchief (General State Archives)
BZ   Ministerie van Binnenlandse Zaken (Archives of the Ministry of Interior Affairs)
KvA Kantoor van Arbeid (Labor Office)
MD   Ministerie van Defensie (Archives of the Ministry of Defense)
OvSI Oostkust van Sumatra Instituut (East Coast of Sumatra Institute)

1

Introduction:
Plantation Perspectives

> One [of the principal questions] is the character that
> colonization will assume; i.e., whether it should be [in the
> form of] laborer-colonies, in the spirit of the factory villages of
> van Marken in Delft and Krupp in Essen, or whether one
> should endeavor toward settlements of agriculturalists like
> those established on some West Indian estates.
> [An estate official in East Sumatra, Lulofs 1920:5]

Lulofs's 1920 statement voices concerns that were to become central to
the politics and policies of labor control in North Sumatra for the next
sixty years—and that in turn provide the focus of this study. At issue
was what proved to be the key to North Sumatra's plantation success;
namely, a labor force that was cheap, socially malleable, and politically
inarticulate. In essence, this pivoted on attaining a state of affairs in
which the semblance (Lulofs's euphemistic "character") of peasant life
was welded to a starker economic reality, the material basis of which
was continually monitored and undermined. But as Lulofs's remark
shows, the decision to opt for ersatz peasant settlements over ersatz
Krupp factory villages was not self-evident.

Simply noting that the planters took such monumental decisions
as theirs already says a lot about North Sumatra's history. In fact, the
option of securing a labor reserve modeled after either Krupp's factory
villages or peasant communities bordering West Indian estates was in
reality never that of the planters alone. These two seemingly superficial
observations go a long way toward capturing much of the history that is
to follow. Strategically, our concern here will be to identify the forms of
labor control and confrontation, the relations of force and resistance
that structured the course of plantation agriculture in North Sumatra
and landscaped that of the Javanese laboring communities now densely
stretched out along its borders.

Over the past century North Sumatra has been the site of one of the
most intensive and successful pursuits of foreign agricultural enterprise in the Third World, and of overt—sometimes violent—confrontation between capital and labor throughout that expansion. Under Dutch
rule, the plantations located in Sumatra's *cultuurgebied* (or "plantation 1

belt") were virtual laboratories for technical and social experimentation. They were also microcosms of the colonial capitalist effort, at once compact and enormous ateliers in which racial, class, ethnic, and gender hierarchies were manipulated, contested, and transformed. This study is concerned with certain of these changes—processes that proceeded unevenly, to varied registers of resistance, and in a multiplicity of forms.

Unlike the plantation companies of Java, whose expansion thrived on a work force drawn from surrounding villages (where a critical portion of that labor power was maintained and renewed), on Sumatra's East Coast, initially Chinese and later Javanese workers were imported by the hundreds of thousands, housed and fed in estate barracks, and bound by indentured status. How, where, and in what form they and their descendants would be allowed to live, work, and reproduce was a pivotal issue of colonial capitalism and its 1945 postindependence transformation. Not surprisingly, the contemporary social, economic, and political space of North Sumatra owes much of its contour to how these issues of land and labor were accommodated, if not resolved.

Today, the juxtaposition of trees and factories—mile after mile of rubber—trimmed with small strips of wet-rice terraces is one striking testimony to North Sumatra's colonial history and the predominant role of the estate industry within it. The area of contemporary North Sumatra (the province of Sumatera Utara) covers about 71,000 km², but it is specifically Sumatra's East Coast that bears this colonial imprint most clearly. This region, referred to in Dutch as the *cultuurgebied*, or alternately as Deli (though this latter was really only the proper name of one small district), includes 30,000 km² of rich alluvial, lowland plains, of which more than 10,000 km² was concessioned before World War II, leased, and brought under the control of the foreign estate industry.

Situated between Aceh in the north, the Tapanuli and Karo highlands in the west, and the Straits of Malacca in the east, the plantation belt has well-marked ecological and social boundaries. Its fertile volcanic soil makes it eminently suitable for the cultivation of tobacco, rubber, and palm oil. Extending over an area reaching inland 50 to 70 km and stretching out 250 km on its north-south axis, today the *cultuurgebied* includes about 265 plantations of more than 700,000 hectares. In its heartland plantation borders continue to abut one another, as they did when the estate concessions were initially leased to planters by the Malay sultans in the late nineteenth century.

The social, ecological, and historical rending of Deli from its tropical rainforest and highland environs is immediately apparent to even a casual observer. From the air, the *cultuurgebied* appears as an enormous nursery of manicured shrubs, whose regularity is effaced only by clusters of buildings dotting the checkerboard pattern of rubber and palm. Approaching by train, we see that these clustered dots are huge, modern factories hugging the railroad lines (actually it was the railroad line which was built to hug them). From this ground level, we might well be in a strangely metamorphosed and vaguely unfamiliar Gary, Indiana, the acrid odor of half-processed rubber and fermenting palms replacing the fume of coke furnaces; flatbed cars loaded with scarlet palm fruits stand in the place of those stacked with iron ingots; and instead of steel girders, here we see tanker cars of oil palm whose half-processed cargo is destined to become soap, cooking oil, and industrial lubricants for markets in Euro-American cities, like Gary, Indiana.

The reordering of the natural environment is perhaps most striking when seen from the road, at close range. Everywhere, the sense of commercial mastery is apparent in the symmetry of plantings and the precision with which the height of palms is controlled and the distances between rubber trees are calculated. The sizes of the estates render them deceptively quiet and empty, dwarfing the huge amounts of human labor that they demand, all the more so today since the proportion of workers who actually live on the estates is far smaller than it was in earlier periods. Still, an estate's core continues to be its *emplasen*, where the miles of footpaths, miniature railway lines, and truck tracts crisscrossing the plantation complex all converge. This core consists of factory, offices, staff homes, and—set somewhat apart—the *pondok*, or workers' dwellings. On most estates, the plush homes of the former European planters are still standing and in use. Built in the heyday of Deli's expansion, the head manager's, or *Tuan kebun's*, house is skirted by those of the higher supervisory personnel in smaller and more modest replica. In contrast, the *pondok* consists of identical single- and two-family structures, laid out in tidy, compact rows with token gardens between them. On some estates these are wooden houses with earth floors; other more lucrative companies provide concrete and tin-roofed buildings. In either case, the *pondok* are uniform, spartan, and ordered.

Not everyone in the *cultuurgebied* lives in this regulated atmosphere. Ethnically, North Sumatra is one of the most heterogeneous regions of Indonesia, its rural population including indigenous Malays, Karo, Simalungun, and Toba Bataks, ethnic Chinese, Indians, and a large number of immigrant Javanese. In 1880 East Sumatra's population was estimated at somewhere near 100,000. Fifty years later—with the inflow of Javanese, Chinese, Europeans, and Indians working for the estate industry or in its service sectors—it had reached 1·5 million

(Dootjes 1938/39, 2:50). By 1930, Javanese immigrants, for the most part plantation coolies, made up nearly 50% of the native population, far outnumbering any other single group (*Volkstelling, 1930* 1935:91). In 1980, out of a total population of more than 8 million (Ginting and Daroesman 1982: 54), at least ½ million, almost all of Javanese origin, were directly employed by, or dependent on, the estate industry.

As noted above, a much smaller percentage of plantation workers still actually resides on the estates. Most live in villages squeezed between the companies' original concession borders, on land seized by squatters during World War II and the early years of independence. These are undeniably *Javanese* communities, and in almost every visual aspect they differ from the regularity of the plantation *pondok*. By the same token, architecturally, linguistically, even in terms of the plants one customarily finds in a house garden, they are clearly distinct from neighboring Malay and Batak settlements. For all intents and purposes these could be villages in Central Java.

My focus in this study is the economic and social contours of these Javanese communities on the plantation periphery today, where the encounter of their residents with past and present modes of labor control, and their defiance of them, have taken a very specific form. Nearly everyone in the communities, made up mostly of the first, second, and third generation Javanese who originally came to Sumatra as contract coolies before independence or after World War II as government-sponsored migrants, has at one time or another worked for the estates. But it is especially the older, usually first generation, estate workers who have spent the past fifty years attempting to disengage from that status. For many of them this effort has centered on attempts to establish independent homesteads for small-scale agricultural production on the plantation edges, or on land seized from the estates.

For their descendants, on the other hand, employment as a permanent estate worker is a prize position, coveted by many but accorded to only a small percentage of the young, healthy, often unmarried men—and often then accessible only by greasing the appropriate palm. For them, these villages are not agricultural centers at all but residential districts housing them and their dependent parents. The remaining majority of the village members, male and female, old and young, appear to straddle both worlds with a firm footing in neither. Many are estate workers but employed on a temporary basis, receiving a fraction of the wages and none of the social benefits accorded to their permanent counterparts. Temporary estate workers both disclaim any real ties to the plantations and, especially among the youth, scorn—and systematically avoid—work on the small agricultural plots of their parents.

The fact that most Javanese communities on the plantation periphery trace their origins back only a few decades to illegal squatter settlements on estate lands has meant that most of them have always confronted their reproduction as an economic—and in some cases political—struggle for survival. For the plantation companies these squatter communities have represented a critical asset as a well as a threat. Both economically and politically their existence and growth have always been of central concern to the colonial, local, and national elite and directly tied to the corporate policies of labor control. This understanding makes reading Deli's agitated agrarian and labor history far more clear: capitalist expansion depended not only on the industry's access and control over land and labor but, as an essential corollary, on the assurance that "its" labor force would have only contingent access to estate lands and only limited access to any others. This was hardly specific to capitalist expansion in its North Sumatran variation.

Despite the unusually vast and rapid injections of capital and labor that accompanied this process, the Deli experience was not unique; the viability of capitalist ventures in Indonesia never depended on the ubiquity of capitalism per se, but on the selective accommodation and submission of antecedent social and economic systems to the logic of its reproduction. The contemporary coexistence in North Sumatra of communal and private property, wage labor and reciprocal labor exchange, collective versus atomized community work and life suggests that the nature of subsumption to capital and of confrontation with its bearers has been uneven and complex.

For some coastal Malay peasants, the coming of the companies entailed their enrichment and transformation into a quasi-rentier class, living off land leased to those Javanese and Chinese immigrants otherwise denied legal rights to it. For the upland Karo Batak it meant drastic community and agricultural reorganization, the disappearance of communal property (but with a strong preservation of communal ties), and rapid expansion of cash cropping in which they had been involved at least since the early nineteenth century. For the Simalungun Bataks situated more squarely within the *cultuurgebied* it engendered not only the invasion of the estates, and later Javanese ex-plantation workers spilling over their borders, but a massive influx of Toba Bataks practicing wet-rice cultivation where Simalungun's inhabitants had traditionally grown dry crops in swidden plots. Among these Bataks and Malays the commoditization process is relatively easily discerned in changing patterns of landownership, settlements, agricultural technique, and ritual life. The internal relations within these groups, however, are not the subject of this analysis. I deal with them here only inasmuch as their actions and the agrarian restrictions imposed upon them affected the relationship between the estate economy's reproduction and that of the Javanese laboring population tied to it.

Labor Control and Modes of Defiance

Accounts describing plantation systems throughout the world, be they of the nineteenth-century American South, colonial Latin America, postslavery East Africa, or contemporary Southeast Asia in some form or another, all allude—and seek some analytic resolution—to the fact that plantation industries (perhaps more so than other capitalist ventures) have reproduced the conditions for their existence, rarely by transforming a particular population into a full-fledged proletariat but more commonly by allowing—and more to the point frequently by enforcing—some degree of self-sufficiency on the part of the laboring poor. Thus Sidney Mintz and Richard Price note that in the American colonies slaves "were forced to grow some part of their own subsistence" (Mintz and Price 1973); during several economic crises, plantation coolies in Sumatra were allocated plots that they had to cultivate in their "spare time"; and in Zanzibar slaves were allowed subsistence plots in exchange for a rent in labor (Cooper 1980: 80).

Some students of plantation economy (and of underdevelopment more generally) have viewed this part-proletarian, part-peasant positioning of workers as an ingenious cost-cutting device on the part of capital; indeed functional theories of imperialism are far more numerous than any other kind (Kahn 1980: esp. 202–05). Nonetheless, others have interpreted the presence of estate workers in this part-wage-worker, part-farmer status as a bid for self-sufficiency, an assertion of independence under different systems of labor control. From this perspective peasantization may be an expression of *resistance*—not compliant accommodation—mounted by workers themselves. Thus we read of clandestine slave gardens on the estate periphery in the American south (Genovese 1976: 535–40); of house and garden compounds intentionally established *outside* the plantation confines,[1] and underground rural marketing networks in Jamaica stocked with produce from squatter plots (Mintz 1974: 180–213).

Sidney Mintz has suggested that this effort at agrarian self-sufficiency gave rise to some of the "reconstituted peasantries" of the Caribbean whose communities emerged "as a mode of response to the plantation system and its connotations, and as a mode of resistance to its imposed styles of life" (ibid. 132). Such resistance showed most clearly in the maroon communities made up of runaway plantation slaves. In defiance of the planter aristocracy, jungle villages were established whose inhabitants lived off hunting, foraging, cultivation of plantains, and estate theft. In French Guiana the authorities labeled these maroon settlements the "gangrene" of plantation society, and in Colombia their self-sufficiency was considered politically dangerous and a menace to a crucial source of plantation workers. According to Richard Price such runaway communities in the jungles of Brazil, Colombia, Cuba, Ecuador, Jamaica, Mexico, and Surinam "struck directly at the foundations of the plantation system, presenting military and economic threats that often taxed the colonists to their very limits" (1979: 3, also 1–30).

This is not to suggest that all the peasantries of the Caribbean reconstituted on this basis, and even less so that Javanese on the plantation periphery today represent a modern variant of *marronnage*. On the contrary, turning back to the question of agrarian self-sufficiency as an essential component of the estate industry's system of labor control, in the North Sumatran context we will look at some of the reasons why, as a vector of resistance, this type of action enjoyed such equivocal success.

This history has remained virtually unattended. In the Indonesian context, studies of popular protest have been confined, for the most part, to peasant millenarian movements and to those social groups— and especially their leaders— at the vanguard of the anticolonialist struggle. Falling squarely into neither category, the Javanese plantation poor in North Sumatra have been largely neglected. North Sumatra as a region has not suffered the same lack of attention. An abundance of colonial and subsequent research has centered on the social organization of indigenous (particularly Batak) ethnic groups; in some, the Javanese communities have figured prominently in wider discussions of agricultural development, internal migration, ethnic diversity, and regional politics.[2] While some aspects of estate development have been treated in detail (e.g., Pelzer 1978, 1982, Thee 1977 and Sayuti 1968), no study has concerned itself with the Javanese estate communities specifically or with the history of estate labor relations through which these communities have been molded and transformed.

The omission is surprising on a number of counts. In the colonial period, Javanese immigrants in North Sumatra provided the labor power for the single largest source of foreign currency and profits in the Netherlands Indies. At the same time, the notion that the Deli estates were a hotbed of radicalism, insurgency, and unrest was widely held. During the Japanese occupation and the independence movement that followed, the estates were a critical resource to all armies in both conflicts. During the 1950s the estate labor unions in postindependence North Sumatra were reputed to have the single largest and most mili-

tant membership of any Indonesian labor organization and were responsible for the majority of labor actions during that period. And after
the 1965 coup, the largest foreign loans granted in Indonesia funneled
into North Sumatra's plantation sector. Thus, in one form or another,
the Javanese workers on Deli's estates have occupied one of the more
charged arenas of racial, ethnic, and class confrontation, often at the
center of regional and national contests for power.[3]

Most accounts of North Sumatra's contemporary history acknowledge the central role of the estate industry in exacerbating regional and
ethnic conflict. But the connection between these tensions and the
industry's policies of labor recruitment, settlement, and control has
been largely ignored. The plantation economy thus becomes a back-
drop for understanding regional and ethnic-based issues rather than the
other way around. Viewing the *cultuurgebied's* history from the latter
perspective demands a wide-angle—if somewhat distorting—lens. Our
focus is drawn to the Sumatran estates as repositories of international
capital, to the conflicting interests of corporate and state authorities,
and to the domination of capitalist enterprises and the labor force contesting that control. A preliminary account of Deli's labor history thus
requires both attention to the structural features of capitalist development and to how these structures were manifested, experienced, and
altered by those living within them.

A Conceptual Clarification of Labor Control

Eric Wolf pointed out more than twenty years ago that,

wherever the plantation has arisen, or wherever it was imported from the
outside, it always destroyed antecedent cultural norms and imposed its own
dictates, sometimes by persuasion, sometimes by compulsion, yet always in
conflict with the cultural definitions of the affected populations. [1959: 136]

The varied forms of persuasive and compulsory measures used to
secure the estate industry's successful expansion serve as a starting
point for understanding the specific forces of domination and resistance that developed on Sumatra's East Coast. As we shall see, coercion and persuasion did not develop in linear progression but existed
side by side (in stronger or lesser relief) in different moments of economic crisis and political repression. Our attention here will be on the
initial absence of a well-honed cultural hegemony as existed in Java,
and the process of its construction. *Hegemony,* as I use it here and as I
think it applies to Deli, includes more than the imposition of a dominant ideology expressing and serving the interests of a ruling class but

"its acceptance as 'normal reality' or 'commonsense' by those in practice subordinated to it" (Williams 1980: 118), the crucial component being that it "does not just passively exist as a form of dominance. It has continually to be renewed, recreated, defended and modified. It is also continually resisted, limited, altered, challenged by pressures not at all its own" (Williams 1977: 112). This entails identifying not only a particular vocabulary of domination but also a set of material and ideological constructs employed to secure its (partial) acceptance. Sometimes this called for direct coercion, other times subtler subversion. These two modes of domination, a *violence ouverte* and a *violence douce*, were not mutually exclusive; both were envisaged as imperatives of a new order, simultaneously and alternately invoked to ensure its success.

I am not suggesting here that *hegemony* serve as a facile gloss for domination *tout court*,[4] and that corporate power indiscriminately permeated every facet of laboring life, but rather that it did so repeatedly in certain spheres, affecting in turn how the relationship between capital and labor was expressed. How are we to identify the boundaries of corporate control or even the spheres into which it permeated? What do we include in the delineation of labor control? Undoubtedly we could demarcate arbitrary and a priori categories of our own making, distinguishing between "political" and "social" impositions, or between those that operated at the site of production versus domestic quarters. But this risks losing what we might gain from a more careful reading, namely, an understanding of the fluidity with which "economic" and "social" boundaries were crossed, modified, and manipulated, the frequency with which the "private" and "public" converged under different labor policies.

For this reason I have chosen to keep close to the authorities' concerns, using their "biases" to see how and why certain "facts" were produced. Colonial and company archives were not concerned with social relations and conditions per se, nor would we expect them to be. What inspires and patterns these reports is an overriding concern with profitability and "law and order." Corporate management and government officials had an acute sense of what would ensure the industry's viability—and this was certainly not limited to production quotas, prices, and yields per hectare. Profitability depended on the continuing cheapness of the work force, its availability, and its submission—not necessarily in that order. Each of these imperatives was guaranteed by a number of reinforcing legal and institutional mechanisms, dividing and defining the laboring community according to a set of social and economic categories that in part structured the community and the productive and reproductive possibilities of families within it.

These concerns, which crop up only at certain times, identify the density of discourse, clustering around the interests of the corporate elite and the "issues" that threatened their dominance. In the Dutch colonial record, these themes are clearly marked off, labeled as *vraag-stukken* or *kwesties* (problems/issues), signaling the nodes of contention between management and workers, within the ranks of labor policy tacticians, or between them and their social critics.

This is not to suggest that all the malignant maladies of estate life were identified in boldface type or that we can directly read from the rulers' record the entire corpus of workers' experience. But, by and large, these debates recurrently focus on matters that are close to this core—and in an idiom that is far less circumspect than it might be today. They are concerned with the maintenance of order and the economic efficiency of the methods employed to ensure it. Company and state archives in turn maintain a meticulous regard for signs of *disorder* such as gambling, prostitution, violence, theft, and usury—all of which were at the very least enhanced in the *cultuurgebied's* frontier atmosphere and by the industry's socially stratified labor system.

The politics of labor control will, in part, orient this analysis. Taken neither as a factor of production nor as the combined "choices" made by those in power,[5] this notion here will serve as a heuristic device in that the parameters and methods of control were continually responsive to the resistance mounted against these strategies,[6] and thus tied to how exploitation was experienced by those subject to it.

Focus on this particular interface of management–labor relations has several advantages: it allows us to remain attentive to critical social transformations in the labor process even when the fundamental social relations of production remain unchanged; second, neither are the spheres of activity in which labor control operates fixed a priori nor can its parameters be statically defined. In Sumatra's estate industry, those elements conceived as essential to labor control have changed in both scope and content. Corporate policies designed to regulate the labor supply have been implemented by readjustments in the size and composition of the labor force, by mapping out living arrangements and residential patterns for workers, managers and their families. These policies have impinged on conjugal and sexual alliances, domestic organization, and community ties. In short, labor control has always been defined with reference to the labor process, but through forms of social organization ostensibly tangential to it. In each of the subsequent chapters I examine how the structuring of gender, ethnic, and racial conflicts were embedded in company efforts to enforce—and workers' efforts to resist—the industry's hold on workers' lives.

Our starting point then is a relationship of contestation and change, not one of institutional stability and cohesion. Although there are a number of studies that take a similar approach, a great deal of the anthropological research on plantations has simply ignored popular modes of resistance—and their consequences.[7] This, in part, may be due to the fact that these studies have taken as their primary object an understanding of the failed or successful *adaptation* of traditional cultures to capitalist enterprises. Obviously this does not mean that cultural confrontation has been altogether ignored; but what has been emphasized is disruption, not culture as political resistance.[8]

The combined effects of hegemonic and coercive control, pervasive in plantation systems past and present, has meant that expressions of labor resistance varied enormously, ranging from physical assault and organized collective action to muted, subterranean, and not always easily identifiable forms of expressed discontent. In addition, workers themselves often view the latter as strategies for survival, not politically motivated acts of protest. Chapters 2 and 3 describe how and why the estate laboring population in North Sumatra appealed to such expressive modes when it signaled to management that it could and *would* not reproduce itself until certain basic social conditions of existence were met. And in chapter 6 I examine why theft of estate produce, graft, and other illicit pursuits tied to the estate economy are a modus vivendi for those subject to an economic system outside their control— and an expression of their cognizance of and anger with this fact. In much the same way that we will be looking at varying spheres of labor control, and changing discourses about it, we will be looking at diverse registers of resistance, those manifest in overt organized action as well as those in more restrained, and sustained, form.

Some of the neglect of confrontation and protest may also reflect the very concepts by which plantation economies have been defined. In an effort to deal with the specific features that distinguish plantation agriculture from other forms of capitalist enterprise, some observers have accorded the "plantation type" an intermediary, nonclassifiable position between feudal and capitalist production systems. Thus, plantations have been characterized as "feudal-capitalist" enterprises, and, in a study of Guyana estates, as neither (E. T. Thompson 1975: 30; Mandle 1973: 12). On the other hand, Mintz, Wallerstein, and others debating the plantation slave's proletariat status have forcibly argued that plantations, and slavery in particular, are "the heart and essence of capitalism as a mode of production" (Wallerstein 1980: 218; see also Mintz 1978 and Beiguelman 1978).

The confusion is compounded by the ambiguous positioning of estate laboring cum food producing farmers on the plantation peripheries of Latin American, Asia, and Africa today. Eric Wolf referred to their "double lives . . . with one foot in the plantation way of life, while keeping the other foot in the peasant holding" (1959: 143). Mintz thought this cultural straddling was not a transitional mode at all but a state of "flux equilibrium," advantageous to management and labor alike (1959: 43). More recent studies such as that of Taussig's on Colombian estates, on the other hand, call these peasant-estate laborers "liminal beings," "neither what they are, nor what they will become" (1980: 103), neither proletariat nor peasant, whose ambiguous experience of dependence on two antithetical modes of production is ultimately revealed in their cosmology (ibid. 113). As we shall see, arguments for the articulation of two modes of production or contrasting economic spheres do not necessarily follow from this ambiguity and they do not necessarily resolve it. In North Sumatra at least, subsistence farming and wage labor are part of a single economic system with multiple ideologies, reflecting the divergent interests of those implementing and contesting labor policy.

We should look for a moment at the lines along which the feudal–capitalist distinction has been drawn. Most students of plantation history agree that in the fields of marketing, investment, and corporate management, large-scale plantations are, and have been for some time, decidely capitalist. But the fact that the organization of labor has been dependent on indenture and other "extra-economic" forms of coercion is considered a critically mitigating factor. In other words, it is in the sphere of labor recruitment and control that the "noncapitalist" features of plantations are said to be located. Along the same lines, the "feudal" characteristics of the enterprises or the deterring weight of "paternalistic" patronage is invoked to explain the absence, presence, or forms of estate labor protest.[9]

If we turn away from "feudal"- and/or "tradition"-based impediments to protest, and compare the tactics of plantation control and confrontation to those cited in modern industrial labor history, some critical points of similarity emerge.[10] Drawing on studies of modern working classes, analyses of industrial labor history in the United States and (especially the mining centers of) the Third World, two themes stand out: the vital role of the state and organized labor in the enforcement of labor control where workers' struggles were curbed by both unions and the state.[11]

In North Sumatra the colonial state apparatus figured prominently in support of corporate hegemony by its participation and acceptance of coercion, while in the postindependence period, the state forced the unions—in the name of nationalism—to assume responsibility for a well-disciplined and productive labor force. The merging and diverging interests of state and corporate authorities is an underlying theme of the industry's expansion and is essential for understanding labor's quiescence at certain key moments of it.

This concern for similar obstacles to collective defiance among a plantation work force and its industrial urban counterpart does not mean that there are not gross differences between them. The experience of exploitation and the expression of class consciousness in nation-states formerly under colonial rule remain inextricably tied to that context. This means, for one thing, that class-based interests, discernible in anti-imperialist campaigns, nationalist struggles, and even in socialist revolutionary movements, are rarely easy to grasp. Rather than attempt to extract the purely "class conscious" basis of social practice, my focus is on how racial and ethnic antagonisms were the context in which the social realities of class relations were lived, mediated, obscured, and transgressed. This should allow us to examine the material and ideological conditions under which estate workers became active agents of social change—and why more often they did not.

2

The Early Contours of Labor Control: Corporate Capital and Contract Coolies

> But what was Deli? In any case more than a name for the
> gigantic plantation belt on Sumatra's East Coast. Deli was a
> concept. We remember tobacco and rubber, extensive clearings,
> plantation zeal and a pioneering spirit. As soon as we speak of
> Deli we begin to think in international terms: we speak of
> world markets, world trade, world prices; but we also think of
> masters and servants, big promotions and abrupt dismissals,
> hard work and Japanese concubines, of hari raya (literally "the
> big day," the day off once in every fourteen days), but also of
> coolie brokers, indentured coolies and the penal sanction. We
> see the bright or the shadowy side depending on where we
> stand, to which group we belong, to which norms we subscribe.
>
> Deli was an island, some said a society within a society, a
> particular form of European society, wholly different from
> that in Java. "Java" and "Deli" were entirely different ideas,
> the planter in Deli was an entirely different being. Deli was
> white, Java was mixed. In Deli everything had to be imported,
> the employees as well as the coolies. The staff came directly
> from Europe, the coolies from Java. Deli was a conglomerate of
> white settlements with Chinese and Javanese colonies
> encircling it. But they were all foreigners, no one had roots.
> [Nieuwenhuys 1978:346, 347]

The development of the estate industry on Sumatra's East Coast was markedly and fundamentally different from earlier forms of capitalist penetration in the Indonesian archipelago. While colonial accounts portray an entrepreneurial success story of rough and rugged men allured by risk, adventure, and promises of easy-won wealth, such an account obscures the more telling features of estate expansion, namely, the coalescence of a highly sophisticated organization of corporate capital and a pervasive and coercive form of labor control that together allowed "the Dollar Land of Deli" to emerge as one of the most lucrative ventures of the Western colonial empires. Marshaling internationally procured funds and a massive force of indentured Asian workers, within fifty years the East Sumatran estate industry's production of rubber, oil palm, tobacco, tea, and sisal accounted for one-third of the export earnings for the Dutch East Indies, providing many of the raw materials on which the expansion of industrial capitalism in Europe and America was based.

The present chapter is concerned with the quality of labor relations emerging out of this ethically impoverished, politically volatile but highly profitable combination. The first section outlines Deli's development within the context of Dutch colonial and world economy in the late nineteenth century; we look here to the emergence of the estate industry and conditions set for its expansion, focusing, as the planters did, with a wide-angle lens on what constituted labor control. This perspective allows us to differentiate a strategically distinct set of labor policies that permeated the coolie quarters as well as the workplace—both a coercive and seductive hegemony implicitly defined by a universe broader than the labor process itself and rooted in command over sexual, familial, and social relations at large. Probing one colonial discourse in particular, that concerning the settlement of the plantation work force, underscores the corporate motivations informing changes in land use, family structure, and labor control.

The Entry of Corporate Capital into Deli

Most accounts of Deli's plantation history begin in 1863 with the exploits of Jacobus Nienhuys and those pioneering planters who first opened the area to large-scale export agriculture. While providing a colorful and romantic starting point, it both pre- and postdates more important political and economic developments of which it was a minor part. These included Dutch efforts in the second part of the nineteenth century to bring the Outer Islands (i.e., those parts of the archipelago outside the colonial heartland of Java, Bali, and Lombok) more squarely within its political and economic control. British incursions into Sumatra at the time gave added urgency to the assertion of Dutch hegemony as the imperialist dominions of Southeast Asia were being more vigorously claimed and secured for production and markets (see Wertheim 1959:62–68).

"Pacification" of the Outer Islands proceeded with varying degrees of physical and social violence. In Deli, where the Dutch were unwilling or unable to allocate the necessary troops and funds (ibid. 67), the European planters were given a temporary carte blanche to pursue and protect their interests as they saw fit, the assumption being that this would promote the interests of Dutch rule. As it turned out, these interests were not always the same, a fact that became increasingly clear as the planters' transgressions of indigenous land rights threatened to undercut the very subsistence base of Sumatra's native inhabitants. The colonial state found itself maneuvering a dangerous course, allowing the planters sufficient—and what was in fact enormous—leeway to encourage investment, but hopefully not at the expense of popular peace.

Deli's expansion was thus also tied to a second shift in colonial policy. State revenues were now to be raised by opening export agricultural production to the private sector. Thus 1870 marked a critical turning point in Dutch colonial rule. After years of a state monopoly on agricultural extractions, an "open door policy" was adopted to encourage foreign investment, codified in the Agrarian Land Law of the same year. Although pertaining only to those regions directly controlled by the Dutch, that is, Java, the general wave of entrepreneurial freedom hit the shores of Sumatra as well; here, in the *zelfbesturende landschappen* (indirectly ruled territories) of Sumatra's East Coast, local rulers rather than the Dutch East Indies government granted long-term concessions (of dubious legality) to foreign firms.[1]

The availability of leases of up to seventy-five years over extensive tracts of land attracted investment in slow-maturing, but highly profitable perennial crops and in the factories and processing plants that they necessitated (Allen and Donnithorne 1962:68). Furthermore, such long-term contracts justified and facilitated procuring loans and credit from trading companies and investment banks. Trading houses, with activities previously limited to handling imports, began financing and shipping produce from plantation firms. European-based investment banks became interested in this speculative market. Among the most powerful and active in Deli was the HVA (Handelsvereeniging Amsterdam), established in 1879 by a group of Dutch bankers and traders. Another was the NHM (Nederlandsche Handel Maatschappij), founded in 1824, which had "transformed itself from crown's agent to private investment firm, half bank and half planter" (Geertz 1968:85), controlling 17 sugar factories and plantations throughout the Indies (Allen and Donnithorne 1962:188).

For the first fifteen years of the new agrarian policy, the majority of estates stayed in the hands of individual planters. But with the economic crisis of the mid-1880s, the prices of coffee, sugar, and tobacco drastically fell, and many planters lacked the financial resiliency necessary to weather out the depression. Well-endowed investment firms such as HVA and NHM quickly bought out and consolidated the fledgling companies, thereby securing for the first time direct control over production as well as trade.

Nowhere was the replacement of pioneering planters by corporate management swifter and more striking than on Sumatra's East Coast. Only a few years after Jacobus Nienhuys had arrived and secured a long-term (99 year) lease from the sultan of Deli, the Deli Maatschappij was

established in 1869—the first limited liability company in the Indies—
backed by NHM, which held 50% of its shares (Volker 1928:13). In its
wake numerous smaller tobacco firms were set up, not only on the rich
and suitable soil of Deli, Langkat, and Serdang but as far south as
Asahan. When the tobacco marked collapsed in 1891, many of the smaller companies and individual planters went bankrupt; between 1890 and
1894 more than 20 plantations disappeared. In addition, since it was
really only the volcanic soil surrounding Medan that produced the fa-
mous Deli wrapper leaf, many found themselves working land totally
unsuitable for tobacco cultivation. Some planters shifted to coffee, others sold their land outright. Of the 179 plantations existing in 1889, 101
were left in 1914, and only 72 by 1930 (Thee 1977:12). Eventually almost
the entire tobacco region was consolidated and merged into four powerful companies (and their subsidiaries), leaving only about 20 smaller
ones.

By 1884 there were 688 Europeans of different nationalities in Deli,
but the tobacco industry was and remained a Dutch monopoly. This was
not the case for the network of estates proliferating soon after 1900 on the
basis of perennial crop production. These companies were not only to
surpass the tobacco companies in area and export earnings but, in virtue
of their size and multinational involvement, drew Deli further into the
international vortex of capitalist expansion.

Multinationalism on Sumatra's East Coast

The emergence of corporate capitalism in the Indies could be (and has
been) construed as a phenomenon that flowed largely out of the peculiar
nature of Dutch colonial policy and the demands of local agricultural
production. In fact, it was a considerably less parochial development,
part of a worldwide shift toward agribusiness, which had already made
its appearance in the British West Indies, the southern United States,
Ceylon, and Malaysia (Beckford 1972:102–13). In each of these areas the
recent "abolition of slavery, technological change, crop disease, and
violent price fluctuations all contributed to make the financial position
of the individual planters precarious and set the stage for the rise in
importance of corporate capitalism" (ibid. 110).

Rapid price fluctuations not only squeezed out small planters but
also served as an incentive for European and American-based processing and trading concerns to secure their own sources of raw materials
(ibid. 112; Gould 1961:82). Southeast Asian production sites gained
appeal as political movements, and the abolition of slavery in parts of
the Americas made these locales less attractive depositories of Western
capital; at the same time, the opening of the Suez Canal in 1869 allowed a

faster and more direct route between the East Indies and European markets. North America's escalating demand for rubber in the auto and manufacturing industries set off a search for areas offering both cheap labor and a strong colonial government.

One of the first non-Dutch companies to arrive in Deli was a British firm, Harrisons and Crosfield, established in 1844 as a wholesale dealer in coffee and tea. The company later became active as managing agents and plantation proprietors in Ceylon and Malaysia; in 1907 unusually high profit from rubber encouraged further expansion to include Sumatra's East Coast. Several concessions were leased in Deli for tea, coffee, rubber, and tobacco, and in 1909 operations were extended to Java, where two more subsidiaries were formed. While the exact figures concerning Harrisons and Crosfield's holdings during these early years are unavailable, we can get some sense of scale from the following:

Through amalgamation with other concerns it acquired interests in Borneo timber and in the tea trade of China and Formosa. In Japan associated companies were engaged in the purchase of tea, silk and other goods. Its branches in North America, Australia and New Zealand . . . later came to deal with many other types of business. . . . In 1956 Harrisons and Crosfield were agents for upwards of 225,000 acres of rubber in Malaya, and 135,000 acres in Indonesia. It was then acting as secretary to a number of tin-mining companies and it had interests in a rubber factory and an engineering works. [Allen and Donnithorne 1962:47]

This was no small enterprise. Some years later its holdings were estimated at 2 million acres in Malaya, North Borneo, Indonesia, India, Ceylon, and East Africa (Fryer 1965:87).

Despite large British holdings, it was the influx of North American capital that quickly earned the East Coast its title as "the Dollar Land of Deli." The interest of U.S. rubber manufacturers in Sumatra was triggered by new production possibilities in the United States, and, in 1910, by a sharp increase in Brazilian rubber prices (Gould 1961:82). When a faltering Dutch company near the town of Kisaran put its concession up for sale, U.S. Rubber Company, an American trust, bought the rights to 35,000 acres and established in 1911 a subsidiary, Hollandsche-Amerikaansche Plantage Maatschappij (HAPM), later to become part of Uniroyal. The addition of 37,000 acres in 1913 brought the total to nearly 76,000 acres, the single largest rubber complex in the world. By 1926 the holdings of U.S. Rubber totaled over 100,000 acres, covering 150 square miles of the East Coast.

HAPM's factory engineers, laboratory chemists, and foresters were all imported from the United States but the supervisory personnel were of different nationalities. The HAPM complex, on the other hand, was (and is) uniquely American, sporting a plush staff club, tennis courts, a golf course, and a forbidding pillared head office all reaffirming the sound durability of U.S. investments in the Asahan jungle. In 1916 Hawaiian Sumatran Plantations Ltd. became the second American venture in Deli with a total of 12,000 acres, and a year later Goodyear followed suit, leasing 16,700 acres of the Dolok Merangir estates. Ten years later 28,000 acres was added and in 1932 another 10,000 acres was cleared to become the [Goodyear] Wingfoot estate on the far southwestern border of the plantation belt.

Among these pioneering consortiums the Franco-Belgian SOCFIN (Société Financière) corporation was a primary force behind the introduction of palm oil cultivation to Sumatra and the major conduit for Franco-Belgian investments throughout Southeast Asia (Allen and Donnithorne 1962:11). In 1909 SOCFIN established itself in Deli and leased additional holdings in Java and Malaya, organizing "an elaborate supervisory service to cover all these territories" (ibid.). SOCFIN's vital interests were inextricably tied to palm oil (with which they had long experience on their west African estates), and therefore to Sumatra, whose highly conducive climate allowed it to become the largest single supplier for the world market.[2]

Other foreign investors in Deli, including the Japanese, Germans, and Swiss, played relatively minor and ephemeral roles. In contrast, managerial personnel included nationals from nearly every Western, and some Eastern, European countries. Thus what distinguished the expansion of Sumatra's cultuurgebied was not only its multinational corporations but its multinational and multiethnic resident population, two attributes which set it apart from previous (and contemporaneous) plantation enterprises in others parts of the East Indies. By 1930 more than 11,000 Europeans were living on the East Coast, directly or indirectly involved in the estate industry. For the first time, personnel, capital, sites of production, and processing plants drawn from, or situated in, different parts of the Western and colonized worlds were pulled together under single, but notably distinct, corporate structures.

Specialization by corporation and nationality was far more evident in the early years. In 1913 (see Table 2.1), the Dutch invested in tobacco, the British monopolized the tea estates, the Americans confined themselves to rubber, and the Franco-Belgians concentrated on their specialty, palm oil. Twenty years later, as more land was allocated to the two principal industrial crops, these lines were less clear. Changes in Dutch capital investments in particular reflected this shift (see de Waard 1934:257). Such agricultural banks (cultuurbanken) as HVA played an important role in financing and encouraging the expansion of these newer crops introduced after the turn of the century. In 1916–17 HVA acquired large concessionary rights in Deli after having changed its orientation from simply marketing to managing plantation production. By

Table 2.1. Capital investments by nationality on Sumatra's East Coast, 1913 and 1932

		Tobacco (%)	Rubber (%)	Tea (%)	Palm oil (%)	Sisal (%)	Total (%)
Dutch	1913	79.5	33.0	3.0	—	—	48
	1932	96.4	36.2	61.3	56.9	100	53.7
British	1913	16.7	34.3	97	—	—	29.4
	1932	—	26.6	31.5	4.0	—	18.1
American	1913	—	16.1	—	—	—	10.0
	1932	—	18.0	—	—	—	11.0
Franco-Belgian	1913	—	15.0	—	97.0	—	10.2
	1932	3.0	12.1	—	33.8	—	12.0
Swiss	1913	2.1	1.0	—	—	—	1.2
	1932	1.0	1.0	—	—	—	1.0
Japanese	1932	—	2.4	—	2.6	—	1.7
German	1932	—	1.0	1.0	3.6	—	1.6
others	1913	1.6	1.0	—	—	—	1.0
	1932	—	2.0	—	—	—	1.0

Source: De Waard, 1934: 257.

the 1920s this single *cultuurbank* controlled more than 49,000 hectares of cassava and sugar estates in Java, another 50,000 hectares in Sumatra, and employed a total of 170,000 workers on both islands (see Brand 1979). Banking firms with their centralized and European-based financial networks provided secure channels for transferring capital from Europe to the Indies—and of course back again. According to some estimates, in 1928 12% of the national income of the Netherlands was directly or indirectly derived from the Indies, and between one-fifth and one-tenth of the Netherlands population in the 1930s was dependent on or had financial interest in the commerce of Indonesia (Allen and Donnithorne 1962:288).

Dutch control over more than half the operating estates in North Sumatra, however, was not enough to ensure their predominant influence and authority—in part because the markets (and thus the indirect capital expenditures in Deli) were outside Amsterdam's control. In the 1920s and the 1930s almost half (45%) of the East Coast exports were destined for the United States (Dootjes 1938–39). In 1925 the United States directly imported U.S. $45.5 million worth of estate produce and another $20 million indirectly (Gould 1961:32). Prior to World War II, more than 75% of the palm oil imported to the United States was supplied from Sumatra, and 46% of Sumatra's rubber was channeled into American automobile and related industries (Dootjes 1938–39:130; Volker 1928:151). The staffs of U.S. companies in Deli seem to have kept a low profile, but American influence in the organization of the estate economy was strong. As evinced in the postwar period, personages such as the King of Kisaran (the contemporary term of reference—not address—for the American manager of U.S. Rubber's Asahan estate) exercised disportionate influence on policy decisions in the planters association of AVROS (Algemene Vereniging van de Rubber Planters ter Oostkust van Sumatra, General Association of Rubber Planters on Sumatra's East Coast).

During the 1920s and 1930s it was British rather than American interests that alarmed the Dutch estate community. Some argued that the government's "open door policy" had been too liberal, threatening the very basis of Dutch domination (Dinger 1929). Whether this was true, it is clear that multinational investments created a new set of problems for the colonial state. With foreign executive boards beholden neither to authorities in the Hague nor to any in Batavia, the pressures traditionally exerted on companies of Dutch nationals were far less effective. Non-Dutch companies were interested in high-quality production, cheap labor, and whatever system best suited these ends. As a staff member of U.S. Rubber Company wrote in 1925:

The indentured [labor] system is still in vogue in Sumatra and it is to be hoped, in the interest of both laborers and planter, that the present system will not be interfered with by legislation. [Hotchkiss 1924:3]

These concerns were not dissimilar to those of their Dutch counterparts, the only difference being that the long-term policies to ensure *Dutch* hegemony and maintain popular peace in other parts of the colony were lower priorities for companies whose home base was not the

Netherlands. As such the state and corporate oligarchies were neither isomorphic nor necessarily complementary in their efforts and their aims. The prolonged contest between the colonial state (for control) and the plantation companies (for autonomy) was ample proof of this.

On several accounts then the nature and magnitude of the capitalist venture in Deli was new to the Indies, as were the means by which that venture was secured and controlled. Planters themselves referred to the estates as a ship whose coordinates located it in East Sumatra, but whose course was steered by the corporate interests of London, Brussels, Amsterdam, and Ohio concerns. To a large extent this was true. Ultimate control did rest in these distant places, but in the early years implementation of estate policy, defining the limits of land and labor relations, were local affairs. Far from the seat of the colonial state in Java, in Deli's formative years the *cultuurgebied* was a veritable "state within a state" with a planter aristocracy exercising de facto control. With the planters assuming what Karl Pelzer counted as the multiple roles of being, "their own lawyers, policemen, public prosecutors, judges, and diplomats" (Pelzer 1978:89), a pattern was set of invoking some government regulations while systematically opposing or ignoring others.

Land Shortage and Collusion: The Planter and Malay Aristocracy

Land acquisition by the early planters was greatly facilitated by an ongoing power struggle among local Sumatran adversaries. At the time of Nienhuys's arrival, Deli's coastal region was dominated by a number of Malay monarchs, with the most westerly interior regions being the kinbased territories of several culturally distinct Batak groups. The Malay rulers—even without their own productive base—controlled the region in virtue of their strategic position on the Straits of Malacca, at the crossroads of international commerce. As mediators and traders between indigenous feuding communities and between these groups and outsiders, the coastal monarchs gained access to the economic and military strength of their less well-situated Batak allies.[3]

This "parasitic" sovereignty and long history of contact and cooperation with foreign traders made the Malay sultans eager and accommodating allies when it came time to establish European rule. Reid writes:

For planters . . . the Malay rulers offered the further great advantage of what appeared to be a domain principle—a claim to have the right to dispose of all land within their jurisdiction. . . . this provided an uncomplicated means whereby vast tracts of virgin forest could be alienated to tobacco estates on the basis of modest royalties to the raja. The four dynasties of the *cultuurgebied* which emerged most successfully from the scramble of the 1860s—Langkat,

Deli, Serdang and Asahan—were rewarded by the Dutch with the title of Sultan, enormous wealth, complete security, and enhanced control over both their Malay vassals and the neighboring Bataks.[4]

These negotiations between planters and Malay monarchs resulted in a social and agricultural configuration that retains much the same form today,[5] while the immediate consequences of these negotiations set the stage for agrarian and labor conflicts that were to play a central role in plantation history.

The Malay sultans greased the way for estate expansion while the colonial state apparatus devised a land classification scheme that conveniently accelerated the same process. Since most of East Sumatra was either jungle or in swidden cultivation and thus not permanent fields, the greater part of the region fell under what was legally termed "waste land" (woeste land),[6] despite the obvious and well-known fact that only a small percentage of swidden fields could be cultivated at any one time. As land contracts came under closer government supervision more legal lip service was paid to indigenous land rights, with little change in practice.

Take for example the Model Contract of 1878. Here it was stipulated that only "residents" (i.e., those whose homes were located within the estate concession borders at the time of the initial agreement) should be allocated plots of 4 bouw (2.8 ha); under the prevailing swidden system this was grossly inadequate for a household's subsistence needs. At the same time the planters cleverly offered these same farmers access to harvested tobacco fields (jaluran) for growing rice on a rotation basis.[7]

Wrongly assuming that a land shortage was not in immediate sight, farmers invariably chose to take the jaluran, which allowed temporary use rights to 8 bouw (5.6 ha) and thus "more tangible and immediate benefits" (Pelzer 1978:73). But this arrangement eventually proved disadvantageous to both parties. The farmers were severely limited in what they could plant and how often they could do so, and as the population grew, the planters were confronted with a barrage of farmers and estate workers who claimed to have legitimate jaluran rights. Over the next few decades these model contracts were modified and refined with more intricate legal loopholes further limiting who could be considered a rightful claimant.

A 1918 map of the cultuurgebied (see map 1), drawn when company holdings were still being consolidated and enlarged, already reveals that as far south as the present day district of Serdang, there was little unclaimed land outside the estate borders. While in the tobacco area around Medan indigenous residents had some access to harvested tobacco land on this jaluran rotation basis, in the more sparsely populated southern cultuurgebied, estate encroachment followed a different

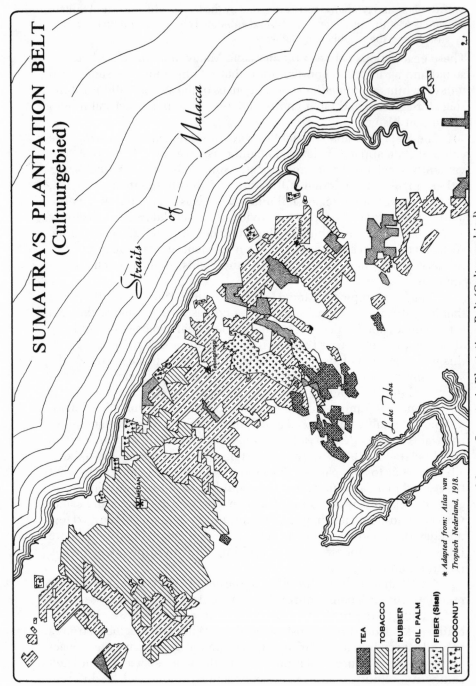

SUMATRA'S PLANTATION BELT
(Cultuurgebied)

Straits *of* Malacca

MEDAN

Lake Toba

* *Adapted from: Atlas van Tropisch Nederland, 1918.*

TEA
TOBACCO
RUBBER
OIL PALM
FIBER (Sisel)
COCONUT

Map 1. Sumatra's Plantation Belt (Cultuurgebied)

course. Here there were no *jaluran* contracts since perennials (rubber, tea, sisal, and palm oil) rather than tobacco dominated the countryside. With far fewer established villages to circumvent, the initial leases to plantation companies were often made in a checkerboard arrangement of uninterrupted concessions with contiguous borders. New leases for oil palm and rubber estates in the 1920s and 1930s further filled out the total area under foreign control.

By 1903 there was already talk among informed authorities of a land shortage attributed to the greed of Malay sultans who had leased out too much of the East Coast (since their revenues were immediately tied to the estate contracts) without setting any aside for the local, much less incoming, population (Bool 1903:50). By the turn of the century we read reports of illegal squatter settlements cropping up along estate concession boundaries. These were peopled with estate workers, Toba Bataks from the highlands and even Malay villagers whose legitimate claims to land (under the existing law) were ignored.[8] The land remaining outside the estates was already deemed inadequate for the subsistence requirements of the current population, very few of whom were in households eligible for the 3–4 ha granted in the tobacco area to residents. Omitted from this scene was an immigrant plantation labor force, growing by tens of thousands every year, whose candidacy for land allocations was rarely considered at all. This was no oversight in planter–sultan negotiations but an integral component of labor recruitment and control.

Indentured Labor

The myth of Deli as a geographic waste land awaiting the pioneering zeal of Western enterprise had its social counterpart: the engineering of a new society where, from colonial and company perspective, none had existed before. In Java, hundreds of years of extraction of land, labor, and produce had molded a mediating native elite and an "absorbent" village structure, one on which the production of commercial crops such as sugar was ecologically and economically superimposed. Despite the use of rural land and labor for export production, peasants remained village residents whose contact with the colonial apparatus was cushioned and muted by a layer of native civil servants. Within this context, traditional institutions were brought within the vector of colonial authority while also serving to check intrusions on, and direct control over, rural life.

In Deli, such subtle ways of subverting culture and extracting labor were unavailable. Deli's sultans had land to offer but not labor since the native Batak and Malay population could be neither cajoled nor compelled by local or foreign authorities to work for the estates. Thus the planters were forced to look elsewhere for their personnel; first to the

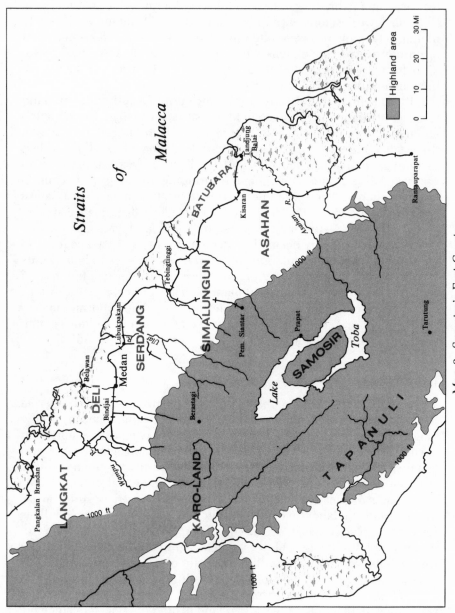

Map 2. Sumatra's East Coast

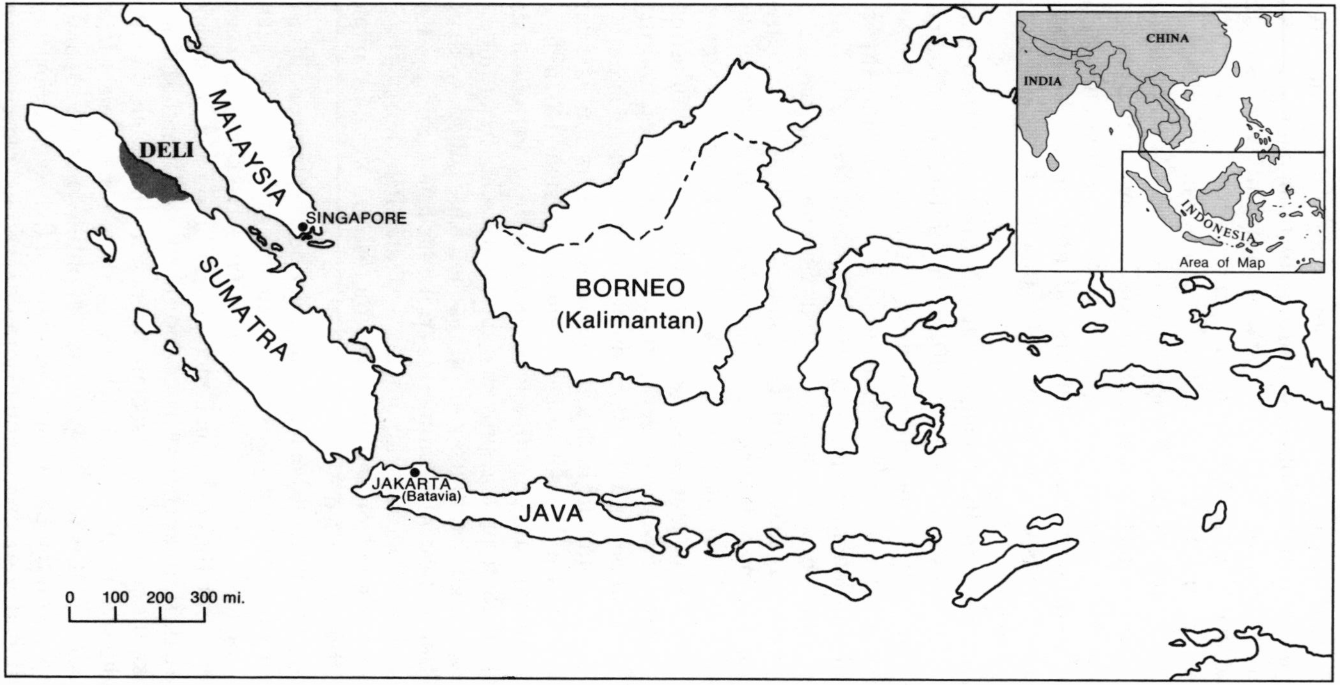

Map 3. Indonesia

Straits Settlements and China, and then to the impoverished villages of central Java for their coolies, to Europe for their managerial staff. As throughout most of Southeast Asia, recruitment was done through "coolie brokers" until the planters began organizing their own convoys direct from China; in the case of Java, workers whose contracts expired were given "home leave" to recruit more workers from their natal villages, thus allowing the companies to avoid the increasingly exhorbitant costs of dependence on coolie brokers.[9] Even by this method recruitment and transport were costly affairs and the planters—and their bankers—made extensive efforts to assure that their initial investments would be secure.

Slavery was legally abolished in the East Indies by 1860, but indenture was not. To support the "pacification" of the Outer Provinces and the development of the estate industry, the government issued the "coolie ordinance" of 1880 (followed by a series of others) pertaining specifically to labor contracts in which coolies were to be transferred overseas. This ordinance stipulated that in exchange for passage to Deli, a coolie was obligated to work for a specific number of (usually three) years. Considering nonwork as a punishable breach of contract,[10] a strict penal sanction (*poenale sanctie*) was enforced; laborers who ran away, refused to work, or otherwise transgressed the rigorous rules inscribed in their contracts were subject to imprisonment, fines, and/or forced labor above and beyond the duration of the initial agreement.[11]

In addition, anyone harboring runaway workers could be punished with heavy fines and prison terms. Ostensibly designed to protect coolie as well as planter, these ordinances provided the government stamp of approval on coercion and provided the legal backbone of the planters' power. Although "contract coolies," as they were called, were not confined to Deli—the coolie ordinances applied to estate, mining, and other development industries throughout the Outer Provinces—the system was really designed for Deli and it was there that it was most intensively and effectively applied.

Various terms have been used to describe the poor conditions of life and labor on East Sumatra's estates in the early twentieth century, among which *slavery* and *forced servitude* have certainly been most prominent. But these slippery metaphors should not be taken as an accurate descriptive account. They describe the *tenor* of the labor system and evoke the physical and social violence involved but do not define the productive relations themselves. Workers were subject to a harsh penal code, but this was only one aspect of the coercive apparatus that kept workers on the East Coast. We shall see that even when indenture was abolished, the extraeconomic forms of coercion remained as much a part of late colonial capitalism as the more "ethical" policies for which that period was better known.

The rapid and iniquitous alienation of Sumatran land and Javanese labor only partially accounts for the strained labor relations that developed on the East Coast; there was also an intensely rigid racial and ethnic ranking enforced and manipulated in the service of maintaining sultanate and planter control. This was particularly clear in administrative matters, where the spheres of direct and indirect rule were meticulously defined; immigrant estate labor was, in all cases, directly subject to Dutch colonial and planter authority while the indigenous population was governed through the Malay administrative and juridicial structures.

In consequence, the vast population of estate workers—by 1930 30% of East Sumatra's total population—and their European overseers were legally subject to the Indies government and economically liable to none but the companies that brought them there. They were outside the jurisdiction of any native elite and found the colonial modes of conduct traditionally applied in Java largely inapplicable to race and labor relations in Deli. Both masters and their subjects had to leave much of their cultural baggage behind and in this (artificial) vacuum a new hegemony was fashioned and transformed.

The European and Asian Recruits

According to period novels and the memoirs of early planters, the European estate administration—especially in the early years of expansion—was staffed with a motley assortment of inexperienced personnel with little or no preparation for their tasks and with a common goal: to make their fortune. Among them were the scions of failed business families, runaways from ill-fated love affairs, destitute aristocrats, fortune-seeking adventurers, or young men trying to pick up the pieces of recent financial disasters.[12] This vision was doubtlessly overly romanticized, harping more on the disportionate number of social marginals and fugitives than on the majority of lower-middle class unemployed for whom the Indies offered the hope of financial improvement.

For Asian workers, the expectation was not all that different, though more modest. Despite indenture, Deli was billed as a paradise where money, land, and women were in abundant supply. Labor recruiters descended on Javanese villages luring the young, poor, and even the landed with tales of gold, land, and high wages. Many were simply enticed by "free" cash advances, and only later were they to learn that these were to be deducted from their monthly earnings. Former "contract coolies" in Sumatra today tell largely the same tale; they were duped by dishonest recruiters, seduced by spirits, and fed potions to make them senseless and compliant. However apocryphal these stories, they express a vivid memory that life in Deli bore little resemblance to what it was said to be.

In the late nineteenth century, Chinese workers were especially coveted for their diligence and skill but recruitment costs, even under indenture, made this source increasingly unattractive. This was all the more true as it was realized that an even cheaper Javanese source was close at hand. As the companies diversified into tea, rubber, and palm oil more Javanese were channeled onto the estates. Gradually Chinese recruitment was phased out. Although there were still 26,000 Chinese workers in 1930, they now made up 10% of the total labor force rather than 90% as they had in the last century (Broersma 1919:247; Thee 1977:39).

Javanese were not excluded from the earlier years of Deli's growth; in 1911 alone more than 50,000 contract coolies were imported from central Java to fill the urgent labor demand on the *cultuurgebied*'s new rubber estates (Stibber 1912:23). Recruiting agencies mushroomed in Java, particularly in the large coastal cities of Semarang and Batavia, drawing labor from the densely populated principalities of the Vorstenland (comprising Jogjakarta and Surakarta), and from the areas around Banjumas and Purworedjo farther to the west. As recruitment efforts expanded on Java, fly-by-night "immigration agencies" reportedly took on the air of wholesale markets dedicated to the sale, not recruitment, of labor. In the contemporary Dutch press, sandwiched between news of animal auctions, public notices advertised the guaranteed delivery of "strapping healthy young men and women" at the "modest" cost of 60 guilder per head (van den Brand 1904:41).

The reasons the Javanese descended on Deli, and continued to for the next 80 years, are easily seen from reading any of the government reports on the "declining welfare" of the native population at the turn of the century. Some may have remained in Deli after their contracts expired "by preference" (Pelzer 1978:61) but many had no choice. The measures used to keep them there were implemented, in part, through gender-specific policies of recruitment, wage payment, and job allocation.

Women and Labor Control

> *"They are whores by nature"*
> *[A Sumatran planter quoted by van den Brand in 1904]*

Pioneering was considered a "man's job," but not all the plantations' needs could be met by men. All the initial Chinese workers were males and the Javanese coolies included only a smattering of women. During the first decades of expansion, married candidates were rejected for the European managerial staff, and even long after, many companies maintained strict rules prohibiting accompaniment by wives and children.

At the turn of the century female coolies made up only 10–12% of a labor force that totaled 55,000 Asian workers. By 1912 there were nearly 100,000 more men than women employed on Deli estates, and of the nearly 100,000 who were ethnic Chinese nearly 93,000 were men (Broersma 1919:39; de Bruin 1918:3). With this highly skewed ratio, those women who did come were considered a scarce resource and became a focal point of conflict between Chinese and Javanese and the excuse for violent assaults on European management by Asian workers.

The female coolies were young, almost all Javanese, and if not openly coerced to prostitute themselves were given few other options. Servicing the sexual and more general domestic needs of male workers and managers was more of necessity than of choice, given that women's wages in 1894 were half those of men and were inadequate to meet daily dietary requirements, let alone other necessities.[13] Two scathing criticisms of the *poenale sanctie* dating from the turn of the century gave detailed attention to the proliferation of prostitution and venereal disease within the estate population. Although van den Brand's *De Millionen uit Deli* (1902), its sequel (1904), and van Kol's *Uit onze Kolonien* (1903) are frequently cited works, their testimonies concerning this aspect of estate labor conditions have largely been ignored.[14] In van den Brand's tour of several East Coast estates he described the following:

Everyone—the planters most of all—knows that they, the girls I mean, don't have enough to eat. When an estate manager from one of the largest companies took me on a tour of his plantation and showed me the housing of Chinese and Javanese male workers I asked him, where do the unmarried Javanese women live? Reluctantly he finally answered, they have no housing but end up staying anywhere they can. [van den Brand 1904:70]

Other sources concur that every year hundreds of young women recruited as contract coolies ended up supporting themselves by servicing the large population of single men in the Chinese coolie barracks.

Women were kept available and "willing" to perform these services by careful design; in a heated debate between planters and their critics the former argued that coolie women were "whores by nature" and would spend their "extra earnings" only on "diversions and cheap ornaments" (van den Brand 1904:70; Mulier 1903:143–45). Domestic (Dutch) social critics cited high rates of syphilis (a Deli doctor reported that more than half the women in one estate district had veneral disease) (van Kol 1903:98). And from an estate in the southern cultuurgebied, a manager complained to his head office that 35 of his 60 female workers were hospitalized with syphilis (AR).[15]

Granted these are meager statistics to go on. Most medical reports on coolie mortality and illness omitted such scandalous entries, but the few references available leave little doubt that the problem was widespread. Van Kol, for instance, described his visit to a Deli hospital, especially for prostitutes:

In the hospitaal voor prostituées one finds a revolting assemblage of victims of our social system. In foul air, I found a score of Chinese, Javanese, and Japanese women and even several mixed bloods. . . . In one ward syphilitic women lay together with dying malaria sufferers, swollen beri-beri patients and lepers. . . . A young, still very young Javanese girl lay flat on her belly, her body ulcerated with venereal sores. [van Kol 1903:103, 106]

Some officials pointed out the connection between this situation and the abysmal wages paid women, but others attributed such epidemics to the moral turpitude of the women themselves, evinced by the high incidence of child neglect and frequent sale of coolie children (AR).[16] As late as 1917, attempts by the Labor Commission to bring about legislation giving pregnant workers the choice of either continuing to work or returning to Java were protested in planters' circles; they argued that "deficient parental feelings of the Javanese lower classes" would result in the abandonment of more children if women were given such a choice [the assumption being that the mothers would leave their children behind in Sumatra] (ibid., Nov.1918).

The companies' position on female workers pivoted on several local requirements of estate expansion. Female coolies were part of the bait that was used to allure male workers to Deli and part of the palliative that was supposed to keep them there. Prostitution was also considered a lesser evil than the alleged sodomous acts performed by Chinese workers when women were absent altogether.[17] On the other hand, an estate population racked with venereal disease and a large number of illegitimate offspring incurred hospitalization costs that many companies preferred not to bear.[18] Although some responded by refusing to employ women, the boycott never gained much support since they still provided the cheapest labor source.[19] In addition, a heavy and profitable traffic in women—financed by managers, foremen, and male workers—was already well established.

Székely-Lulofs's novels in particular detailed a rigid hierarchy of race and seniority invoked in deciding who should be allocated a "wife" when each new shipment of Javanese women arrived. In *Koelie*, for example, the story of a young Asian woman sold to an old coolie upon her arrival, the heroine is chided by a foreman for prostituting herself to the Chinese workers. She answers:

I've nothing to be ashamed of, those who gave me away to some man have no shame do they? I was given away like you give away a dog. Parman isn't my husband. I'm only living with him because I have to, because my name is "*orang kontrak*" [contract coolie]. So he's ashamed—I couldn't care less. So I'll be a Chinese whore! If I feel like it, I'll go to the Chinese barracks. Where else could I earn money? By hoeing? You've got to be kidding! [1932:100]

Székely-Lulofs's popular novels are romanticized and voyeuristic, but they do corroborate evidence from less aesthetically motivated sources.

In creating a society in which prostitution was the norm rather than the exception (for Asian and Europeans alike), the companies had not reckoned on all its consequences. *Vrouwen perkara*, disputes over women, frequently turned into deadly brawls between Chinese and Javanese. And many assaults on white personnel were attributed to irate fathers and jealous husbands whose daughters or wives had been summoned to a manager's house and had not returned. Whites, of course, always enjoyed rights to the first "picking." Van den Brand cites one particularly vivid example: an administrator who decked out a small room in his office with a couch, table, mirror, and washing things, and here chose from among the newly arrived women those "who seemed most amiable—as he euphemistically put it" (van den Brand 1904:53).

Under such conditions "coolie contract marriages," as they were disparagingly called, had little chance of survival. Family life, in fact, any lasting social ties, were all but absent in a situation where workers lived in barracks and were being continually shifted from one division to another without regard to conjugal or family ties. Consequently both married and unmarried women prostituted themselves, cooked for the unmarried work force, or became the "bed-servants" of the white colonial staff. Not all Javanese women were subject to this fate. Many either deserted or returned to Java when their contracts expired. Others continued to work sorting tobacco, harvesting tea, and tapping rubber, subject to the same maltreatment as their male counterparts. But, for the most part, sexual harassment prevailed in the fields and factories as well as in the barracks. Thus, despite the tenuousness of marriage (and concubinage) at least it offered some modicum of defense against the economic and sexual vulnerability to which women without a resident male protector were subject.

At the same time, for many male workers payment for female services made a large dent in their own meager wages, helping to keep them in debt—and indentured. Other inducements to remain in Deli included "unlimited" credit from company stores, where prices were notoriously higher than in the surrounding rural markets. On the tobacco estates, labor contracts were usually renewed en masse after the harvest; during these periods gambling was informally licensed (and actively encouraged) by management; foremen were given large cash sums by the estate administration to dispense as "unlimited" credit; both ruses usually meant reengagement for another three years until these debts were repaid. Such practices significantly lowered recruitment costs and padded the pockets of the Asian supervisory personnel.[20]

This partial list of the measures used to keep workers in Deli should suffice to indicate the broad outlines of a system characterized by what appears to be ultimately incompatible strategies of labor recruitment and control. On the one hand, there was a multitude of coercive measures used to retain workers; on the other hand, these were coupled with laboring and living conditions that emphasized the transiency and expendability of the same population. Cramped and poor housing, widespread disease, high adult and infant mortality, along with verbally and physically abusive (and violent) labor relations, were features of a system that in the end could not reproduce the conditions for its own existence.

According to van Kol, in 1900 mortality rates ran as high as 238/1,000 workers. Other sources contest this figure, more modestly estimating the rate at between 27 and 60 deaths per 1,000, a rate comparable to (but still higher than) mortality levels for rural Java at the same time.[21] This latter "proof" that working conditions in Deli were not so bad as they were made out to be is questionable. We might well ask whether these rates can reasonably be compared with those in Java. The Deli estate population was neither sociologically nor biologically "normal." Prima facie, there are a number of reasons that mortality rates on the Sumatran estates *should* have been noticeably lower than those for rural Java as a whole.

First, the old and the sick were not accepted for estate work, especially during the initial years of rapid expansion (Schuffner and Keunen 1910:23). Second, malnourishment presumably would be a major cause of sickness and death in a "normal" (read: impoverished) rural population, which included the landless and the very poor. On the estates this *should* not have been a contributing factor since regular wages and subsidized rice payments were guaranteed. Third, the effects of death during childbirth would have been greatly reduced on the estates with their disproportionately large number of male workers. For the same reason, child mortality would have been comparatively lower. In addition, those found to be seriously ill were usually returned to their places of origin because managers preferred to repatriate sick workers rather than pay for their costly and prolonged hospitalization (AR:II:Aug. 1912).

In short, the population on which these mortality figures were based represented a highly skewed age and sex pyramid, clearly affecting the mortality rates derived from it. It is not surprising that death figures were low—they should have been. It is more striking that they were as high as they were. Although some companies claimed to have sharply reduced worker mortality over the years, as late as the 1920s infant death rates were high enough on the Deli estates to warrant a special investigation into the causes (Straub 1928). Eventually efforts were made to preserve the costly labor supply recruited from Java. But it is clear that for several decades after Deli's opening, not only were the majority of companies unwilling to invest in maintaining a healthy and permanent work force, but, as one observer noted on the subject of Chinese recruits, "the planters encouraged a pattern of social and economic relationships which was actually inimical to [it]" (Reid 1970:320).

Ex-coolies outside the Estates

Although regulations specifically stipulated repatriation to Java for workers whose contracts expired, each year hundreds of uncounted Javanese slipped outside the estate sphere, remaining wedged between it and the Malay villages on its borders. We know very little about their activities. Since most were living a vaguely underground existence, legally under neither Dutch nor Malay administration, their lives seem to have eluded the scrupulous reports of both authorities.

What we do know is that before 1900 there were reports of clandestine Javanese settlements on the concession peripheries. By the 1920s nearly one-third of the Javanese living in the dense estate district of Simalungun were reportedly living outside the plantations. Figures from the 1930 census for East Sumatra estimated that nearly half of the more than one half-million Javanese in the region were not living on the estates. Some sources suggest that at least half of them had become part of the urban proletariat in the rapidly growing trading and administrative centers of Medan, Pematang Siantar, Tebing Tinggi, and Kisaran. They supposedly worked as unskilled laborers for Chinese merchants, some even becoming small traders and petty commodity producers in their own right. The latter two occupations seem less likely because small-scale trade was already a kin-based and ethnic monopoly of Malays and Bataks, and artisanal production, or even bricolage, entailed more economic wherewithal than a runaway coolie was likely to have.

Those not in urban centers seem to have made up a new underclass in the hinterland; settled in Malay villages on "borrowed" land as *men-umpang* (literally "passengers"), they performed agricultural work in exchange for board and use rights to village plots. Elsewhere they became sharecroppers to indigenous (usually Malay) claimants on *jaluran* or other agricultural land. This practice must have been relatively common by 1888, since at least one Dutch official issued a ruling forbidding the rental of *jaluran* to Javanese and Chinese estate workers in an effort to avert (1) an exodus from the estates and (2) a greater land shortage than was already the case (Bool 1903:38). Some local rulers eager for additional personal income allotted part of their territories to ex-estate workers, fixing rents at as much as two-thirds the harvested (rice) crop (de Ridder 1935:51). Clearly anyone accepting such conditions was set on leaving plantation labor and gaining access to land at a high cost.

Generally the planters became cognizant of what was happening on their borders only many years after the fact. At the turn of the century, and for even decades after, the concessions represented enormous unchartered tracts (literally tens of thousands of hectares) of virgin forest or dense, uncultivated secondary growth. Under such conditions settlements of Javanese and Bataks could and did crop up undetected on the plantation borders and often within them. Cases of such "newly discovered" five-year-old villages were reported at the turn of the century with inhabitants who were neither easy to oust nor particularily eager to work for the estates (Bool 1903:50). These settlements were certainly not what the planters had in mind when designing the ideal labor settlements of Deli's future described below. The estate industry had emerged on the basis of a captive immigrant labor force. It was now about to begin a new phase of expansion predicated on a still captive, but resident one, no longer legally coerced.

A New Phase: Designing a Resident Labor Reserve

The pioneering spirit that had initially carried the planters was becoming problematic by the second decade of the century. For one thing, the Javanese work force was not sharing this enthusiasm. For them contract work in Sumatra often meant temporary migration or a stepping stone toward acquiring an independent homestead of their own. Each year thousands requested repatriation to Java. In 1915 more than 42,000 new recruits arrived in Deli but more than 15,000 left Sumatra in the same year.[22]

Second, the cornucopia of Javanese labor was expensive to tap and difficult to maintain. As the total area of estate concessions expanded, recruitment agencies were hard pressed to keep up with their increasing demand for labor. Some planters began to complain of a growing number of "dangerous," "extremist," and "undesirable elements" among the recruits. The extent to which these perceptions were in anyway accurate will be dealt with in the following chapter; here the important point is that from the planters' perspective, the apparently "expendable" Javanese coolie was proving too costly to expend. One former Deli official argued that if things continued unchanged, sickness, weakness, and high mortality rates among the workers would eventually "render the estate industry impossible as a profitable undertaking" (Tideman 1919:126–27).

With strong opposition to the penal sanction being pressed from several quarters, it became necessary that Deli's labor system assume a less coercive countenance. In response to van den Brand's and van Kol's exposés on Deli's "outdoor prison" and "modern slavery," a government labor inspectorate (Arbeidsinspectie) was established in 1907 to investigate labor conditions and to check the more excessive abuses of labor contracts. The inspectorate had little success in accomplishing either: estate managers were singularly unsympathetic to its aims, and workers, fearing reprisal, were reluctant to express their grievances—at least through this official channel. In short, planters saw this development as a hostile, liberal, and pernicious threat to their autonomy; although they attempted to court and cow these inspectors out of performing their jobs, the estate staff could not stop the outward flow of information that was later used against them and the penal sanction that they supported.

Under heavy criticism from several quarters, in 1911 the first legislation was passed to gradually phase out the penal sanction and indentured labor. Contract coolies were to be replaced with vrije arbeiders (literally "free workers"), who, though also bound to contract, could not be legally coerced to remain on the estates. As it turned out, vrije arbeiders was a gross misnomer given the actual conditions under which Javanese men and women continued to work.

In the meantime a new theme emerged in the planters' discourse concerned with offsetting whatever corporate inconveniences might result from the abolition of indentured labor. It was often stated in terms of a goal to create a "free and normal labor market," a "permanent laboring population," "labor surety" to be realized by establishing a resident labor reserve on the East Coast. In planters' circles these terms took on a peculiar connotation with normal defining a labor market in which supply far exceeded demand and alternative income sources were severely limited, with the "ideal" result that estate wages would remain depressed.

With the shift from Chinese to Javanese recruitment after the turn of the century, Deli's estate labor force began for the first time to include working families. Thus, this reorientation brought with it the minimal social unit required for the systematic internal growth of the working population, and the first possibility of an alternative to the transient, virtually all male and essentially nonreproducing work force on which the planters were then dependent. By 1903 encouragement of *gezinvorming* (family formation) was already at issue. Some companies saw it as a financial burden and remained firmly opposed to family recruitment. Others emphasized that married women in the coolie population could have a positive effect:

The more marriages and the more family formation, the better the situation will be. A married woman, cultivating a small garden, or as a cook, baker or basket weaver can bring in extra earnings and thus lighten the burden and improve the well-being of the family. [Mulier 1903:145]

In 1903 the cushioning effects of a domestic economy were still negligible since only a fraction of the labor force was married. But this potential for deflecting some of the maintenance costs of workers became an increasingly central concern.

Strategies for securing this local labor pool rested on colonization and the establishment of labor settlements in East Sumatra. The debates detailed the most efficacious means to keep workers available when needed but not wholly dependent on estate wages during periods of slack. Java's long history as the fountainhead of colonial wealth was in part predicated on its ability to provide an abundant labor reserve from its landless and land-poor villagers, who were willing (or through indigenous patronage pressures could be forced) to work when needed for low cash wages but who could ostensibly be easily "reabsorbed" into their villages when not. In Deli such villages had to be created and colonization was considered the most expedient measure. Some details of this debate are worth noting because they make explicit the strategies behind land allocation and labor control as well as the basis on which an artificial distinction was created between the capitalist estate economy and the peripheral "subsistence" sector surrounding that core.

Colonization as conceived in 1902 had a dual purpose: alleviation of population pressure in Java and provision of a local labor pool for plantations in the Outer Provinces. This latter priority was set out in unambiguous terms in 1910 as a "desideratum" to be achieved through a progression leading from population increase, to land shortage, to impoverishment, leaving the "surplus [population] to seek work on the estates."[23] This script remains an uncanny prophecy of what happened decades later. In the meantime such schemes were rejected on the grounds that they could offer little immediate alleviation of the labor shortage that many planters were convinced would accompany the impending abolition of the penal sanction.

In the interim the companies sought a more immediate remedy in the establishment of "labor settlements" (arbeidersnederzettingen), while the central government proposed "agricultural colonization" (landbouwkolonisatie). Although these two plans appeared as variations on a similar theme (with the term colonization often applied to both), they were motivated by different priorities. The latter, pushed by government authorities, was concerned that demographic pressure in Java was heightening political instability throughout the Indies. Under this plan, emigrant families would be allocated tracts of land sufficient for their subsistence, independent of any commitment to perform estate work. The planters, marshaling their expertise on matters Sumatran and their political resources, managed to dissuade the government from adopting and carrying out this plan, arguing that the East Coast had no need and no room for additional agriculturalists.

The planters contended that Deli needed laborers, and the free colonization of Javanese families "undisciplined and unaccustomed to estate work" was unlikely to provide a willing estate laboring population—especially if these families were granted sufficient land to live off:

The result would be that an even greater portion of valuable estate land would be transferred to the natives without the estates receiving any assurance that in exchange they [the settlers] would also do estate work. [Lulofs 1920:15]

Company representatives further argued that in any case there was no room left for such allotment. Land grants, they claimed, would result in more agrarian conflict and "degrade" valuable commercial holdings by transforming them into "unprofitable" rice fields (ibid.).

With such appeals to government interests, the companies stood fast in asserting their sovereignty over land and labor. In the 1920s and 1930s numerous commissions investigating colonization possibilities all came to the same conclusion: however colonies were to be created, the "colonists" must be coolies first and foremost, accustomed to estate work, and subject to stipulations which would assure that they remained economically dependent on, and available to, the estates. A scheme outlined in 1910 stipulated allotting miniscule plots to married workers who would live in estate "villages" under company supervision for the duration of the worker's contract. Later addenda to this proposal decreased the allotment size and increased the company's control over the settlements. Proposed allotments ranged from 700 m^2 to a mere 100 m^2 per family for house and garden.[24] Obviously the planters had successfully blocked any realization of agricultural colonization.

To get some relative notion of what this amount of land would mean for a family of four, we can compare this figure to the contemporary guidelines for rural Javanese households. In 1976 2,000 m² was the estimated minimum necessary for a family to subsist given *double* cropping and labor intensive cultivation (Stoler 1977b:695). Since much of the Deli land under consideration could produce only one crop a year, it is clear just how far from meeting subsistence needs these planned allocations were. In fact, the labor settlements that were built were often no more than corporate euphemisms for an alternate housing arrangement to coolie barracks. Nominal land allotments represented both a rationale for depressed wages and a relatively cheap means of providing the semblance of village life.

In the 1920s most of these attempts remained halfhearted. Planters complained that workers were unwilling to tend their private gardens (in their "free time" after what was then a ten-hour workday), and since workers were transferred frequently from one division to another they often had no chance to harvest what they had planted and tended (Versluys 1938:171). Other companies argued that health care and labor discipline would be more difficult to maintain with workers dispersed in individual dwellings that used *seven times* more land than the prevailing barrack system (Tideman 1919:127).

In the end such objections won out and the "development of family life among the coolies" was kept slow until the depression (KvA 1927:18). Such material deterrents were reinforced with social restraints; marriage fees for workers were kept very high and some employers simply refused to grant marriage licenses, pleading that such unions would raise their operating costs (ibid. 47). Also, the companies did little to rectify the uneven ratio of men to women, a major and long-standing grievance—and an obvious and basic requirement for a family-based labor force—arguing that "the costs related to transport, housing and medical treatment . . . would be greater than the advantages accompanying the creation of a more normal sex ratio" (KvA 1928:61). Thus while the long-term interests of the industry and the government favored family recruitment and a domestic climate to encourage it, the shorter term interests of individual companies militated against such a change. Fostering family formation was still a prerequisite for a resident labor reserve; thus the debate remained heated and open.

With agricultural colonization abandoned, the location of the proposed labor settlements—on or *off* the estates—became the issue in question. Settlements within estate borders meant that in time of crisis the companies would be burdened with a work force for whom they could not provide work and for whom they preferred not to be responsible. Although a land-lending scheme of sorts was carried out on a number of plantations, most firms refused even to try such a costly venture. Labor settlements *off* the estates (*randkolonisatie*) were also considered a risky undertaking because they threatened to destroy what some authorities saw as Deli's primary asset: an uninterrupted expanse of estate concessions allowing for *united* foreign control (KvA 1932:43). Nonetheless, during the depression such colonies were established as a "crisis measure" to maintain a minimal local labor force without "endangering the vital interests of the country" (KvA 1939:39–44).

The reams of paper generated over these proposals belie the fact that most of these schemes never got beyond the experimental stage and were certainly never implemented on a region-wide basis. The largest concentrations of such efforts came at critical economic junctures—during World War I, the economic malaise of 1921–23, and the depression of the 1930s: that is, when it became mandatory to reduce labor costs, in part through massive dismissals of managerial and coolie personnel, in part by allocating more of the maintenance costs of labor power to the workers themselves.

These projects thus had another objective closely tied to the fact that East Sumatra was one of the most serious food-deficient regions in the Indies. Local food production was hardly sufficient to feed the native inhabitants, much less the estate industry, which was totally dependent on imported rice. Plantations located far from urban centers were particularly vulnerable, and during World War I many allocated part of their concessions to essential food crops in case an embargo cut off their supplies (AR).[25]

An early example of this dates from 1918, when rice shipments from Rangoon were stopped because of a food shortage in the British Indies, prompting the government to decree that estates set aside 3.5 ha/100 workers for corn, cassava, and dry rice cultivation (KvA 1919:34–35). From the companies' perspective such schemes were a waste of valuable land and labor. As a preferred solution some allotted workers small plots to cultivate in their "spare time" outside working hours. This had the obvious advantage of reducing the estates' (labor) costs for the cultivation of emergency food stuffs. Temporary land grants were one component of this semi-self-sufficiency program and a convenient way to keep a core labor force fed and active until the crisis passed.

Measures to keep low operating expenses in the estate industry devolved on a cut in labor costs as in the schemes above, and on a general wage policy that guaranteed against significant increases. The planters were the first to point out the dissimilarities between Java and Deli, but their notions of what constituted a "normal labor market" were unequivocally conceived from a Javanese paradigm: a labor force economically dependent, socially malleable, and politically inarticulate—

and one for which wage levels remained independent of the market mechanisms of supply and demand. Low wage rates were ensured through several measures. The powerful planters' associations of AVROS and DPV (the Deli Tobacco Planters' Association) set a uniform wage standard that avoided competitive wage wars between the companies. Second, wages were paid in cash and in kind, the latter usually in the form of subsidized rice. A confidential report from an estate manager to his head office in 1912 suggests the rationale behind this wage form:

Losses are still considerable because of the high price of rice in the last six months of 1911. It seems preferable, however, to bear this loss, since . . . the government would otherwise deem it necessary to increase the coolie [cash] wages, which would certainly be more costly for us. The high price of rice is only temporary, but once [cash] wages are increased it would not be easy for us to lower them again. [AR][26]

Subsidized food payments thus helped to prevent wage increases; even the impending abolition of the penal sanction served as a rationale for keeping wages low. More than a decade before its abolition, planters argued that wage increases must be avoided in anticipation of wage hikes that would presumably accompany the introduction of "free" labor. From 1894 to 1920—a highly profitable period for the industry— real wages of estate workers improved little, despite the strong demand for labor during most of these years (BZ).[27]

We can conclude that a general food shortage was not the major thrust behind the various land allocations and lending schemes described above as the colonization debate makes clear—as does the radical change in labor policy that the 1930 depression prompted. Despite the panic this worldwide crisis caused, in Deli the planters were able to put it to remarkable advantage, using it as an excuse to revamp the structure of the estate labor force—economically, politically, and socially—as they saw fit. First of all, on the eve of the crash Deli's plantation workers numbered 336,000 and although the companies were operating at full potential they were also supporting a massive, imported work force bound to contracts for which the firms were liable. Second, increasing occurrences of collective labor protest and physical assaults on management (though never with the organizational sophistication, frequency, and political inspiration that the planters claimed) in the late 1920s, coupled with calls for the abolition of indenture from many quarters, were conspiring to force the industry's hand.

It had further become clear that the creation of a resident labor reserve required a form of hegemony in which overt coercion could play only a partial role. It demanded a social environment in which Javanese working families, as the planters put it, would be "content" (senang) and "feel at home." It demanded a housing situation that would encourage marriage and propagation, as well as medical care and social facilities that would allow regeneration.

Consider the changing view of health care that accompanied the industry's interest in fostering local population growth; this new priority brought with it the recognition that population increase would necessitate that workers maintain themselves and reproduce a healthy generation of future workers. A study of child mortality in the late 1920s made explicit "that through an improvement in child mortality our goal of [local] population increase can be more quickly attained" (Straub 1928:9). The investigation showed that more than 50% of estate coolie children in the HAPM estates died by the age of three, and that on the Deli Maatschappij plantations the same percentage were dead by the age of fifteen (ibid. 31). Infant mortality rates on Java during the same period averaged between 225 and 250 deaths per 1,000 births (Nitisastro 1970:113); on the East Coast the rate was 370 per 1,000. Respiratory infections were cited as the main cause of infant mortality, amoebic dysentery as the primary cause of adult deaths. Both these afflictions were found to be far more prevalent on those estates with barrack housing and cramped, dark living quarters. A doctor working on the Senembah Maatschappij estates corroborated these findings that the shift from barrack housing to individual family dwellings resulted in a much more rapid population increase (ibid.). Only ten years earlier, family housing had been opposed on hygienic grounds, but now with a change in company outlook, scientific research confirmed the prevailing priorities.[28]

Policy Changes of the Depression

What did the planters do? Like most industries caught in the depression in Europe, America, or the Third World they fired workers on a massive scale. But in Deli this was done by first activating the abolition of indenture (legally authorized but not enforced for two decades).[29] Fearing a dangerous spread of "pauperism" on the East Coast, the government strongly backed the planters' move by decreeing that the vast majority of dismissed coolies would have to be repatriated to Java. Between 1930 and 1933 the work force was reduced from 336,000 to 170,500 workers— thus nearly 50% of the work force was fired and their contracts were terminated. Those contract coolies who remained on the East Coast were replaced with *vrije arbeiders,* in practice often one and the same person, released and rehired again at 25% his or her former wage (O'Malley 1977:134). For the workers who were retained, a system was introduced that provided work for half-days at half pay and frequent unpaid "holidays." According to the companies, these workers could recover their lost wages by using their increased "free time" to grow food crops on land made available by the estates.

In the meantime the 150,000 workers who were to be dismissed were chosen with care, according to the industry's revised specifications. The rationale for dismissal selected for a family-based population. Thus single males were among the first to be returned to their homelands in China and Java. On the same principle married women were fired but *not* repatriated; with their jobs sacrificed to "household heads" (i.e., men), they were allowed to remain in Sumatra as dependents of their employed husbands (KvA 1932:43).

In 1934 as production possibilities revived, what was previously felt as a cumbersome excess of workers was now experienced as a labor shortage. And with this shift, plans for colonization and land-lending were shelved. Recruitment incentives were given renewed priority with an emphasis on married couples—including working or nonworking wives.[30]

The plan to create labor colonies was long given up, but some salient features of it remained, one of which was to fashion a living situation bearing an evocative resemblance to Javanese village peasant life. Karl Pelzer, writing of the "pseudo-colonies" in 1945, noted:

The planters were . . . willing to furnish each laborer of good standing with only a tiny garden plot of one-tenth of a hectare—large enough collectively to provide the atmosphere of a *desa* [Javanese village] but too small to grow food stuffs for the families. At the same time the planters reserved the right to evict a laborer if he did not work regularly. [1945:201]

And *good standing* meant a male household head with more than five years of loyal service to the estate. One attestation to the efficacy of this new family policy was that by 1940 nearly 74% of the labor force was locally recruited (Boeke 1953:55); and by the late 1930s estate managers and civil servants were applauding the "social tranquility" of family-based workers "accustomed to regular estate work and discipline" (KvA 1937:54).

The Social Parameters of Labor Control

This chapter has dealt with some of the constraints defining the changing nature of estate labor relations on Sumatra's East Coast. The issues raised are those that the state and companies themselves argued, those deemed essential to the priorities of the new industry. In each case, this order, as implemented through regulations for recruitment, housing, and wage forms, entailed an element of social violence—reconstituting sexual, familial, and labor relations, where possible, around the new and changing imperatives of expansion.

Among the more controversial issues relating to labor control and discontent were those that devolved on, and were resolved through, control over sexuality and the gender-specific roles entailed. A short list of salient *arbeidersvraagstukken* (labor problems) suggests that sexuality, as Foucault suggests, was an "especially dense transfer point for relations of power" (1980:103): prostitution, venereal disease, sodomy, illegitimate offspring, brittle marriage ties, a scarcity of women and families. All, in one form or another, were social "disorders" tied to the companies' and state's efforts to impose their control and authority over the intimate life of men and women.

In turn these "problems" sanctioned a more detailed scrutiny of the workers and further intrusions into their lives. Women married as long as fifteen years were subject to obligatory checkups for venereal disease, and menstruation leave was granted only after a medical examination to which most women would not submit. The "breeding patterns" of the estate population were placed under a microscope, yielding data that allowed for further control over (or at the very least more efficient adaptation to) the productive and reproductive proclivities of this laboring population. Sexuality and knowledge of it were not the sole vectors of labor control but they seem to have been charged with "instrumentality." Essential to this process was the malleability of a domestic organization and a set of social relations that could be severed and reinvoked to comply with the changing labor requirements of the estates. Backed by a strict penal code that severely punished those who would not acquiesce, this cultural violence was rationalized as an imperative of pioneering, progress, and the increased productivity necessary for an expanding capitalist industry.

Several important themes that have emerged here inform much of Deli's subsequent labor history. For one, we have seen that coercion, in its direct and subtler forms, was not an anachronistic or a transitory method of labor control but an integral part of colonial capitalism even in its late expansion. Following from this, we have seen that the distinctions drawn between "indentured" and "free wage" labor marked neither the exit from a "precapitalist" system nor the entry into a capitalist one; there was virtually no change in the working conditions or the productive relations that prevailed on the Deli estates. The penal sanction was simply the legal component of a much more widespread system of manipulation, whose corpus permeated social relations within and outside the labor process—long after the penal sanction itself was abolished.

The planters' discourse has allowed us to see what initial steps were taken to introduce on the plantation periphery the appearance of peasant independence and, in essence, a dual economy. We have looked at some of the ways in which this spatial and social universe was constructed. The "villages" established to house estate coolies in Deli, the plots they were offered to work in their "spare time," the social benefits supplied to encourage "family formation" and to give the semblance of community life did not mark the emergence of an autonomous set of productive relations on the estate periphery but dependent relations squarely rooted in the corporate strategies of labor control. More evidence for this interpretation will be offered in the following chapters, which look at the lives of workers in villages on the estate periphery today. I anticipate this argument here because of the strong continuity between the industry's goals of the early twentieth century and what transpired decades later—and because the sources themselves clearly reveal how these constructs were made, rendering superfluous any academic "translation."

One might argue that I have presented the planters as omniscient and omnipotent in a situation in which they were neither; that I have assumed they schemed and plotted with acuity and success, when in fact what they attempted to manipulate was not always malleable. Often they did not plot at all but were themselves subject to constraints and forces outside their control. The planters did not have the choice to employ those systems of labor control most conducive to profit maximization and the smooth extraction of surplus value. Their actions—and reactions—were strictly circumscribed, not only by external pressures (international and state intervention, social criticism and the nationalist movement), but from within the ranks of the plantation labor force itself.

In Deli the changing strategies of control reflect this confrontation; by incorporating new spheres or realigning and reconstituting old ones, these strategies were continually responsive to the state of labor relations and worker resistance. This does not mean that these methods simply *reflected* the intensity of popular protest. In the following chapter we see the extent to which *potential* danger and violence from the coolie quarters was used to justify (and indeed did promote) new modes of repression and exploitation.

3
Plantation Workers in Protest: The Politics of Violence

Deli's contract coolies were never known for their docility. Disengaged from the ties that bound them to Java, they were also disencumbered of a cultural baggage that nurtured acquiescence, silence, and submission.[1] By the 1920s, assaults on white personnel had escalated to such a level that Sumatra's East Coast became infamous throughout the Indies—and an embarrassment in this Dutch realm of *rust en orde* (law and order). The last chapter in part portrayed Deli as a capitalist success story; the present chapter deals with labor's challenge to that tale. Here we are concerned with the nature and intensity of labor protest in the estate industry's prewar expansion, with the conditions that bred a concentration of violence and an accompanying concentration of debate about its causes. Here the discourse is something more than a commentary on the prevailing practices and attitudes of a ruling class; it represents one of the active agents in fomenting fear and promoting repressive measures in response to it. Distinguishing appearances from the actual incidents of labor action should bring us closer to specifying the form and content of popular resistance in colonial East Sumatra.

To the chagrin of many Sumatran planters, the Javanese in Deli were an unfamiliar breed. Planters complained of the poor quality of recruits and the preponderance of "undesirable" and "dangerous" elements among them, lamenting that these immigrant Javanese lacked the virtues of passivity and obedience. Some planters complained that only social dropouts and marginals were willing to migrate, among whom were vagabonds from the urban centers of Semarang and Batavia, murderers, petty criminals, and thieves. Others saw the change as a more general consequence of displacement. The author of a 1913 handbook for new estate staff members offered this analysis:

[The Javanese worker] feels himself detached from all the old formality and customs, placed in surroundings which are totally foreign to him, in a land where people do not speak his language, where his customs are unknown; slighted by his own countrymen, among comrades who have cast aside all etiquette and submissiveness such as he learned in Java, he is an entirely changed being. No wonder that his way of doing things doesn't remain the same. No wonder that he, the "little person" from Java, as a contract coolie in Deli, is no longer recognizable to the Europeans.[2]

A profusion of ideological constructs gave credence to this portrait of the Deli estate worker and added weight to the argument that coercive measures were needed to control him. In a recent study on the ideology of colonial capitalism, Syed Hussein Alatas argues that the image of the indolent Malay, Filipino, and Javanese native was a product of colonial domination used to "justify compulsion and unjust practices in the mobilization of labor" (1977:70). Within this idiom *indolence* referred to those unwilling to perform plantation work and *industriousness* applied to those who easily became the companies' chattel. *Indolence* thus connoted an image of passivity, threatening at most the Calvinist (or more generally Protestant) colonial ethnic, but essentially a "harmless" form of resistance. Although this indelible image of the "lazy native" certainly helped to rationalize indenture, it alone would have been insufficient. Alatas's account lacks not that part of the native (in the planter's eye) which withdraws from, avoids honest work, but that part which actively resists, drives him to violence, and necessitates the big stick to prod—and restrain.

In Deli the two images converged. On the one hand, estate workers are said to be "industrious" and hardworking; on the other hand, they can unpredictably go amok, become unfathomably violent, incited by external forces or obscure notions of revenge. Here it is not violence per se that justified armed police, intelligence networks, a penal code, and physical force, but violence of a particular sort, stripped of its validity and exposed as the response of irrational and rapacious elements. It had to be shown as something outside rationality: as an unreasonable response according to the canons of Western thought. And where it was (seldom) granted that some rational motive lay behind a worker's attack on an assistant or a foreman, the victim was chided simply for misunderstanding the strange workings of these unsophisticated minds, thereby reaffirming with condescending concession the curious and superstitious norms of the Asian mentality. But there is a twist in this psychology: the coolie is considered childlike, his cultural eccentricities must be pampered, but he is also a man-child whose temper tantrums are both rash *and* dangerous. In any case this caricature attributes an impetuousity to the male worker (and by extension to the female coolie) that had to be guarded against.

The credibility of this image was sharply reinforced by a structure of labor relations that assigned young white staff members an economically and a socially vulnerable position within estate society. Fresh from Europe, they were not only unschooled in plantation agriculture but often less knowledgeable than their underlings in the unstated rules of interracial conduct. The "newcomers" (or singkeh as they were contemptuously called) were excluded from the social circles of the older planters, ridiculed for their ignorance, mocked as "greenhorns," and allocated the most arduous task of management: daily confrontation with the native labor force.[3] Subject to the same ten-hour day as their coolies, which started with the predawn roll call in the workers' barracks and often ended with the supervision of obligatory overtime, ultimately they were held responsible for whatever was done or not done by the approximately 500 workers under them. Clear-cut indicators of superior status were particularly important for these white staff members, the "assistants" who ranked among the plebians of planter society and were themselves in a thankless position. With base salaries set extremely low, the major portion of their earnings came from bonuses (tantiemes), which always depended on the performance of the coolies with whom they were charged.

Below the various grades of assistants (usually differentiated by seniority) were the Asian supervisors, Chinese overseers (tandil), and Javanese foremen (mandor) charged with the work gangs of their respective ethnic origin. Although chosen from the workers' ranks, these native servants of capital were the most direct agents of labor control. The corporate elite only set the general policies for production; it was the Asian staff who were delegated the daily task of enforcing submission to these regulations with penal punishment for those who would not obey. Thus they and the assistants were the main targets of dissatisfaction—both from above and below.

Given the ethnic diversity on the East Coast, market Malay, not Javanese with its multiple and intricate forms for marking social status, became, by default, the language of the plantation. Learning to give orders in this coarse, broken, stepchild of Malay, the new assistants adopted a stiff and an unadorned mode of communication, more conducive to blunt imperative than gentle command—and invariably accompanied by physical rather than verbal emphasis. Although in later years some companies urged intensive language training for their European employees, it is clear that the use of this crude creole was only one component of a conscious distancing between the races.

There were other methods far more explicit. In Székely-Lulofs's novel, *De Andere Wereld,* a new assistant is given this advice by an older colleague:

And now while we're at it I'll teach you a few things, the ABC's of our relations with the natives. . . . Every native must get out of (or step down from) his vehicle when encountering a white, a company building, office, shed, or house and not get on again until he is at least 10 meters distance. . . . You may find this somewhat excessive, but you must not forget that we whites stand alone against the masses, and we can only maintain ourselves by such rigid regulations which must function as a form of discipline and restraint. Do you see what I mean? Because the first necessity of the planter is to have the natives in your grip, the rest will take care of itself. [1946:101]

Relations of dominance, codified between people and personified in things, went far beyond the hierarchy of the labor process. One had to learn not only how to manage a labor force but how to act as a young raja, how to preserve and recreate the prestige of the planter oligarchy—no matter how subordinate one's present position within it.

Implicit in these lessons was always the threat, the fear, that with a loss of prestige, the whites would be shamed, and violence against persons and property would follow; that order would give way to chaos, that the world might be turned upside down, putting white supremacy—and capitalism—at stake. Sartre's observations of South Africa might well have been written with Deli in mind:

Propaganda had to reflect this universal violence, and reflect his own violence to the colonialist as the simple manly courage, resolute in all things, of an embattled minority; and it had to present everyone with with the *other-violence* of the natives as constantly endangering the colonialists everywhere. That is to say, it struck permanent fear into the colonialists and presents this angry fear as pure courage. [1976:726]

From this perspective, the persistence of fear (or its better mask, courage) was not a measure of the actual frequency and severity of assaults on whites. Whenever such incidents did occur in Deli they were invariably labeled first as acts of personal revenge or political acts of insurgency, and responded to accordingly. The former were "manageable" irritations, the latter threatened foreign rule. In the early years of estate expansion, great effort was made to deny the political basis of violence since during this period it would have been particularly compromising, both materially and ideologically, to request armed government support. Such an admission, that the coolies were not under control, would have been reason for further state intervention in estate matters—something the planters were trying scrupulously to avoid.

Sometimes the companies did complain of insufficient government backing; in 1877 planters charged that theft and murder were more frequent now, under the paternal eye of the government, than when judicial matters were in their own hands (Anonymous 1925:71). But the colonial state's attitude was in large part of the companies' making. Having enjoyed relatively free rein for the first few decades of Deli's opening, they were hardly willing to relinquish this autonomy. The companies wanted state assistance to enforce indenture, without restricting their own practices. The government, for its part, tried to maneuver a narrow course, allowing the planters sufficient leeway to encourage investment but not at the expense of popular peace.

Given this rather delicate situation, the companies adhered to a single interpretation of popular violence—that it was criminal, personally motivated, and certainly not an expression of resistance to the companies themselves. Thus in 1876 an estate inspector wrote: "Once again the cause of the assaults is not political, but based on personal revenge and rapacity" (Anonymous 1925:15). In the same year, the secretary of the Gedong Johore estate reassuringly reported that the European enclave was calm despite numerous assaults on its members since these acts were obviously matters of personal vengeance (ibid. 15). This bicentennial volume of the Deli-Batavia Maatschappij, a long and confused commentary on the issue of "danger," concludes with this summing up of the events of 1870: "Repeatedly, people were uncertain as to whether an assault should be considered as 'hostile' or indeed only as 'rapacious' and 'cut-throat,' although people lost lives and goods in both cases" (ibid. 11). In any case, most estates had their own detachment of soldiers stationed to protect them from the fear, if not from the danger, to which they were subject.

In Deli's colonial record, multiple motifs alternately deny and fixate on the subjects of "peril," "danger," and "risk." The assertion of danger was one pervasive theme. Its counterpoint was vaguer and subtler in content. Here the planters downplayed the danger, even denied its existence, because news of such "disorder" in Deli would deter future investments and discourage potential European recruits. This discourse presents a braver mien, an echoed laughter in the belly of the beast. Estate administrators, eager to reassure their executive offices (and themselves) that all was secure and under control, reported of planters' clubs being built, tennis courts in the making, and other accoutrements of the (fortified and) healthy white enclave. Here disturbances in the social order were cited in the past tense, as evils overcome, not as omens of the future.

These juxtaposed themes, one variant overstating, the other muting, the dangers, were neither mutually exclusive nor historically separate— they coexisted (and reproduced each other) throughout most of North

Sumatra's modern history.[4] In Deli the focus on danger and the denial of fear alternated as methods of coercion and responses to it were modified. In either case the solution was always the same: never a relaxation of control but displacement of the spheres in which it was exercised. We see below how the profusion of inquiries into labor conditions on the East Coast altered the mechanisms of control and settled new power on those with more access to that knowledge.

Under Deli's conditions passivity had not traveled well. Although planters were convinced that "undesirable elements" were a Javanese export, more evidence shows that such "elements" were a creation of Deli's own social and political environment. In the absence of a well-honed and inbred cultural hegemony such as the one that prevailed on Java, the *daily* reproduction of dominance (and resistance to it) played a more essential role. A French colonialist remarking in 1910 on the success of Deli's penal system lauded the construction of vast modern prisons and the swiftness with which the Deli planter had carried out the prime duty of a colonizing people: the maintenance of law and order by establishing a solidly based police force and system of justice (Guyot 1910:197).

The coolie ordinance of 1915 (in effect through the 1920s) unambiguously outlined the infractions that were deemed an offense against this ordered peace. Workers could be imprisoned and fined not only for refusal to work, desertion, and "other willful violations" of their contracts, but for virtually *any* act deemed threatening to the "safety of persons and peace and order on the estates" (Bool and Fruin 1927:34). "Insulting a superior" was punishable by a fine of 25 guilder or a maximum of 12 days in prison. "Threats by word or posture" liabled the accused to 1 to 3 years in prison. And "resistance" without inflicting serious injury was punishable by a maximum of 3 months in jail. As with all these violations, *resistance* was loosely defined and more loosely interpreted to include any gesture that might endanger the "good order on the estates" (ibid.) With such stipulations written into both the legal and social codes it should not be surprising that offenses against the coolie ordinances ran into the thousands. Between 1917 and 1926 there were 8,000 to 13,000 infractions annually; in other words on an average 5 to 10% of the work force was guilty of at least one offense per year (KvA 1926:46; Middendorp 1924:37).

Physical abuse of workers and bodily assault on managerial personnel were part of estate labor relations from its earliest years. Statistics from the DPV and AVROS planters' associations, however, indicate that such incidents continued to rise throughout the early part of the twentieth century, culminating in such high frequency before the depression

that the European community was reportedly thrown into unprecedented alarm. From 1925 to 1930 alone reported assaults on overseers
(whites and Asians) rose from 31 to 220, and the number perpetrated
specifically against European personnel more than doubled for the same
period.[5] In all the Outer Provinces, nowhere were they more numerous
and widespread than on Sumatra's East Coast.

That such incidents fell off sharply during the depression when the
penal sanction was lifted was construed by some observers as proof that
the penal sanction was indeed to blame for what had been "amiss" in
Sumatra's plantation belt. This interpretation ignores the significance of
other simultaneous forms of labor protest manifest in demonstrations,
petitions, and riots against company practices that were directed at
many more injustices than those of the penal sanction alone.

At the same time that the penal sanction was abolished, the government and estate industry responded to these expressions of labor unrest
with rigorous and effective measures to repress them. They contended
that the estates were being infilitrated surreptiously by communist agitators, "extremist" elements, and nationalist troublemakers who were
allegedly turning the coolies on a radical bent. Ill-trained personnel and
greedy Asian overseers were also given their share of the blame, with the
implication that their "misbehavior" was somehow anomalous to the
"normal" tenor of labor relations rather than part and parcel of it.

Indies Political Movements in the Early Twentieth Century

Increase in labor unrest on Deli's estates was concurrent with important
political and economic changes in the Netherlands Indies and in the
plantation industry in particular. For one thing, the political climate in
Java had little in common with what the Deli planters had idealized it to
be in their nostalgia for tempoe doeloe ("the good old days"). On Java,
resistance to foreign rule manifested itself in organized and collective
action soon after the turn of the century.

Such organizations as Budi Oetomo, and Sarekat Islam (ostensibly
religious and educational associations with no overt political program)
had formed during a brief period of relaxed restrictions on civil liberties.
In 1908 the first Indonesian-based labor union was formed, which, under the influence of the zealous Dutch socialist Hendrik Sneevliet, actually concerned itself with "improving the lot of the unskilled and impoverished Indonesian workers" (McVey 1965:14). In its wake, tens of
other unions were organized among dockworkers, drivers, pawnshop
clerks, and other government civil servants. By the end of 1919, Sarekat
Islam had united 22 trade unions with a membership of 77,000.[6] In 1919,
sugar workers organized, and in 1924 the first union of estate employees

was founded, the Sarekat Buruh Onderneming. Generally, 1919 marked a particularly active year of organizing and activism. The large profits for foreign capital stood in sharp contrast to the diminishing real wages for indigenous workers. Strikes proliferated and in 1920 as many as 84,000 workers participated in labor actions (McVey 1965:173).

Overt signs of labor unrest in Deli came with a rapid expansion in estate size, accelerated labor recruitment, and thus a greater flow of newcomers—and communications—from Java. As such, news of, and experience in, acts of labor protest presumably would not have been contingent on the arrival of strategically placed "agitators" as the planters claimed. Politically active and informed recruits could have arrived with each new shipment of workers to Deli. In this sense, estate agitators could have been from "outside"; but for that matter so was the entire plantation community. The fact that an increasing number of indentured workers brought with them some awareness of their legitimate right to contest their working conditions hardly implies that the *causes* of their discontent were imported as well.

In Sumatra, indigenous organizations of a nationalist and socialist bent were also emerging, though in somewhat muted form. In 1908 Budi Oetomo established a Medan branch and Sarekat Islam and Taman Siswa soon followed (Langenberg 1976:118–20). By 1920 some sources suggest that a "widespread and energetic anti-colonial movement was afoot" (ibid. 127). Unfortunately, evidence concerning the specifics of how, where, and when plantation workers participated in that movement is extremely tenuous: To what extent were assaults on whites and collective forms of protest in this period signs of popular politicization? Or were these events independent episodic "outbursts" of little political consequence? Were these nascent forms of a left-wing nationalist labor movement taking shape or merely isolated incidents with little pattern or effect?

The secondary sources to appeal to are few, aside from some general references to Deli's estate workers in studies of indirect concern. For example, a noted Sumatran historian, Anthony Reid, suggests that plantation coolies were marginal to the political and social drama played out in the prewar years on the East Coast, on the grounds that they were effectively quartered off from political activity by the repressive apparatus of the coolie ordinances and penal code (1979:43). George Kahin, on the other hand, wrote that in the 1920s communist strength was particularly visible in East Sumatra's plantation belt (1952:85). Langenberg also points out that in the 1930s Taman Siswa and the Indonesian Nationalist Party (PNI, Partai Nasional Indonesia) marshaled much of their support from the large Javanese population in the *cultuurgebied* and on the estates proper (1976:135). Other sources indicate that in the same years

Iwa Kusumasumantri, a well-known Medan lawyer and Communist party member, had success in organizing estate workers initially through chauffeurs, and later directly on the estates.[7] These somewhat contradictory but tantalizing references offer little to substantiate their own claims or those of others.[8]

Standard sources on the prewar labor movement basically ignore Deli's estate workers altogether. Since the classic works of Blumberger, Pringgodigdo, and Sandra were concerned with *organized* labor, the seemingly ad hoc actions occurring on the East Coast were outside their domain (Blumberger 1931, 1935; Pringgodigdo 1950; Sandra 1961). Only Pluvier refers to the fact that, "in Deli, where an oversupply of labor power did not exist and workers thus had to be brought in from outside, the Penal Sanction hindered the emergence of a powerful labor union movement" (1953:155). There are more references to the organizations of Budi Oetomo in its early years, Taman Siswa, and the PNI later, all of which advocated the abolition of indenture and improvement in estate living conditions. But the indisputable fact that many such groups championed the cause of estate workers is not evidence for the actual participation of the workers themselves in any nationalist, much less radical, anticolonial struggle.

Given the constricting labor contracts to which workers were bound, the prohibition on strikes, and the strength of the legal apparatus used to enforce both, we would hardly expect to find that estate workers were collectively and consciously incorporated into these organized movements. They did, however, constitute a social force in their own right by threatening—with potential and actual violence—the industry's profits and in turn by directly affecting corporate labor policy and the strategies of labor control. Analyses of the Deli labor situation by government and company officials hinged on a definition of the *political*, which was always equated with that which was *externally* induced. More evidence, which we turn to below, suggests that this "external" scapegoat masked the racial and class conflicts embedded within and generated by estate labor relations themselves.

In the absence of any prior sociological attempts to map out Deli's estate labor history through either oral or written accounts, we begin with the available primary sources: reports of labor inspectors, chronicles of the planters' associations, government reports filed in Holland, and newspaper accounts from both the native and European press. That each of the groups represented in these sorts of documents promoted singular interpretations of labor unrest and were often in hostile and open confrontation with one another over its causes provides a pivotal focus of this analysis.

An aggressive long-standing discourse between the European and indigenous press in Medan, for example, hinged on the presence of communist and nationalist agitators on the estates. Another prolonged dispute, between government and planter authorities, was over where to lay blame for the increase in riots and murders in the plantation belt. By examining where these accounts overlap, contradict, and bypass one another, we can begin to question the credibility of certain interpretations and identify the more blatantly fictionalized accounts. Questions concerning the relationship between political activism and labor unrest (as with the question of gender discrimination in chap. 2) are not ours alone; these issues were central to both those upholding and challenging foreign rule. Whether the fact of "external agitation" can now be written off as a "red herring" is beside the point. This issue nourished a dialogue rich in the details of working conditions, giving texture to the social confrontations in plantation life.

References to *gevaarlijke elementen* ("dangerous elements") and *koelieaanvallen* ("assaults by coolies") date back to the earliest accounts of Deli's opening, when they were few and far between. Before 1900 the estates were far more isolated; assaults on coolies, and by them, were rarely reported. These incidents, we learn from later sources, were usually handled on the estates and hushed by administrators who preferred not to have it known that their coolies were not "in hand." From the *Deli Courant*, the principal news organ of foreign investors, we know that disturbances were not infrequent; ransom notices appeared offering rewards for the capture of workers who had murdered whites (Said 1976:35). Elsewhere references are made to "dangerous elements" and roving bands, sometimes of ex-contract coolies, attacking the estates by night and living in the jungle by day (Anonymous 1925:66). In 1903 van Kol refers to the fact that *moordaanslagen* ("deadly assaults") on Asian overseers were by no means rare. The number of workers prosecuted for such offenses rose from 148 in 1894 to 209 in 1902, or "two per thousand coolies" (van Kol 1903:99). Van Kol called for abolition of indenture to alleviate the situation, while others sought the solution in stricter police control--and an armed white staff.

In support of the latter proposal, the former assistant A. Hanegraff offered this incident:

In Kisaran, the N.A.T.M. estate was recently the the site of a bloody drama. An assistant, Heer O., when making his way at 5 in the morning to his work, encountered a group of coolies who assumed an unwilling posture. While he was speaking to the men and giving them their orders, he suddenly was dealt a hard blow with the shaft of a hoe, whereupon he fell in a ditch. Forthwith several of these fellows flung themselves on top of him, of course not with all too friendly intentions. Luckily Heer O. was armed with a revolver, and he shot his fierce opponent smack dead. Instead of being deterred, the rest of the band assumed such a threatening stance that the assaulted assistant was forced to make use of his weapon again with the result that a second assailant lost his life and a third was seriously wounded. Only then did the rest finally beat a retreat. [1910:18–19]

Such accounts raise more questions than they answer: Why the "unwilling posture" of the workers? Was the attack premeditated? Were the workers intent on killing the assistant? And why did he think he had no recourse but to commit two murders? All we know is that from the assistant's perspective and the community that supported his case, this was justified self-defense. The fact that he was armed and thus got away with his life is given as proof that more white staff should be distributed weapons.

Some estate managers recognized that a gun-wielding supervisor could provoke more violence than he prevented, but not all white employees were willing to give up this security. In a 1913 report from an Asahan estate manager to his head office, an assistant's dismissal was explained on these grounds:

In retrospect, it seems that Heer E. never went around to inspect the work of the Chinese coolies because he was afraid of their violence if he criticized their work. His lack of personal courage, despite his physical strength, is well-known in Deli. Even among the Hakkas, with whom we have never had trouble, he never went to the fields [where they worked] without very visibly bearing a revolver. [AR][9]

Even if we are to believe that Hakka coolies in the remote areas of Asahan were no trouble, this was not the case elsewhere. Reports of an increasing number of assaults on white personnel appear in the same year from other parts of the East Coast. One local member of the planter community questioned whether there were in fact more assaults or only more reported to the authorities. Arguing the case for the latter, he suggested that formerly such incidents were not divulged and certainly would not have been brought to the attention of the local press (Dixon 1913:59). Increase in the number of assaults *reported* may have had less to do with the incidents themselves than with the existence of a new scapegoat on which to blame them. Reportedly almost as soon as the Deli branch of Sarekat Isalm opened in 1913, it was charged by the European papers with engineering coolie attacks on estate personnel. Mohammad Said, in a history of the North Sumatran press, notes that "depending on how the Dutch press saw the problem, that's how they arranged the news" (1976:43–44).

There was another whipping boy closer at hand. While planters lobbied for more police control to counter *koelieaanvallen*, a team of government-appointed labor inspectors was busy combing the plantation belt to investigate working conditions made infamous by van den

Brand and van Kol ten years earlier. The planters responded to this invasion of their sacred domain by accusing the labor inspectors of undermining both estate discipline and white prestige. Such accusations escalated in later years as the bureau expanded its personnel and its inquiries. In 1913 the indictments remained opaque and circumspect, directed for example at the Arbeidsinspectie's practice of having workers' complaints lodged through overseers and interpreters, who, the companies claimed, distorted the facts and added to the tensions between labor and management (Dixon 1913:62).

In the early years the Arbeidsinspectie had minimal impact since the information they were given access to was carefully limited. Although inspectors supposedly made efforts to talk to workers directly, most managers made a point of being present during these sessions, thereby imposing heavy censure on any complaints. In such situations the workers, for example, would deny that the roofs on their homes leaked despite the obvious fact that they were studded with holes (KvA 1913:8). Those workers who did speak up were severely reprimanded or quickly hushed by their overseers. In other cases they were simply demoted to lower paying jobs (ibid. 87). Still, information did trickle out about maltreatment, forced overtime, bad housing, and various means by which overseers withheld or appropriated their workers' earnings.

The Arbeidsinspectie was an information-gathering service, not a vehicle for change. Skeptical of its efficacy, some estate workers chose to file their discontents through more direct methods. The following is condensed from a somewhat long-winded 1913 account of such an incident:

Several years ago during the tobacco sorting season several ringleaders threw the estate into total commotion. The entire Chinese coolie population numbering 300–400 strong stopped work and marched to the manager's office complaining that they were inadequately paid and demanding that the books be reexamined. The accountant said the books were in order and admonished them in the name of peace to return to their work. On the following afternoon the workers went back to their jobs and received their pay. When they went home at 5 in the evening, nothing untold had yet occurred. It seemed that they were still not well enough organized to undertake an action.

It was early morning, still dark, when the Bengalese nightwatchman came to tell the manager that the head overseer was there and wanted to speak to him. The plot was betrayed. He now knew the names of the ringleaders—a group of 6 dangerous fellows who especially had it in for the manager. On the signal of one of them everyone [in the tobacco sorting shed] was to rise up and go for the manager. That night a chicken was slaughtered to seal their pact. The coolies figured that in the commotion no one would see who actually made the assault and thus no one would be punished. The next morning as the coolies entered the packing shed the ringleaders were picked off [by the estate police] one by one—

and when the rest of the workers realized that their leaders were gone, they lost their lust for the action and simply went on with their work. [Dixon 1913:52–58]

What can we learn from such an account? First that the Asian overseers played an instrumental and subversive role in averting the action; two, that recourse to violence came only *after* the first nonviolent protest proved ineffective. And three, by the very way in which the incident is described, we are led to believe that mass support for the protest was conjured up by only six "ringleaders" who "had it in for the administrator." In later accounts this invocation of the personal was repeatedly used, denying the consenual nature of the demands.

In the next few years, government-sponsored inquiries into the alleged increase in assaults and labor unrest continued. In 1915 recommendations were made to (1) stop assistants from striking coolies, (2) use a more careful selection process to assess the suitability of prospective staff, (3) make sure that assistants are well-versed in labor regulations, (4) strictly control the activities of overseers and foremen so that workers do not become financially beholden to them, (5) improve workers' wages, and (6) strongly forbid relations between European assistants and female contract coolies. In this connection the ban on married European personnel was abolished.[10]

Although improved working conditions for the Asian work force were nominally included in such recommendations, we can see that more attention was placed on "quality control" of European assistants. Several years earlier the Union of Deli Assistants (Vakvereeniging van Assistenten in Deli) was formed in the face of strong opposition from executive boards in Europe. One high government official in Java referred to the union as a sign of "degeneration" in estate relations, bordering on "*chantage*" (OvSI 1917:39). What this "blackmail" actually consisted of is unclear. In *De Planter*, the news organ of the assistants' union, grievances were frequently aired concerning wages, bonuses, furloughs, legal protection (in cases of assaults on workers), and general working conditions; still, there is little to suggest that these demands were ever translated into labor action or that the union represented any real challenge to the corporate elite. Nonetheless, the European enclave's "united front" in Deli was—in spirit at least—weakened.

In 1917 and 1918 official inquiries were renewed into the causes of frequent assaults on supervisory personnel. Once again assistants were reprimanded for their "hot-tempered" and "tactless" behavior vis-à-vis their workers, for the "rude" and "harsh" fashion in which they addressed their Asian subordinates (Heijting 1925:56). Although some informed observers seemed to be suggesting that a well-trained, experienced, and "tactful" managerial staff was a necessary and *sufficient* condition for creating harmonious labor relations, the majority of planters were not so easily deluded. More preventive and coercive measures were taken against those "elements among the workers who could be compelled to perform their duties only by fear of punishment" (OvSI 1918:66)—and by ensuring that none had arms. In the 1916 report of the East Coast of Sumatra Institute we read:

It would be advisable to forbid coolies to bear pointed weapons at work. I think this prohibition is a very necessary measure and it is regrettable that it is left to the discretion of estate personnel as to whether they choose to enforce it or not. Many planters do not [enforce it] because they want to show their workers that they are not afraid. This is an entirely misplaced boldness and it would be preferable that the directors make their wishes known to the estate managers that this ruling should be strictly enforced. [OvSI 1917:36]

In the following year this advice was heeded. The *pisoblati verbod* (prohibition on weapons) legally forbid contract coolies to bear weapons (or pointed objects of any kind) during working hours without the employer's permission.[11]

While such efforts were made to alter the nature of the confrontation between assistants and coolies, more immediate measures were sought to avert the confrontation altogether. Predawn roll calls (on which occasion many assaults took place) were abolished (OvSI 1917:35), and work orders and other directives from above were now to be transmitted only by Asian supervisors, putting them, rather than Europeans, in the cross fire (ibid. 57). In addition, initial plans were made to establish *tussenpersonen* (go-betweens) to mediate management–worker relations, chosen from among those workers deemed reliable and trustworthy by the managers (ibid.).

For the most part, these measures were palliatives, as many observers noted at the time. In a sobering report of the Arbeidsinspectie from 1918, we find a striking shift in explanation: not merely a preoccupation with "disorder" and physical assaults but an attempt to consider the structural features of violence embedded in the relations of production themselves. Commenting on the tenor of labor relations, the author writes:

In short, the relations are the following: on the one hand, well-organized employers with aides, the assistants; on the other hand, a large mass of workers, still unaware of their strength, who lack a means of defense, and for whom the penal sanction is their foremost weapon for legal protection of their rights (not their interests); the right to strike is forbidden them.
    We see that the former group is powerfully organized into two large planters' associations which are bound by law to certain regulations concerning labor time, services, and minimum wages, but within these bounds, has the right to

increase the labor intensity of its unorganized workforce as much as possible, and to maintain wages as low as possible. . . . so long as the employers strictly adhere to the stipulated labor contract, the coolie can neither avoid nor resist the greatest possible demands placed on him, because he has neither the right as an individual, nor in a group, to refuse the legally enforced demands on his labor. [van Lier 1919:202]

Under such conditions, workers took recourse to forms of resistance that effectively impaired production without using the strike weapon: The report continues:

What is to some extent in his power, and fully utilized, is a passive resistance against the employer's demands by working slowly, badly, or carelessly, by not following directions, by ruining the produce (for example, by mixing water into the latex); in short by various means which advance and strengthen his personal interest, i.e. an absolute minimum performance of actual labor for an absolute minimum wage. [ibid.:202]

Few other contemporary accounts described with such precision the conditions that fed labor conflict and, at the same time, encouraged increased production output. Earnings for the assistants were based on two primary components: an extremely low base wage, and *tantiemes*. These bonuses fluctuated enormously each year, reflecting changes in the world market price of estate products but more closely reflecting variations in the labor performance of the approximately 500 workers under each field assistant. Thus the Arbeidsinspectie recognized that an improved base wage for assistants would do nothing to alleviate labor tensions since "*relations* between the coolies and their employer, in practice, will still remain unchanged" (ibid.). New protective measures improved the general living conditions of the assistants and checked excessive demands on *their* labor, but a more important structural component of the relationship remained unaltered, namely, that "the financial interests of the assistants demand that the labor performance of the coolies remain as great as possible" (ibid. 209).

Promotions and increased earnings for assistants clearly rested on increased exploitation of coolie labor; at the same time, such inordinate labor demands created more resentment, often manifesting itself in violent and deadly assaults on the assistants themselves. Caught in this double bind, the assistants were willing to ease up the pressure on their underlings only "in the most extreme border-line cases of excessive labor demands" (ibid.). That is, in those cases where the assistants *felt* that heavier exactions would threaten their own lives,

one can expect some relaxing of the existing labor relations, but the present *system* itself will, in essence, remain unchanged [since] these labor relations arise from the unjust manner in which the coolies' labor power is used, on the basis of a labor contract which subordinates their labor power to the needs of the employers. [ibid.]

On Java an organized labor movement was emerging in part through an alliance of European and Asian workers, but in Deli such a threat to corporate hegemony was quickly averted. By introducing new rulings to improve the lot of the assistants, the firms more strongly sealed the alliance on their side. Assaults on their lives, however, continued. In 1924 it was calculated that an assistant in fifteen years of service had a 3% chance of being killed by a worker and at least a 50% probability of being physically assaulted (Middendorp 1924:4).

Statistics concerning the number of assaults on European and Asian supervisors are scarce, and when figures from two different sources are available they rarely agree. Figures for assaults on Asian overseers were not even collected until 1925; for European personnel they are somewhat more complete but still problematic. For instance, one source states that 13 Europeans were assaulted in 1919, another sets the figure at twice that number. Between 1914 and 1923 the number ranged between 25 and 35 attacks at a time when the labor force totaled about 200,000.

The proliferation of texts, articles, and reports on estate labor unrest bore little connection to the number of assaults within the plantation enclave itself. Not surprisingly, attention to this issue related more to the general increase in anticolonial, nationalist, and radical political activity *off* the estates, and to the fact that indictments against the penal sanction were becoming more pronounced. While the 1916 *Kroniek* of the East Coast of Sumatra Institute could mention 12 native organizations and dismiss them as posing "no threat to Dutch authority" (OvSI 1917:54), in the succeeding years they were not written off so lightly. Particular attention was drawn to those associations whose apparent "economic motives" were found to be "politically based" (OvSI 1918:41). Special note was made of the profusion of Chinese and Malay language newspapers expounding "revolutionary and socialist ideas," and of articles "which had no business being written" (OvSI 1918:47).

In 1920 a strike among the Deli Railway Company workers gave the planters more cause for worry because contract coolies as well as free laborers had been involved. The strike was broken, in part because the contract coolies withdrew from the action when threatened with enforcement of the penal code. But the fact that they had participated at all made the plantation industry seriously question the possibility of such a situation arising in their protected domain. In this regard the 1920 Arbeidsinspectie wrote:

The possibility is not excluded, that such labor conflicts in the long run could even happen with contract workers, taking into consideration the fact that with this kind of workforce desires and passions could easily be aroused; in which case, confrontation with the employers would be unavoidable. In general the so-called "power position" [machtspositie] of workers has increased in recent years, and it is not at all inconceivable that the plantation workers' "power position," which still lies dormant, will also emerge. [KvA][12]

In analyzing the causes of the railway strike, the Arbeidsinspectie took a line that it reiterated in later years; namely, that the workers' economic demands should not be accepted as the underlying and "real" reason for the strike action. A similar warning is offered vis-à-vis the estate coolies:

Taking into account the indifference and docility of the Javanese, other reasons than obtaining a financial improvement of their lot would have to be at the root of the strikes. The workers' desires in this [financial] respect are not very great, so that other factors must come into play. Often workers take part in a strike on the instigation of someone from outside the laboring population who for some reason deems it in his interest to incite such an action. And it is where workers feel discontent with their treatment that such a leader will have easy success. . . . It is therefore of the utmost importance that employers pay attention to the grievances of their workers. [ibid.]

And so they did to a greater, but still limited degree. The Arbeidsinspectie of 1920 is the first to enumerate the number and causes of assaults by workers on management—and vice versa. It gives a list of 39 estate managers prosecuted for infractions of the coolie ordinance due to, inter alia, inadequate housing and irregular or withheld wage payments. In addition, 90 cases of "blows inflicted" on workers by supervisory personnel are cited.

The Deli railway strike provoked other strategies for defusing a potentially dangerous situation. The earlier proposal to establish tussenpersonen formed the basis for setting up "labor councils" where carefully selected worker representatives, so-called vertrouwensmannen (liaison men) would meet monthly with the estate administrator (in small committees "to avoid political intentions") to discuss the workers' complaints. The plan had little success. On the Adolina estate the experiment was stopped on the workers' request, and on the Laras estate the employer was informed by his workers that only 2 of the 13 vertrouwensmannen had any notion of what they were supposed to be doing (KvA 1923:28). After several such failures, the idea was shelved, reappearing in another form—as an estate intelligence network—some years later.

The number of assaults on white personnel remained relatively constant throughout the early and mid-1920s, but violent manifestations of labor unrest were apparently on the increase for the same period. In

1924 references appear to a greater number of labor riots, in which workers collectively marched on tobacco (sorting) sheds, estate offices, and homes of European personnel, damaging the buildings or threatening the lives of the occupants: "One of the many examples of such mass protest was the bombardment of the office and the fermenting sheds at the end of 1922 on the Tandem estate, after which that same night tens of coolies were imprisoned for up to three months" (Middendorp 1924:23). The mid-1920s mark a turning point in the nature of government and company response to labor protest and popular resistance in general. Although the shift toward more repressive strategies of labor control was signaled by an Indies-wide curb on civil rights and political expression, the particular form it was to take on Deli's estates was so fierce that in later years it did successfully block most forms of plantation-based protest.

Labor Protest and the Legal Mechanisms of Political Repression

As early as 1854 suppression of civil rights had been written into the Indies legal code, strictly prohibiting any political associations or assemblies considered dangerous to the public order.[13] In 1915 a new provision formally recognized the right of assembly and association, but it was only three years later that its specifications were defined and the law was put into practice. This 1918 decree, however, strictly forbade any clandestine organizations and meetings. While allowing for closed (i.e., for members only) outdoor meetings without permit, it forbade all public, open-air meetings without prior permission of the local authorities. In 1919 a further qualification allowed that "officers and employees of the police" were to have freedom of admission, and for closed meetings notification had to be made 5 days in advance. In addition, as in 1854, the governor general was invested with the right to proclaim illegal any association that he deemed in conflict with the public order.

Given the political nature of the labor movement on Java during this period, the legal code amounted to a virtual ban on any form of collective action. Commenting on the use of the 1915 penal code during the strikes of the 1920s, a U.S. Department of Labor report noted: "The provisions of the Penal Code applicable to trade unions were vague, leaving wide discretionary powers to the enforcing authorities. Even a first attempt to organize a strike to combat just grievances could thus be prosecuted" (U.S. Dept. of Labor 1951:134). Over the next few years numerous specifications were appended to further restrict political, and thus labor, actions of any kind. In 1923 the government responded to the wave of strikes that broke out in Java (where the coolie ordinance, i.e., the penal sanction, was not in effect) with an amendment specifically prohibiting *the instigation* of strike actions.[14] Known as the *artikel karet* (the rubber article) because of the elasticity with which it could be interpreted, this Article 161 *bis* became a primary tool used to halt labor protest and left-wing demonstrations and to further curb freedom of the nationalist press. Ostensibly meant to hinder radical political agitation, it had far greater consequences.

The government's refusal to distinguish political agitation from criminal offense, or labor actions from political incitement, meant that anyone actively participating in a work stoppage by verbally supporting it (for example, by simply addressing the workers) was subject to criminal prosecution. For estate workers, refusal to work had long been considered a serious infraction of the labor contract under the coolie ordinance. In the 1920s, economic demands were labeled as political actions and treated as criminal offenses. In referring to the implications of Article 161 *bis*, Virginia Thompson wrote:

Any labor agitation that tended to disturb public order or contravene a labor contract was liable to penalization. Theoretically this legislation aimed to prevent political agitators from vitiating economic issues, but in practice its terms could be applied to prohibit any organization of strikes. [1947:160]

Ruth McVey similarly questions the government's conflation of political and economic issues; here, in regard to the railway strike of 1923 she noted: "The government justified its severity by arguing that the strike was inspired by political and not economic motives. . . . It could hardly be claimed that the strike was pushed upon the workers by their leaders, since, as the government's own report pointed out, the reverse was patently the case. Union demands had been nonpolitical and were in most cases justified" (1965:153).

This blurred administrative vision of what comprised political agitation, economic grievance, and ergo criminal offense provided a base for government repression of anticolonial resistance in Java. In regard to the issues that arose in Deli during the mid- and late 1920s, it is important to keep this legal and ideological justification in mind. It colored the tenor of labor relations and the interpretations of imagined insurgence and real confrontation.

Planters on the Alert

In 1925 the communist-led dockworkers' union staged strikes in the Javanese port cities of Semarang and Surabaja, and at the Belawan harbor outside Medan. All three were basically defeated, resulting in a blacklisting of alleged communist participants and a government decree denying the right of assembly to communist-based organizations. But the International was sung in Deli and the 3,000 or so women and men marching on the governor's office were given extensive coverage in planters' circles and by the local press (Said 1976:126). Remarking on the harbor strike, the *Kroniek* of that year concludes: "It was not an economic strike, rather one of a more or less political nature, instigated by communist elements, and it must have been mostly fear of these leaders which caused the strike's quick spread" (OvSI 1926:29).

This is the first year in which the *Kroniek* allots a special section to "political agitation and disturbances of the peace." Communist propaganda is reported on several estates where the alleged perpetrators were immediately returned to Java. In Langkat and Siantar a number of estate clerks are dismissed because of "communist tendencies" (ibid.). And the estates of Bekioen, Klambir Lama, and Kwala Binjei were the sites of serious riots during which a police commandant, among others, was wounded; anti-British sentiments are reported to have been demonstrated on the Tandjong Bringin estate, where an English assistant was assaulted. These are the only cases specifically mentioned, with the following general observation:

Disturbances of the peace occurred on other estates, but it is not clear whether the more fundamental causes were political; since the riots took place within several days of one another on different estates, one could surmise that this was organized agitation, but the facts suggest that they were only isolated incidents. [The disturbances] had to do with some vexation over an assistant's remark about their work in the tobacco sheds and resentment at police interference during a gambling party. [ibid.]

For the same year, the Arbeidsinspectie gives a somewhat more substantial description of the nature of the disturbances but with no reference to communist influence of any kind. Of the 30 reported assaults, 6 were *massa-aanvallen* (mass attacks). Here, for the first time, a collective refusal to work is labeled as a "strike." Refusal to work on one estate had followed a grievance against a foreman who had blocked the marriage of two contract laborers. On another estate a riot followed after the wages of one Chinese laborer had been cut; his work was supposedly below standard quality, but the worker refused to accept the assistant's decision and along with several of his comrades assaulted the assistant and the head overseer. Police, called in to restore order, killed one worker in the process. Elsewhere, several laborers walked off their jobs in protest against an assistant whose orders were invariably accompanied by repeated beatings; the assistant was transferred, and the workers returned to their jobs. On another estate a crowd of workers hooted and hurled bricks at an assistant whom they complained was unduly harsh.

On two tobacco estates serious disturbances broke out among Chinese workers in protest over their diminished earnings that year. After a short scuffle with the police, order was reportedly restored. On another estate the workers simply refused to accept their wages until the administrator and a recently appointed overseer were dismissed. Here the workers armed themselves with knives, axes, and truncheons, but again order was restored by the police. Here was the only case in which the riot was attributed to political issues, supposedly instigated by a recently dismissed foreman. The final incident mentioned in the Arbeidsinspectie report was a riot on a tobacco estate where several new Chinese workers had supposedly spread a rumor among other laborers that one of them was going to be killed by an assistant who had recently been assaulted. Here too, "peace" was quickly restored but not before a great deal of damage to company property.

The Arbeidsinspectie report suggests several things: first, a disproportionate number of the incidents of labor protest were perpetrated by Chinese workers, who, at the time, made up only one-tenth of the work force but committed one-third of the assaults on supervisory personnel. Second, most of the riots seem to have occurred on the tobacco estates in the older districts of the plantation belt, where most of the Chinese were employed.

This concentration of incidents seems to relate closely to the fluctuations in the average price of tobacco during these years. Between 1925 and 1929 the price of Deli tobacco halved on the world market, the most dramatic decline since the last century; with it the wages of tobacco workers fell for the first time in several decades. The tantieme earnings of assistants also diminished, creating added tensions within (and therefore between) both parties.

Moreover, incidents of labor unrest were more likely to be reported near Medan, where the government-judicial bodies were closer at hand. In any case the preponderance of such incidents among Chinese workers on tobacco estates calls into question the assertion made by many company spokesmen that disturbances were more frequent among Javanese newcomers. The latter were usually recruited for the rapidly developing estates in the outlying districts, not the older center encircling Medan.

Complaints and requests lodged by workers during 1925 were more frequent, but unchanged in content. They concerned obligatory overtime and transfers of workers to other estate divisions without their families, exhorbitant prices in the company stores, and, as always, physical maltreatment by staff members. The Arbeidsinspectie considered most of these complaints unfounded, lodged "by persons who are under the influence of others who prefer to keep out of harm's way" (KvA 1926:63).

In 1926–27 attention to labor unrest and assaults on the estates is minimal in both the Arbeidsinspectie and the Kroniek, although the actual number of attacks on Asian overseers rose dramatically (from 24 to 61). These were years of strong opposition to the penal sanction, and the increasing number of reports of *klapzaken* ("blows inflicted by supervisors on coolies") must have added weight to the case of those seeking the penal sanction's abolition. From 1926 to 1927 the number of *klapzaken* increased by 70% (from 303 to 548). The *Arbeidsinspectie* attributed this to the large number of *slechte elementen* ("bad elements") among the newly recruited workers, thus whitewashing the assistants of the blame.

But one case, thoroughly exposed in the Malay language press, made it more than clear that atrocities were going on that even the planters could not ignore. The "Pulau Mandi scandal" involved the brutal maltreatment of workers by a Japanese assistant on a rubber estate in the Asahan district. The entire court proceedings appeared in serial form in *Benih Timor* (a Medan Malay-language newspaper) during October 1926, revealing the following facts:[15]

Assistant Kozo Oriuchie was tried and found guilty on 12 counts: for repeatedly beating his workers with a rotan stick and ordering his overseers to do the same; for locking up workers for weeks on end (except to leave for work) in a 2 × 2 × 2m hut. A number of workers testified to being stripped, having their bodies smeared with horse manure and having been force-fed manure and human feces. The assistant was dismissed by the company and the planters' association immediately ousted Pulau Mandi from its membership. Several companies issued circulars to their estate divisions warning that an assistant found guilty of such maltreatment would be fired. [OvSI 1927:32] Oriuchie's original 3½ year sentence was shortened to 2½ years, and eventually he paid a fine in lieu of serving the full-prison term after the outrage had died down. [Said 1977:153]

To cleanse Deli's tainted image in the outside world, several months later the planters' association sponsored (and paid for) a visit of Javanese regents to examine the living conditions of estate workers. As planned, they publicly lauded the exemplary material conditions in which the workers were living. *Pewarta Deli*—a nationalist Medan paper started in 1910 with an audacious, witty, and sharp-tongued editorial staff—challenged the objectivity of these particular observers, suggesting that perhaps a more informed contingent of *bumiputera* (natives of the Indies) with knowledge of and familiarity with the estates, but with "absolutely no connection with the companies," would have undertaken a more realistic appraisal of the situation (*Pewarta Deli*, 15 Mar. 1926).

In the meantime, most of the government's energies in Deli and elsewhere in the Indies were focused on the "communist threat." In April 1926 a new provision was added to the penal code, Article 153 *bis* and *ter*, further limiting freedom of the press and stipulating even harsher punishment, up to 6 years imprisonment, for those who "intentionally express in word, writing or illustration be it obliquely, conditionally or in disguised terms, approval of disturbances of the public peace, or overthrowing or interference with the established authority in the Netherlands or the Netherlands Indies or who create an atmosphere favorable to this" (quoted in McVey 1965:326). Invoking this new artikel karet, authorities formally disbanded the Indonesian Communist Party (Partai Komunis Indonesia, PKI) in May of that year, and those labor unions on Java which would "have provided the major revolutionary thrust were in a state of collapse" (ibid. 327). A communist revolt—whose failure was virtually assured before it began—was squashed and by December the mass arrest of all those persons known and alleged to be communists ensured the movement's (temporary) decline (ibid. 345).

As news of the Javanese uprising spread to Sumatra, Deli's power elite, comprised of state officials, police, planters, and sultans, went on their qui vive;[16] "intelligence services were doubly vigilant" and house searches and arrests yielded tens of "communist agitators." In the Serdang district a communist propagandist was sentenced to one and a half years imprisonment, and in Binjei ten communists were sentenced to prison terms of two and a half to four years. But on the estates proper there were few incidents of political agitation. In January, three alleged communists were arrested in a tobacco shed of the Deli Tobacco Company and returned to Java; elsewhere, several workers of the same company were fired for spreading communist propaganda (ibid. 34).

Despite, or perhaps because of, the increasingly repressive measures taken to round up communists and bridle the local press, Pewarta Deli came out with more daring articles than ever. One, titled "Further curbs on the mouth of the press," openly criticized Article 153 bis, and another entitled, "Which is more dangerous, those suspected of being communists or thieves?," unabashedly mocked the activities of the local rechercheurs (police agents). Relating the story of a barber and a small shopkeeper arrested on scanty evidence for being communists, Pewarta Deli (1926) writes:

What puzzles this writer is whether they were arrested for being communist or for reading something in a newspaper which is said to be communist? If the latter is the case, it is the same as saying a person who talks about a theft can be accused of carrying out a robbery. Astounding!

Noting that police agents were paid bonuses of 25 guilder for every communist captured, Pewarta Deli suggested that this was fine incentive for labeling just about anyone a communist with no evidence to go on. These arrests were only the initial stirrings of a full-fledged vigilante movement that really only began to mushroom in 1928, more than a year after the communist movement in Java had been successfully surpressed and forced underground.

Reassessments of Labor Protest, 1928–29

In 1928 assaults on white personnel rose from 36 to 54 and complaints lodged by workers against Asian overseers mounted considerably. In contrast to earlier years the *Arbeidsinspectie* and the *Kroniek* were quick to point out that the causes could (and should) not be attributed to the ineptitude of the supervisory personnel alone. The *Arbeidsinspectie* related the increased complaints against Asian overseers to "the fact that workers in this region were less willing than formerly to remain silent about their grievances, that the workers are possibly staging attacks themselves to give vent to their resentment against a foreman who, for one reason or another, they dislike" (KvA n.d. *Dertiende*:99). And concerning the assaults on white personnel,

> Except in those cases where the attackers are directly or indirectly influenced by extremists, *in which case the assault has absolutely no relation with the labor situation*, the deeper reasons for the majority of assaults lie in the labor performance of the attackers, which is, in terms of quality and quantity, below what is expected of them. [ibid. 95, emphasis added]

The *Kroniek* too alleged that these attacks were rarely connected to the assistants' behavior but resulted from "other, deeper causes" (OvSI 1929:45) (what these were exactly still remained uncertainly defined). The European press also expressed fear that some new current was rippling through the plantation populace. *De Planter* (published by the Union of Estate Assistants), which had often argued that the coolie attacks were not always the workers' fault, became more and more convinced that "destructive outside influences" were now at play (Said 1977:160). And the staunchly conservative *Deli Courant* now claimed that the assaults no longer could be dismissed as matters of personal revenge but as the consequence of a new "consciousness" incited by external sources (ibid. 161).

Matters were made worse (or, as some contended, *made*) by the arrival of Iwa Kusumasumantri in Medan in early 1928. Sumantri, a well-known proponent for nationalist independence, had been educated in Leiden and was an active participant there in the radical student movement. After leaving Holland, he spent 1925–26 in Moscow teaching at a school for Asian revolutionaries and writing political pamphlets on, among other subjects, imperialist exploitation and peasant movements in the Indies (McVey 1965:221, 241). Arriving in Medan, Su-

mantri set up a law practice, began organizing workers within and outside the estates, and soon became identified by the European
community as an insidious and influential provocateur of labor unrest.
By Sumantri's own account he not only championed the cause of estate
coolies but actively attempted to recruit and organize them. The vig-
ilance of local authorities made this no easy task. Rather than making
contact with estate workers directly, Sumantri strategically worked on
unionizing drivers who had free and easy access to the estates in virtue
of their jobs and thus could act as convenient messengers, carrying
information from one district to another.[17] Sumantri's tenure in Medan
was short-lived. In July 1929, during an Indies-wide roundup of nationalist leaders, he was arrested. The time he did spend in Deli coincided, not so much with an increase in assaults per se, as with an alleged
general increase in estate-based collective violence—and the European
press was quick to draw a causal connection.

With or without Sumantri the estate workers of the 1920s were
recognized as a different breed from those of ten years earlier, more
aware of their legal rights and more quickly prepared to physically and
verbally express their discontents. While still deliberating the precise
connection between labor unrest and extremist agitation, the government and planter establishment initiated a joint effort to weed out dis-
ruptive elements throughout the East Coast.

In 1928 the two powerful planters associations of DPV and AVROS
in coordination with the Indies Intelligence Bureau (Politieke In-
lichtingsdienst, PID) devised and implemented a cooperative scheme to
keep a closer eye on political activities of the estate population. The
arrangement allowed for estate intelligence agents to be invested with
the official authority of regular police under the PID but with funds
provided by the plantation companies. It was an amenable and a convenient plan for both parties; the government had neither the human nor
fiscal resources to maintain surveillance of the expanding political activities of East Sumatra, and the planters welcomed an official guise for
their spy network (Said 1977:159). In addition a more systematic fin-
gerprinting system for recruited estate workers helped block "undesirable elements" (who had been sent back to Java) from returning again to
another estate. Prison facilities were expanded, and numerous alleged
communists were imprisoned or exiled to Boven Digul in New Guinea
(OvSI 1929:27–30).

Despite numerous allusions to outside influences acting on the estate labor force, most of the 1928 Kroniek's reports on communist roundups provide little evidence of political activity on the plantations proper. Among those listed were two "extremists" working as contract
coolies along with a press rumor that new communist activities were

being planned—of which nothing materialized; and a coolie riot of 200 workers on the Kloempang estate, where police came in to restore order. In the latter , no reference was made to a political motive.

The Arbeidsinspectie's reports on disturbances for that year reveal most to have been based on minor grievances and minor demands, such as 100 Javanese workers marching on a controller's office protesting that they had not received their proper pay. When it was learned that the estate in question had recently changed ownership and had closed its accounting books two days earlier under the new proprietor, the incident ended. On another estate a secret association of Chinese workers (whose ostensible purpose was mutual aid but whose motives were found to be "less innocent") was disbanded and the "ringleaders" were returned to China. Elsewhere a group of 35 Chinese workers refused to follow planting orders; when it was found that an overseer had instigated the action, he alone was punished and returned to China. On yet another tobacco estate a team of Chinese laborers refused to work until their usual bonus was paid. As the bonuses had been withheld because of the poor quality of the work, the agitators were punished and returned to China.

We should note: none of these events was specifically tied to "outside elements" or political motive. Given this background, it is difficult to understand the 1929 explosion of concern and panic among Deli's European community over "insecurity on the estates." The profusion of newspaper copy and of government reports and circulars connecting estate labor unrest to extremist agitation in volume alone far exceeded what had been produced in the entire preceding ten-year period. For example, a quick survey of *Pewarta Deli* in 1928 yields only a few articles on the penal sanction and estate-related issues. In 1929, on the other hand, every few days and sometimes daily, some reference is made in front-page headlines to court cases involving, arrests of, and labor actions by the estate population. As *Benih Timor* had done with the Pulau Mandi scandal in 1926, *Pewarta Deli* published a blow-by-blow account of a coolie's trial for killing a European assistant. The hanging of another coolie was related in gruesome and vivid detail.

Cumulative lists of coolie assaults appeared in the *Kroniek* and in the *Arbeidsinspectie*. As more information was amassed and information about the labor situation became more accessible to both the European and indigenous literate communities, it became more difficult for either group to plead ignorance as to estate conditions on the East Coast. The *causes* of this proliferation of material are open to question, however, and were seriously questioned at the time. Company and government authorities expressed alarm at the increase in the number of assaults and incidents of mass labor actions, but for the latter, statistics were never collected. For the former, the actual figures vary considerably; some sources cited an increase from 43 to 63 assaults on white personnel between 1928 and 1929, while others placed these figures at 54 and 61, respectively (KvA n.d. *Veertiende*:109). Some of this discrepancy can be accounted for by different methods of calculation. It seems that in later years "threats" as well as actual physical assaults were included in some counts.

In addition, between 1925 and 1929 the estate work force experienced its most rapid expansion, unparalleled before or after this period. In five years it grew by 50%, that is, by 100,000 workers. In regard to the actual ratio of the number of assaults to the total number of workers, the increase between 1928 and 1929 represents the *smallest* change in that five-year period. But those in power were interested in the absolute number of assaults, not relative increase; and no matter what the discrepancy between these various calculations, clearly there were more such incidents in 1929 than ever before. In fact the Arbeidsinspectie noted that the figures provided for 1929 were probably seriously underestimated. At least 24 assaults and 22 threats on personnel later came to their attention that initially had not been reported (ibid. 108).

For the European establishment in Deli and elsewhere, the frequent occurrence of physical violence signaled a more general change in labor relations, and a new threat to the prevailing social order. In a report of that year prepared by the Permanent Labor Commission set up in 1925 to investigate estate labor conditions, the attitude of planters and government was clearly expressed:

The principal cause of the majority of assaults must be sought deeper . . . in the present-day spirit of the workers; a spirit, which is partly unconscious, but also in part intentionally fostered by destructive propaganda through agitation and the Indies press, emanating from Java and in this region itself. [Treub 1929:22]

The authorities paid lip service to a distinction between "common criminals" and "subversive agitators" but in practice both were considered *slechte elementen*, an amorphous category of those deemed an economic or a political hindrance to the estate industry. The advice of the commission continued:

Two elements must be separated. There is the unwilling constantly resisting, criminal element; and there is the changed mentality resulting from a growing consciousness. Insofar as this changed mentality entails lawlessness, an unreasonable refusal to fulfill one's obligations, and insofar as this insubordination manifests in resistance to the employer, the strongest actions should be taken against it. Police and justice must stand shoulder to shoulder; against all which is extreme or excessive, or threatens to have that tendency. . . . Yet insofar as today's coolie demands better treatment, this mentality must be reckoned with.

It goes along with the fact that a coolie will no longer accept treatment which he considered normal 10 or 20 years ago. . . . This changed attitude is a primary factor with which the government and the planter must reckon. However, there is no need to fear for the life of the industry, because if the undesirable and criminal persons are expelled, there always exists a large mass of workers who will peacefully perform their work. But even this scarce breed has become more conscious in recent years. The contract coolie of 1928 is quite different from the one of 1915 or 1920. This means that in the future the coolies must be handled in a different manner than what has heretofore been the case. [ibid. 22]

The latter part of the labor commission's recommendations, at least for the time being, fell on deaf ears. Although police, politicians, and planters were willing to acknowledge this new "consciousness," their examination of its causes were strictly circumscribed, confined to the sparks that ignited this violence rather than the combustible composition of the situation itself.

Thus several major questions remained unanswered. Many sources hint at some strategic realignment of the work force, but was there a qualitatively new form of labor resistance underfoot, different in scope and content from that which occurred a decade earlier? Was there a regional clustering of incidents, a concentration on certain types of estates, or a pattern in the demands or sequence of labor actions? What were the possible bases for a more common self-awareness among workers during these years, apart from outside agitation alone? And finally, to what extent did labor protest encroach upon the planters' power, subvert prevailing economic and social relations, or call for a transformation rather than a mere alteration of them? Despite the extraneous detail and gaping holes, some discernible patterns do emerge from the incidents and discourses around them, which I examine in more detail below.

Labor Protest and the Planters' Panic: Quelling the Red Peril

"Something is amiss in estate labor relations."
[governor of Sumatra's East Coast, 1929]

In January 1929, 9 assistants and 1 Asian overseer were assaulted on the estates of Bahsoemboe, Pagar Marbau, Mendaris, Kenopan Oeloe, Bukit Tinggi, Aek Pamineke, Batang Serang, Sungei Behasa, and Tjinta Radja OvSI 1930:48–51). In February there was a temporary lull, but roundups of various alleged PKI leaders and nationalists continued. In March, 6 assistants and 4 Asian overseers were assaulted on the estates of Lobo Dalam, Klambir Lama, Serapoh, Gedong Johore, Mabar, Poeloe Rambung, and Limau Manis. At Tanjung Morawa estate 33 Chinese coolies attacked and wounded an overseer and on the Soekaranda estate an assistant, Arbman Bergh, was assaulted and murdered. At the end of the same month a "strike" of 11 coolies broke out on the Soengei Putih estate in protest against physical maltreatment by a foreman.

In April, 14 more assaults were reported. At Mariendal an assistant was threatened by a Chinese coolie; at Tanjung Kubu an assistant was assaulted by a coolie, who was restrained with a revolver. At Pabatu and Sempali estates a Chinese overseer was attacked and wounded by a Chinese coolie. At Tanjung Morawa a worker wounded a foreman in a dispute over a woman. At Simpang Ampat and Sungei Behasa workers attacked an assistant. At Bulu Cina a Chinese worker "mishandled" an overseer. At Adolina a Javanese female worker threatened a female overseer but was restrained. At the Kloempang estate 14 Chinese coolies were sentenced to 1½ to 8 years imprisonment for attempting to kill the head overseer. At Bandar Kwala an English assistant was seriously wounded by a Javanese coolie. At Tanjung Jati, Tanjung Bringin, and Bandar Kwala plantations, assistants were threatened by Chinese and Javanese workers.

In May, 3 overseers were threatened or assaulted at Paja Bakong, Simpang Ampat, and Bekiun, and on the Namoe Trassi estate an assistant was threatened by 4 Chinese workers. In June, 6 more overseers and 4 assistants were attacked. In July, 20 coolies threatened an overseer, and at the Parnabolan estate, an assistant's wife was murdered. News of this latter incident spread throughout the Indies and became a cause célèbre of those who had long criticized what they saw as the government's leniency toward the native population. Two assistants from the Adolina and Sempali estates were threatened and assaulted in the same month. In August, 2 assistants were threatened. In September no incidents were reported. In November, 2 assistants were attacked, in one case by a foreman, and 2 overseers were assaulted. And finally in December a Japanese assistant, an English assistant, and an administrator and assistant were attacked, while the head foreman was murdered.

In total 65 estates were the sites of such incidents; plotting them on a map of the East Coast, we find them to be widely dispersed without contiguity, reaching from the northern- to the southernmost borders of the cultuurgebied, with slightly more concentration on the estates surrounding Medan, where, as noted earlier, disturbances were more likely to be reported. Assaults occurred on the old tobacco estates as well as the new plantations of perennial crops, and repeated assaults on the same estate did occur but were not especially common—two incidents were reported on 11 estates but only one plantation reported three attacks. This is not conclusive but it does suggest that repeated attacks were uncommon. On the other hand, these figures drawn from the Kroniek list only 43 attacks on assistants and 30 on overseers in the same year that the *Arbeidsinspectie* sets these numbers, respectively, at 61 and 143; since the *Arbeidsinspectie* neglected to list the estates concerned, this means that at least 18 more assaults on assistants and 113 more assaults on overseers occurred that could have been repetitions on the same estates.

During these months the European and native press selected certain of these incidents and used them to air publically their respective discontents with the existing labor situation. Those advocating the penal sanction's abolition used the March trial of a coolie accused of murdering an assistant, just as the Parnabolan murder was to be used by their adversaries several months later. As reported in the court testimonies, Assistant Arbman Bergh had docked the pay of a worker, Djemadi, for leaving his job a few minutes early on the grounds that a just-revised ruling stated that workers could no longer return home simply because their piecework was done. On hearing of his punishment, Djemadi pulled a knife on Bergh and stabbed him to death.

Like many of the assaults during these years, the *immediate* provocation was seemingly trivial, certainly not warranting murder. Perhaps for this reason, *Pewarta Deli* singled this one out for public scrutiny, publishing the entire court proceedings in serial form.[18] In editorial commentary the paper argued that it was neither the coolie Djemadi who really killed Bergh nor the assistant Bergh who was really in the wrong; Djemadi's outburst was the expression of a more pervasive anger and resentment among many workers at what they rightly saw as an unjust ruling. Reading through *Pewarta Deli*'s headlines on the following days gives some notion of how daringly they leveled their criticism:

IT'S NOT THE COOLIE DJEMADI WHO SINNED BUT THE PENAL SANCTION
THAT KILLED ASSISTANT BERGH

and

THE PENAL SANCTION HAS BECOME THE MURDERER

The European community, however, still contended that the assault was probably due to a "personal issue" between Bergh and Djemadi. *Pewarta Deli* refused to accept this conclusion, arguing that such justifications were frequently invoked by planters to deflect attention from the real issues at hand. In the end, Djemadi was not hanged but sentenced to fifteen years in prison, a decision received badly by Europeans but with gloating approval in the Indonesian community. The day after the court decision was read, the *Deli Courant* admonished Indonesians for their "snickering" approval of the murder. *Pewarta Deli* responded by accusing the European press of distortion, and in an article entitled "Gevaar-lijke Elementen" (intentionally in Dutch, not Malay, meaning "dangerous elements") the European press, rather than certain coolies, were identified by that well-worn label (3 Apr. 1929).

The planters feared the pervasiveness of violence but, more pointedly, the collective nature of it. Still, from the Kroniek's reports it appears that most assaults were carried out by individuals: only in five cases were two to three persons involved, and in eight cases ten people or more. On the other hand, not all the planters' fears were unfounded. There were collective actions mounted by workers, but most often these took the form of refusals to work rather than physical assaults per se. And it was these collective actions—especially those demonstrating sustained protest, as in the case below—that evoked a McCarthy-like conviction among the planters that communists were at the bottom of it all:

In the beginning of April a growing "restlessness" was reported among the coolies of the Tandem estate, located outside the town of Binjei, northwest of Medan. Not less than 37 Chinese workers marched to Medan to protest the arrest of five of their comrades accused the previous year of instigating communist riots. The protesting workers were immediately repatriated to their homelands, while police guards were sent in to patrol the estate. At the end of the month there was still trouble; 103 coolies refused to work until an overseer was dismissed. The court sentenced all of them to one month's detention, after which 60 more workers were sent back to China. When the remaining workers returned to the estate and again refused to work, they were sentenced to three more months' imprisonment. In June, 60 workers again staged a work-stoppage until police forces quelled the action. Finally, after strict surveillance, a "secret organization" was discovered on the Tandem estate and the court sentenced 26 of its alleged members to four years in prison. [OvSI 1930:30–31]

Coverage in the European press of the events at Tandem described it as a hotbed of communist insurgency; Pewarta Deli, however, had a somewhat different interpretation and accused the Dutch papers of blowing up the incidents to suit their own interests. In the article below from June 1929 entitled "Communisme diantara koeli-koeli" (Communism among the coolies), the Tandem actions are described in a different light:

The situation on the Tandem estates these days has become more and more aggravated. Yesterday we reported that a squad of district police were stationed there because the coolies were becoming rambunctious. Scores of workers have been already detained and charged with inciting obstinacy, fomenting trouble, and refusing to work. The Dutch press reports that there are provocateurs from China among the estate coolies. They are supposedly making communist propaganda and organizing a secret society with the intention of inciting unrest among the workers. These provocateurs and leaders have thus far evaded capture and still cannot be identified. The police are now trying to find out who among the coolies is the ringleader, who is urging them to protest. Estate security appears to have been seriously shaken. Although there have been scores of persons detained, the coolies still dare to fight the authorities and are unwilling to work. Quite a number have fled the estate and thus far have not been caught.

Such is the news of estate security. These coolies are social beings . . . they know the difference between well-being and trouble. . . . It's not as if they don't know that if they run away, if they create disturbances as they have been doing, that they'll be in trouble, that they will not be safe in the plantation sphere. . . . Tens of coolies were recently called before the district court. They were accused of unwillingness to work and defiance of orders. The coolies explained clearly that they were not happy working under a particular overseer, and that they preferred prison to returning to work on that estate. The reason they gave was that the overseer liked to beat the coolies, was unduly severe and gave out unsuitable work. The coolies also brought up an accusation that the overseer had once struck a coolie who died from the blow. The murder case was investigated by the authorities, but the evidence was insufficient to indict the overseer. We don't blame the police. An investigation was made. According to the constitution, there can be no sentence without witnesses and evidence. Thus the overseer was not brought to trial. Even if he could not be sentenced, even if there is no proof against him, one thing is sure: the coolies did not want to take orders from this overseer. . . . Sure the coolies are stubborn, sure they are said to fight, sure they are said to have established a secret organization, but one more thing is certain: the reason they mounted this action was because they were uneasy under this overseer.

The coolies were prosecuted; the overseer remained an overseer on the Tandem estate. This is what is at the root of all the trouble. . . . Do all wrongs have to be pinned on the coolies? Do we have to let the estate authorities scot-free of responsibility? If the estate had gotten rid of the *tandil* or had removed him from contact with the workers, it's sure that we would not have heard about communist propaganda on the estate, it's almost sure we would not need to send 25 district police, it's almost certain that the government authorities and police would not have to waste all their time on estate matters.

Almost every single commotion on the estates has a single cause; the coolies are dissatisfied with how they are treated by the assistants, overseers and other managerial personnel. Disturbances occur because these feelings of malcontent go unheeded. . . . The estate managers can ignore the coolies' complaints because they have the power of the penal sanction behind them, because they have enormous power over the coolies. This legal right causes the *tuan kebun* [estate manager] to assault a coolie, and causes the coolie to make trouble.

This is the general situation on the estates and this is what happened at the Tandem plantation. When the coolies' needs are ignored, they become agitated. This feeling grows and is vented in riots. And when these disturbances occur people call it communism. It doesn't take much to be labelled communist in this colonial state of ours! Whether communist, or extremist, or whatever "ist," only justice and truth can bring some peace. That is the "key" to all the trouble. [28 June 1929]

Pewarta Deli's style is exemplary on several accounts, particularly in its play of irony, sarcasm, and bluntness often used (but seldom so deftly) by the native press to make its case against the government and estate authorities. And like its antagonists, *Pewarta Deli* scrupulously hedged the question as to whether there was in fact a communist movement emerging on the estates. Instead, it played on the planters' fear, implying that this was a label employed to divert attention from the injustices of the labor system, but also suggesting and threatening that if the penal sanction was not abolished, the planters might very well find their fear of a communist threat transformed into reality.

Like the planters, *Pewarta Deli* often overstated its case; by arguing, for example, that Tandem would have been free of problems if only the overseer had been properly disciplined. But the major point of the article stands; whatever labels attached to the disturbances, "communist, extremists, or whatever 'ist'," the *causes* of labor unrest had to be sought in the tensions produced by the social relations (of life and labor), not in the phantom of external agitation.

In some limited ways the planters and government officials acknowledged this. Many reports written during this period began with recommendations for better treatment of workers, higher wages, improved housing, more free time—"all naturally within reasonable bounds"—and a closer to equal ratio of men to women (KvA n.d. Vertiende:104). When it was found that many more assaults were perpetrated against assistants with less than three years' estate experience, recommendations were also made for improved training programs so that new recruits could more quickly familiarize themselves with the language, customs, and mentality of the "underdeveloped" laboring population (ibid. 93).

But most of the reasons found for Deli's labor unrest and the solutions sought to alleviate it fixated on the inadequacy of proper labor control and insufficient police protection. In this regard the Arbeidsinspectie came under renewed attack. Since the Pulau Mandi scandal in 1926, the inspection system had become more thorough and intensive, including "surprise" estate visits by inspectors, to which many planters adamantly objected. Managers criticized the inspectors for speaking directly with the workers and thereby undermining the managers' status, especially vis-à-vis the "worst estate elements." The AVROS solution was to ban all surprise visits and to allow no gatherings in which the workers jointly (and more easily) could lodge their complaints.

Reproach also focused on the Asian overseers. A sharp increase in the number assaulted by coolies was accompanied by a more dangerous development: participation by foremen and overseers in assaults on European personnel, a siding with workers in labor actions, and alleged membership in political and secret organizations directed against foreign rule. As go-betweens their loyalty was no longer to be trusted. Some companies suggested appointing Indonesian graduates of agricultural schools in Java who would be responsible to the European assistants and supervise the foremen, thereby distancing the chain of direct command between white managers and coolies one step further. This would also create a more clear-cut class-based division within the indigenous estate population between those who supervised and those who were subordinate.

Pewarta Deli immediately responded to this divisive strategy in a detailed commentary on the motive and implications behind it, warning in no uncertain terms that any Indonesian willing to play such a role would be an accomplice in exploiting his own people and would be classified as a traitor to their cause. Implementation of the system was delayed for some years. In the meantime, solution was sought in a stricter selection process for "higher quality" overseers, and increased wages to secure their allegiance to the interests of the foreign firms.

Even with this slight diffusion of the blame, those in power rarely wavered in their fundamental assertion that demonstration of collective labor actions must have nationalists or communists at their base. Aside from the Tandem affair, several others received special attention. In May 1929, 16 persons were arrested as members of a "nationalist Javanese organization" whose purported aim was to stage an uprising on 1 May 1930. Coverage in the European press emphasized the presence of nationalist provocateurs. In retaliation, *Pewarta Deli* ran the article, "Nationalists on the estates; is that more sensational than communists?," and charged the European press with falsely coloring the situation "so that anyone reading the paper will think that the coolies have already fallen into the nationalist movement and are under Sukarno's influence" (9 May 1929). The article continues:

Whenever there is some small incident, it's generalized to look as if the coolies are to blame . . . and now, on top of this, they [the Dutch press] compound this with the idea that nationalists have spread like wild fire on the estates. . . . The communists are no longer around to blame, so the Dutch press switches to accusing nationalism. This is playing with fire and their hands will be burned! Pointing a finger at nationalism is the same as saying: if you're bothered by rats, burn down the house!

A week later, an article in the *Deli Courant* described yet another case, this one on the Soengai Toewan estate, connecting the nationalist movement to labor agitation. Elsewhere it was suggested that the events on Kotari (the estate mentioned above) and Soengai Toewan were probably related (OvSI 1930:32). The following story appeared in the *Deli Courant:*

Sometime ago an old Javanese woman from Deli settled in a village nearby the Soengai Toewan estate. Often she had such a stream of people coming to her house that people thought a wedding procession was approaching. Every Friday afternoon she gathered the villagers around her to discuss religious matters. But very soon it became clear that it was not religious matters, but the nationalist movement that they were talking about. It came to the attention of the local authorities, but since it didn't seem a very serious matter, they let it go. In the meantime, more information was collected. It turned out that whoever wanted to take part in these weekly meetings had to contribute 25 guilder and sometimes rice, chickens and eggs. The money and profits from selling the produce were to go to the uprising set for May 1, 1930. . . .

When sufficient evidence was collected by the authorities, the head foreman, another foreman, and 14 coolies were arrested. It was indeed surprising that the head foreman had joined the movement since he had worked for the Senembah Company for 27 years and was the *vertrouwensman* of the administration. In addition, it was established that here had been more or less regular contact made with outsiders. Two times, in the middle of the night, an automobile had arrived at the old woman's house, which wouldn't have been very significant if it wasn't for the unusual hour at which it occurred. [15 May 1929]

The old woman was quickly arrested and the "uprising" averted. But the story was used by at least one East Coast official as an "instructive" example to show that "extreme nationalists were not sitting quiet." He had this to say regarding the apparent quiescence:

On the contrary, they are using apparently innocent means to camouflage their actions. . . . let it be a warning to those who opine that there is no longer ferment in the Indies. The government is more vigilant than in 1926; but if they start again and a rebellion breaks out, it will be much more serious than it was several years ago. Things are brewing again; the growing insecurity [for the staff] on the estates is a symptom of it. [Treub 1929:24]

In the following months more secret organizations were uncovered throughout the *cultuurgebied*. In June, 23 "ringleaders" charged with instigating riots on the Tandem Ilir estate were arrested and a secret organization with "communist tendencies" was disbanded. In July, 6 coolies and a foreman were returned to Java as "undesirable elements"; on the Tjoekir estate, 12 coolies were repatriated after being accused of setting fire to a tobacco shed. In the same month on the estates of Kisaran, Bah Jambi, Tinjowan, and Tanjung Bringin (all about 150 km south of Medan), 60 coolies were arrested for communist activities (OvSI 1930:32). In August, 10 "undesirables" on the Bandar Negeri estate, purported to be members of a secret organization, were returned to Java. On the Gedong Johore estate, 51 Chinese coolies staged a strike over a wage dispute. In September there was again trouble on the Kotari estate; this time 29 Javanese workers were arrested for being members of a secret organization. In November, 27 coolies and a foreman were returned to Java from the Kanopan Ulu estate, and in the same month 400 workers from Tanjung Bringin "rioted" in protest against what they saw as an arbitrary deduction from their wages.

During 1929 the number of workers repatriated as "undesirables" had increased twofold from the previous year to well over a thousand persons.[19] According to East Sumatra's Governor van Sandick, most were political undesirables or persons who had come to Deli "on false premises." By July, labor actions and assaults had been occurring with such frequency that AVROS and the DPV sent a joint secret petition to the Indies governor in Batavia requesting, among other things, that the abolition of the penal sanction be further delayed in the interests of security and peace, and that more police reinforcements be sent to Deli.

During the same month the murder of Assistant Landzaat's wife by the laborer Salim on the Parnabolan estate set loose the few repressive mechanisms that had been held in check up until then. The muted panic of the preceding months crescendoed into an Indies-wide scandal; 167 European women in Deli sent telegrams to Queen Wilhelmina demanding protection (OvSI 1930:44; Said 1977:164). And while newpapers in Java speculated on a "Moscow-Deli connection," army troops were sent by the governor general in Java to "restore order." Within a week of the incident Salim's trial started, five days later he was sentenced, and on October 23 he was scheduled to hang.

From the court proceedings (published in the native and European press) it seems that Salim had been transferred to an estate division far from where his wife was living; for days he petitioned to the head foreman and to Assistant Landzaat to have his wife transferred as well, but the request was denied supposedly because she was already pregnant by another man. Salim told the office clerk that he would not work until the issue was settled. In the meantime Landzaat, angry with Salim for making trouble, threatened to have him punished by the police. Three days later, when Salim's wife still had not shown up, he approached Landzaat's house and, finding him not at home, stabbed the assistant's wife to death.

Other versions of the story were also circulated. According to Hasan Noel Arifin, editor of Pewarta Deli (who went to Parnabolan to investigate the situation more thoroughly), Landzaat had decided to take Salim's wife as his own mistress and would not allow her to be transferred to Salim's division (Said 1977:165; also see 1976:157–61). This did not come out in the trial; at the hearings, the foreman testified that Salim's wife had not wanted to return to him, although she was not in fact pregnant.

Pewarta Deli (24 July 1929) was not satisfied with the testimonies. As with numerous other coolie trials, Salim could not argue his own case or give voice to the more general situation surrounding the incident. The paper proceeded to ask questions the court ignored. The prosecution, of course, asked Salim whether he read communist newspapers and belonged to a communist organization. It did not ask why Landzaat was so easily enraged by Salim's behavior, or why the head foreman had already kicked out two other coolies (before Salim arrived) at the new division. These turned out to be not unimportant questions. Parnabolan's administrator was quietly dismissed after the trial when it was found that there had been repeated incidents of maltreatment and general labor unrest on the estate.

The fact that *Pewarta Deli* refused to treat the Parnabolan affair as anything more than what might be expected from an unjust labor system, was met with sharp disapproval by the European community, which was milking the incident dry for its own purposes. At the end of July a secret circular was sent to all the Deli trading houses requesting that they withdraw advertisement from *Pewarta Deli* because of its reportedly cavalier attitude to Mevrouw Landzaat's murder. Soon after, another meeting was held at which it was decided to boycott not only *Pewarta Deli* but "all anti-European publications in the Melayu press." Three days later, *Pewarta Deli*'s editor was brought in for questioning by the police and the newspaper was temporarily shut down. The crackdown was well on its way. Kusumasumantri, who had in earlier months been subject to several interrogations by police intelligence, was finally arrested, this time on the pretext that he had participated in communist activities *six years earlier!* (OvSI 1930:33).

Although the Chief Head of Justice publicly affirmed that the Parnabolan murder was unrelated to extremist activities, this did not deter planters and politicians from using the case as a raison d'être for further repression of civil rights. On July 16, 1929, 2,300 Europeans in Medan held a public meeting deploring the government's weak stance against the situation and demanding that stronger measures be taken to protect their interests (ibid. 45; also see Reid 1979:39). In this spirit, a right-wing and fascist-linked organization christened the Vaderlandsche Club was established in Deli. As in Java its members "held most of the key-positions within the colonial administrative apparatus and within industry and commerce" (Drooglever 1980:348).

Despite police reinforcements and more severe punishments for political agitators, labor actions and assaults continued unabated. Only two months after the Parnabolan incident, the manager of the Aloer Gading estate was assaulted by 20 coolies and murdered. Five workers, including a foreman, were brought to trial. In contrast to Salim's hearing, the witnesses' testimonies were far more revealing of the violent context in which the assault had taken place. According to the accused, the incident had been precipitated by the demotion of a foreman whose "gentle manner" vis-à-vis his workers had been considered inappropriate by the manager, Waller. In the trial the new foreman, who was also implicated in the murder, testified that only those persons willing (and unafraid) to beat coolies were promoted to a supervisory position. Other workers testified to severe beatings and abuse by Waller, who had increased the work load as well as the frequency of corporal punishment since becoming manager. Even with this evidence of "extenuating circumstances," the political climate in Deli was such that the court remained unsympathetic to the workers' case. In October 1929, four workers were sentenced to hang, and one was given a fifteen-year prison sentence. But as in the Parnabolan incident, no connection was found to extremist agitation.

Even in the case of sustained labor protest on the Tandem estate, evidence of political motive, much less outside political instigation, was never offered. There was one notable exception on the Kotari estate, where a mutual aid and ketoprak (popular opera) association allegedly provided the front for the planning and financing of a rebellion against Dutch rule scheduled for May of the following year (Pewarta Deli 16 Nov.; 2–4 Dec. 1929). According to the head foreman (who betrayed the plot) and other workers called to testify, the foreman, Saelan, had organized the associations. During the first meetings, called several months earlier, he had collected dues and said that they would be used to buy rice that would be exchanged for a shipment of weapons from Java to be used in a plot to overthrow Dutch rule. He promised that if they participated in the uprising they would receive estate land, theirs by right anyway, since it was they, not the foreigners, who had labored to open the cultuurgebied.

Saelan adamantly denied the existence of either the open-air meetings or the plot, but a score of workers testified against him and his comrades, confirming that the meetings had taken place and that there were at least 70 members in the two secret organizations with an active leadership of 15 workers. Saelan was sentenced to four years in prison while his 14 coconspirators received sentences of two years each.

Although this case was referred to as a "communist affair" in all the local European papers, there was never evidence brought to bear that (1) Saelan was a communist, (2) the organization had outside support or was the product of outside agitation, or (3) the outside support was from communist sources. All that was substantiated (and all we know) is that on at least one Deli estate there were some workers eager and actively engaged in a political struggle that went beyond purely economic demands.

Several patterns become clear in reviewing the events of 1929. First of all, most of the serious incidences of *mass* assaults and *collective* labor actions singled out by the *Arbeidsinspectie*, the *Kroniek*, and the native and European press show little evidence of communist influence, external agitation, or even internal political motivation. For the state and corporate authorities Kotari was the case that *proved* the presence of communist insurgency. For us, it is the exception that confirms, albeit tentatively, the (converse) rule: namely, that contempt for, and resistance to, foreign supremacy needed no communist prodding. The very fact that Kotari was one of the very few cases in which a veritable plot was acknowledged by workers themselves suggests that most expressions of protest and violence were myopically conceived, centering on estate-based grievance, not fundamental opposition to colonial— much less capitalist—domination as manifest on the plantations or in any other form.

Second, it seems that the majority of the labor actions embodied in collective refusals to work occurred on the older tobacco estates, while assaults were more widely dispersed throughout the entire plantation region. That these two forms of protest were of a qualitatively different order with distinct distributions may reflect the unique labor situations and different economic positions of the tobacco and the perennial-crop estates during these years.

From 1925 to 1929 rubber and oil palm were expanding faster than ever. Land given to rubber had increased from 188,000 to 255,500 ha, and that to oil palm nearly doubled during the same period. As more area was opened, planted, and eventually brought into regular production, the demand for labor increased accordingly. Although the work force swelled by 100,000 workers in the same four-year period (with more than 36,000 new recruits in 1929 alone), AVROS still calculated a labor shortage of somewhere between 40,000 and 60,000 workers (*Pewarta Deli* 14 Dec. 1929). For the new estates in particular, the companies often shifted workers from division to division, and sometimes from one estate to another. With these frequent transfers and a continual influx of new workers living in makeshift barracks, it is not surprising that ties between workers were short-lived and not conducive to collectively planned and sustained action. Assaults, on the other hand, by an individual or a handful of workers usually required little planning or long-term cooperation.

On the tobacco estates the situation was quite different. From 1925 to 1929 the price per bale of Deli tobacco nearly halved from 230 cents to 135 cents. The tobacco area was not expanding, and under these unfavorable economic conditions the companies were under severe pressure to lower their production costs. In such a highly labor intensive industry, this primarily meant lowering the costs of labor. Many actions occurring in the tobacco region during 1929 were precisely related to a decrease in workers' earnings from the year before. In addition the tobacco estates were not expanding their labor force—if anything, they were reducing it—and those employed would hence have been resident on the same estate for sometime. Thus there were new economic conditions feeding discontent, and a laboring population with longer tenure and presumably closer ties with one another.

Finally, it cannot be ignored that many of the larger collective protests involved Chinese workers, not Javanese. This fact was never pointed out or discussed in the written records for good reason; it would have refuted many of the planters' and politicians' claims that labor unrest was a product of *nationalist* and communist propaganda from Java. Differences in national character aside, the tobacco industry (where most of the Chinese were employed) was in the midst of a crisis that permeated labor relations and may partly account for the distribution of varied forms of labor action. The planters had a saying that, despite its somewhat vulgar caricature, did reflect the Chinese workers' recourse (on the tobacco estates) to collective protest and the Javanese workers' recourse (on the rubber and oil palm estates) to violent assault:

You can cut the wages of a Chinese worker but it must be justified—even over a half cent—he'll give you trouble. He has no pride, you can kick him, nevermind. But as for the Javanese, you can't kick him, you can cut his wages, nevermind, another day, another wage.[20]

Casualties of the Depression

Through 1930 labor unrest still showed no signs of subsiding. The total number of assaults and threats on supervisory personnel remained virtually the same as in 1929. Again the *Kroniek* noted that peace was seriously disturbed by political agitation, "yet it is difficult to determine to what extent the assaults on European, native, and Chinese supervisors are related to extremist agitation" (OvSI 1931:36).

In the meantime *Pewarta Deli*'s editorials on the atrocities of the penal sanction became less frequent as censorship of the native press was more rigorously enforced. Coverage concerning the plantation workers shifted in emphasis from open-ended and snide diatribes against European management to more detailed "factual" reporting that spoke for itself. For instance, in March a short article entitled "Latex cup not clean: 12 days imprisonment" needed little commentary on the absurd excessiveness of the punishment. Frequent articles on runaway coolies, beatings, reports of inadequate food rations, and heavy fines for trivial offenses made the similar point that the estate labor system was unjust and needed drastic reform.

But even these articles became less frequent as the effects of the depression reached Deli in the mid-1930s. Labor actions, on the other hand, continued. On the Bah Boetong estate and on several neighboring plantations in the far western district of the *cultuurgebied*, 400 workers participated in a work stoppage, demanding full-time off for an Islamic holiday. On a tobacco estate 40 Chinese workers demanded the dismissal of an overseer; in July, 35 Chinese workers refused to work because of a wage dispute. And on the following day 200 workers rioted in protest against an abusive foreman; upon the arrival of a labor inspector and the police most of the workers returned to their jobs and eventually the foreman was dismissed.

In early August, 65 workers staged a work stoppage, demanding the dismissal of an assistant who had mismanaged their rice rations and forced them to work on holidays; the assistant was transferred and the rationing was readjusted. In August a group of Chinese tobacco workers staged a work slowdown. In September, 11 new Chinese recruits refused to work because of a wage dispute; they were immediately returned to China. Elsewhere, a number of Chinese workers protested the way their cash advances were calculated but returned to work when police arrived to make arrests (KvA n.d. *Vijftiende*:133–35).

While the activities of native political organizations were severely curtailed, those of the right-wing European community were gaining ground. The Vaderlandsche Club, for one, had expanded to 400 members with branches in Kisaran, Siantar, and Binjei. As the severity of the depression became more apparent in mid-1930, other political and economic organizations were established to ensure that government priorities concentrated on safeguarding foreign capital—not the jobs of Asian workers. In December the Colonial Workers' Association was set up to countermand "difficult and costly social legislation . . . which would lead to complete economic disruption" (OvSI 1931:40).

But the depression was a worldwide "disruption" that local planters were obviously powerless to avert. The only question was to what extent the companies could use it to their advantage, and the answer was found in a massive retrenchment of European and Asian labor. In May 1930 the estate work force totaled 336,000; by December, 40,000 workers had been dismissed, and by late 1931 another 62,000 were fired. This trend continued until 1934, when there were only 160,000 workers left (partially) employed on the East Sumatran estates.

The industry was in dangerous economic straits but its control over the labor situation remained clear-sighted and precise. As thousands of workers were repatriated to Java each month, a careful selection process assured that only the most trusted, docile, and hardworking married men and women were retained. As described in chapter 2, the timely implementation of legislation to abolish indenture facilitated this process, as the companies were legally released of all responsibility for the repatriated workers and their families despite the contractual tenure of employment.

In 1931 the number of assaults and threats on supervisory personnel dropped to 113 from 220 the preceding year. The number continued to decrease through the 1930s, reaching an all-time low of only 25 such incidents in 1936. Some of those who had long opposed the penal sanction were convinced (or so they argued) that the decline in assaults was directly related to its demise; others were under no such illusion and saw the reduction in assaults as an obvious result of employing a much smaller number of workers. With a rigorous selection for "good elements" (of submissive character and healthy physique) there was less occasion for maltreatment and less impetus for resistance among those who were fortunate enough to have *any* work during the depression.

Other, more important changes contributed to labor's quiescence. The repressive apparatus of the state and the companies was progressively tightened—along with the belts of the plantation workers. Rather than signaling an easing of control, on the contrary the passing of the penal sanction "brought a certain measure of *military discipline*, proper food provisioning and medical care, whereby physical strength and labor productivity increased" (De Waard 1934:272). In this connection the entire estate industry witnessed a dramatic change in the techniques of production, allowing the companies to realize their profits on the basis of a more "modernized" mode of exploitation; one that no longer rested principally on the extraction of *absolute* surplus value, that is, longer working hours, lower wages, and increased labor intensity—all of which were palpably and immediately experienced by workers as excessive and unjust and warranting violent retaliation. Instead, corporate stategies were shifting to a focus on increasing labor productivity: the extraction of *relative* surplus value, through revised organization and technical factors in the production process. Allen and Donnithorne describe this transformation:

However disastrous the Depression may have been from a financial standpoint, it was certainly instrumental . . . in eliminating waste that had been accepted during periods of high prices. Among the improvements that lowered costs, either immediately or in the long run, were the adoption of new tapping systems, the abandonment of clean weeding, the introduction of high-yielding plants, and the use of more efficient machinery in the estate factories where the rubber was processed. Productivity per labourer grew substantially. At the same time it was found possible by the employment of Asian conductors to reduce the number of expensive Europeans in supervisory work. [1962:124]

In terms of labor relations this meant less direct contact between European staff and Asian workers, and less occasion for volatile confrontation between them. On the other hand the material conditions of estate employment in many cases remained the same or indeed became worse (Langenveld 1978:362). Despite a new coolie ordinance in 1931 which stipulated that the companies must provide a "living wage" for their workers, subsequent calculations made by the Arbeidsinspectie still found wages often to be far below an adequate subsistence base. But earnings were far below that base for thousands of workers throughout the Indies; the fact that estate workers had any subsistence security at all must have meant they were probably somewhat better off than many of the rural poor. Certainly the repressive political climate and generalized state of impoverishment gave little impetus for any group to champion the plight of plantation workers in particular.

In the early 1930s the native press was further censored in a series of new amendments that dissuaded overt confrontation with the authorities. Moreover, no newspapers save Dutch ones were allowed on the estates (Said 1977:173), and many estate schools closed at the start of the depression were not later reopened (V. Thompson 1947:142); by denying workers access to nationalist newspapers and to Taman Siswa schoolteachers who were renowned for their strong nationalist sentiments, the companies further ensured that a literate and an informed opposition to colonial rule, on the estates at least, would not be nurtured.

In the meantime, the local sultans worked closely with the government authorities to repress any form of nationalist or left-wing political organization. From 1932 to 1937 their campaign was successful and what was left of the Sumatran anticolonial movement was well underground. When it did reemerge in 1937 it was formulated in a different idiom, without the penal sanction as its focal point and with estate workers effectively isolated from it.

GERINDO (Gerakan Rakyat Indonesia) was established in that year as the leading organization of an anticapitalist and anticolonial movement. In several areas small farmers (mostly Karos and migrant Toba Bataks) were counted among the local leaders (Reid 1979:173). Although GERINDO supposedly received "strong support from the Javanese estate laborers" (van Langenberg 1976:362), there is no evidence that this support manifested itself in disruption of estate production or serious collective labor agitation on any scale. In the 1930s the reports on mass actions among estate workers were few and far between and seemed to have caused little concern to estate authorities—not enough even to report them as they had so scrupulously done in the preceding decades.

The plantation companies were under fire from other quarters, including, among others, Karo Batak farmers, who were the most vocal in advocating seizure of estate lands. Popular resistance to colonial rule had not disappeared but it had changed in form and content. From the perspective of those in power, we can only assume that their campaign to weed out and quiet "dangerous elements" among the plantation population was temporarily successful enough to ease the planters' fears of (and discourse on) estate-based insurrection.

This account of estate labor protest during Deli's colonial period represents only a small wedge from a history of confrontation reaching far beyond the *cultuurgebied*'s borders. Unfortunately the workers' testimonies have often been erased from the record, drowned out by more articulate and resonant voices—leaving us with garbled grumbling to decipher from the static of fifty years. Instead we have relied on the caustic voice of the native press with its vested interests in suggesting that estate-based political action was often nothing but an inflated phantasm of the colonial elite, and that violence was simply a product of the penal code itself. Or we have the officious voice of the European press and government functionaries, indiscriminately labeling all and any signs of "disorder" as communist or nationalist resistance to the colonial state. In the interstices, where these discourses converge or diverge, the workers' voices emerge more clearly—as something more than peevish mutterings and something less than the battle cry of insurgency.

Here we have focused on one "register" of resistance, on those dramatic manifestations of conflict represented in physical violence, and less frequently collective action. Through the skirmishes between white staff and Asian workers, through these "tracers," we learn which forms of resistant social practice were considered viable and deliberately chosen for (Tilly 1975:248). And from the planters' discourse we learn which of these were conceived as the most serious threat. To call these "skirmishes" is perhaps to underestimate their cumulative impact. In the labor actions in the decades preceding 1929 there is evidence of confrontation (albeit often of a personal and parochial nature) against a form of labor control which attempted to ensure that the individual experience of exploitation would remain just that—isolated and unarticulated.

Looking at the events surrounding these disturbances, we can identify some of the palpable points of conflict between management and labor, such as physical and verbal abuse, arbitrary transfers, dismissals, and wage cuts, thus locating those aspects of labor relations experienced as intolerable and justifying redressive action. Omitted from this list are more generalized grievances that could not be expressed, by Javanese coolies at least, within the prevailing colonial order. The grievances that workers did lodge, as opposed to the criticisms leveled by those championing their cause, were invariably directed against practices that violated their rights under the *existing* labor contracts; these protests left uncontested the validity of the contracts themselves and the terms inscribed in them.

This does not mean that the laboring population left the structure of labor relations unchallenged or unchanged. On the contrary, the shift to family housing, improved medical care, the abolition of the penal sanction, and technical innovations to increase labor productivity were in part responsive to the unstated demands of a labor force that could not and *would* not reproduce itself until certain social conditions of existence were met.

From this perspective the consequences of labor resistance cannot be confined to the arena in which workers consciously—and certainly class-consciously—resisted colonial rule.[21] On the other hand a literal reading of the issues that provoked coolie assaults and work stoppages would produce a vision as analytically myopic as that of those who participated and those who feared the consequences. Braudel went so far as to say: "we must learn to distrust this history with its still burning passion, as it was felt, described and lived by contemporaries whose lives were as short-sighted as ours" (1972:21). Here I have tried to stick close to this "still burning passion," be it fear, courage, or outrage to see how it was produced, what ideas and what material conditions sustained it. This is not to suggest that accounts of these "lived experiences" are a more authentic description of social relations and how they change. On the contrary, I have tried to account for how these realities were structured, how the limits of viable social practice were set, and what conditions allowed specific social classes or fractions thereof to transgress these constraints. In each case specifying how things appeared and why they appeared as they did has meant identifying those structural limitations that fell both within and outside the temporal and spatial purview of those immediately involved.

In short, the daily confrontation between assistant and coolie was not class structure writ-small. If anything, these incidents represent a key to the ways in which class interests were obscured and expressed along ethnic, gender, and racial lines. Conversely, this "lived experience" does not reduce to false consciousness, rendering it analytically trivial. The structural features of capitalist development in East Sumatra defined some constraints on social practice without providing a pre-scription for it. A fuller account has demanded that we ask why experi-ence appeared in such "fragmented and differentiated form" and under what conditions these forms were used and transcended. The following chapter continues this inquiry in the context of the Japanese occupation and national revolution.

Young contract workers boarding a truck at dawn for a palm oil estate 20 km away, 1979.

For relatively big *slametan* (ceremonial feast) women still work together in large groups to pound rice.

Coconut husks or wood collected from neighboring estates is the fuel usually used for cooking. Asahan, 1979.

Aerial view of a Deli rubber estate, ca. 1939. Courtesy of Tropen.

House of the head administrator (*Tuan kebun*) at the Soengai Mentjirien tobacco estate, ca. 1900. Courtesy of Koninklijk Instituut voor Taal-, Land-, en Volkenkunde (KITLV).

Housing for pensioned workers on a government estate in Asahan, 1979.

Pre-World War II *pondok* for Javanese workers on the Anggoli rubber estate in Deli. Courtesy of Tropen.

Rail transport of tobacco to the fermenting sheds, ca. 1920s. Courtesy of KITLV.

Main office of the Uniroyal (formerly HAPM) estate complex in Asahan, 1979.

Sumatran tea factory, 1979.

Javanese workers threading tobacco leaves onto rods for drying, 1927. Courtesy of KITLV.

Although there are no women rubber tappers in North Sumatra today, this was not the case during the colonial period. Courtesy of Tropen.

Harvester carrying bunches to a
loading point on a palm oil plantation
in Simalungun, 1979.

Children are often hired by harvesters
to collect the *brondolan* (individual
palm kernels) that fall from the
ripened bunches during harvesting.

Almost all the work of weeding (*garuk*)
and cleaning under and around the
palm trees is done by women through
labor contractors. An Asahan palm and
rubber estate, 1979.

Estate watchmen were usually Bengali
Indians during the colonial period.
Courtesy of KITLV.

Deli planters at the manager's house, ca. 1880. Courtesy of Tropen.

Deli planters with Chinese, Indian, Batak, and Javanese workers, ca. 1880. Courtesy of Tropen.

The production of Deli tobacco. Courtesy of KITLV.

Javanese women sorting tobacco leaves. Courtesy of KITLV.

Chinese workers in sorting rows of a tobacco fermenting shed. Courtesy of KITLV.

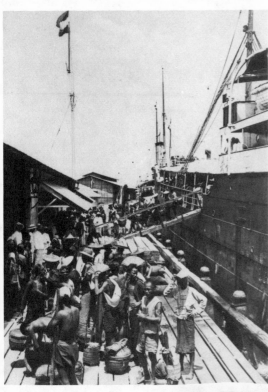

Chinese coolies disembarking at the port of Belawan on Sumatra's East Coast, ca. 1905. Courtesy of Tropen.

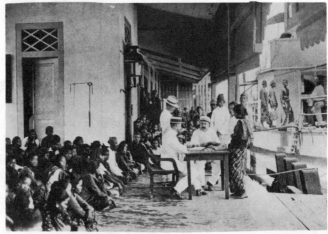

Inspecting the papers of Javanese women and men embarking for Deli as contract coolies, ca. 1905. Courtesy of Tropen.

Cooking facilities in the Javanese workers' quarters on the Senembah Company tobacco estate, ca. 1940. Courtesy of KITLV.

At work: overseeing the monthly cash transport on a Deli estate, ca. 1890. Courtesy of Tropen.

At home: drinking beer at the end of a workday. An assistant's bungalow in the plantation belt, ca. 1890. Courtesy of Tropen.

Planters from the Medan estate with their concubines and offspring, the Chinese majordomo, Indian watchmen, and Javanese domestic servants, ca. 1880. During the early years many companies forbade their European employees to bring wives. Courtesy of Tropen.

At play: A successful hunting party in the jungle surrounding the Deli estates, ca. 1920. Courtesy of Tropen.

4
War and Revolution: A View from the Estate Barracks

The two preceding chapters have outlined some of the structural features defining the nature of corporate hegemony in colonial Deli, and the contrasting social realities of those living within and contesting its constraints. The present chapter tries to identify the experience and fate of the estate population during the wartime occupation by the Japanese and the subsequent period of Indonesia's national revolution. For several reasons, this will not be an easy task. Instead of a profusion of sources aimed specifically at the contours of estate labor conflict, here we have a fragmented, less focused record in which the role of Sumatra's estate workers in the political and armed struggle for independence remains ambiguous and opaque.

Although archival and secondary sources detail the machinations of community-based Karo Batak resistance, Toba Batak militancy, and Malay sultanate collaboration following the Japanese surrender,[1] the movements of the Javanese estate community, which had 200,000 workers on the eve of World War II, are far less clear.

Not surprisingly, both contemporary accounts and later analyses have concentrated on the activities of those individuals and social groups at the forefront of the national and local resistance movements, rather than those caught by the undertow of political and economic disorder. But the estate workers fit well in neither category. As the pariahs of Deli's colonial society and as immigrants with as yet tenuous roots in (and claims to) Sumatran soil, they were unlikely candidates for revolutionary militancy. We have already described (in chap. 3) those labor policies applied by the companies in the 1930s that weeded out contentious elements, retained and rewarded those who toed the line. This revamping of the labor force (in size, composition, and political 93 sentiment), in hand with a more repressive stance toward civil liberties by the state, gave little room for labor activism on the estates and little opportunity for contact with the nationalist underground outside their borders.

At the same time, it was precisely among members of the plantation community that subjugation (and dependence) under colonial rule was most palpable and apparent, where nationalist sentiments supposedly had once thrived, and where proximity to the heart of the colonial machine and access to a finely webbed communications network might have allowed for rapid politicization and mobilization. In fact, neither occurred.

Regardless of any general notions we might otherwise entertain on peasant/proletarian passivity or combativeness, the history at hand demands that we bring evidence to bear showing why some of the basic social hierarchies of the prewar period remained so firmly intact. If we look to how workers' experience was structured during the war and revolution, it should be easier to locate the estate population's strategic but constricted position within the critical geographic and political space of the nationalist movement. For the very reason that control over plantation land, labor, and produce was to become a central focus in the contest for power in North Sumatra, the plantation populace was shoved to center stage. But occupying this charged position was a far cry from playing a pivotal revolutionary role; more often the workers were the *objects* of struggle, not its agents.

By most received accounts the Japanese occupation wreaked havoc on the colonial order, clearing the path for and setting the initial course of Indonesia's quest for independence, declared in 1945 and granted five years later. As in most other parts of Indonesia, the Japanese occupation of North Sumatra accelerated the possibilities for both the dissolution of foreign hegemony and the mobilization of a mass-based and viable social revolution. Most students of this period agree, however, that in the end neither occurred. Economic independence was forfeited for political sovereignty, and the initial thrust toward a social transformation of Indonesian society—glimpsed in the regional "social revolutions" of 1946—was thwarted by a nationalist leadership which despite its revolutionary rhetoric acted on the belief that popular and spontaneous demands for political power were dangerous impediments to the success of the nationalist struggle.[2]

The political settlement that was eventually, though by no means unanimously, agreed upon rested on a protection of foreign economic interests and a cautious nonantagonistic stance toward American and Western European powers. The consequence of this ultimate reliance on concessionary diplomacy (*diplomasi*) rather than armed struggle (*per-*

juangan) was reflected throughout Indonesian society. Nowhere was the hostility to, and reliance upon, foreign capitalist enterprises more evident than in North Sumatra's *cultuurgebied*. Popular actions manifest in illegal seizure of estate land and attempts at establishing workers' control over estate complexes were viewed by the newly formed government as subversive actions and a threat to the diplomatic agreements on which independence was contracted. While the constraints placed on Deli's estate workers were significantly greater than those imposed on the rural masses in general, their awkward position of reliance on, and resistance to, foreign capital was in many respects a position paralleling the dilemma of the nascent state as a whole.

The strategic importance of the plantation complexes and their workers is already clear during the Japanese occupation. The following section examines the redistribution of these resources and its effects on the racial, ethnic, and class hierarchies of estate life.

Plantation Policy under the Japanese

The Japanese landing in Deli in March 1942 was not altogether unexpected either by Indonesian nationalists, who initially welcomed its coming, or by the estate companies, who had been fearfully preparing for it. The East Coast's precarious dependence on overseas rice shipments to feed its burgeoning estate and urban population had already become a primary concern of colonial authorities, and various measures were taken in the years immediately prior to the occupation to build up local food stores. In 1939 a compulsory cultivation ordinance was issued that "called for an intensification of food production by peasants and compelled planters to take down their "no tresspassing" signs and in other ways facilitate the cultivation of some of their lands for subsistence purposes" (Pelzer 1978:119). By early 1942, in the densely populated estate districts of Langkat, Deli, and Serdang, 42,000 hectares of tobacco land was temporarily assigned to plantation workers and indigenous inhabitants for cultivation of rice and other food crops (Dootjes 1948:14). In addition, another 37,500 hectares of perennial-crop estate area was allocated to food production, either under the direct supervision of the companies or through allocations to individual farmers living on the estate periphery (Pelzer 1978:120).

The planters' associations of AVROS and DPV required their member estates to maintain rice stocks sufficient for three to six months. Many estates planted quick-yielding corn varieties, and corn seedlings were distributed as an emergency measure to be planted when and if rice shipments were blocked (Dootjes 1948:14). These measures helped to ward off a serious food shortage throughout most of 1942 but not for much longer. More importantly, they set a "dangerous" precedent for squatter cultivation of estate lands (Pelzer 1978:119), and by providing adequate food supplies in the initial months of the occupation, Japanese authorities could concern themselves with continued commercial crop production. Thus throughout 1942 a sizable plantation area remained intact.

Although estate production was suspended just before the Japanese landing, during the first two months of the occupation many estates continued to pay their workers. This, along with the fact that food provisions were available on the estates proper, ensured that the coolie labor force "in general behaved itself very well in these disturbed times" and that estate property would remain temporarily protected. Looting was reported in towns and larger urban centers, but it seems that the Javanese estate dwellers took no part in these actions (Dootjes 1948:17).

Control over the estate population was further secured by the fashion in which the occupied territories were organized. Although all of Sumatra, Malaya, and Singapore came under the jurisdiction of the 25th Japanese army command with headquarters in Singapore, only plantation lands were directly under military administration.[3] The Deli estates were to provide an important source of revenue and raw materials for the Japanese war effort and, at the start at least, every precaution was made to ensure that estate workers stayed at their posts. In May 1942 East Sumatra's military commander of the occupying forces established an estates advisory board, the Noyen Renggo Kai (NRK), with various key estate administrators from such large companies as HAPM, SOCFIN, and HVA acting as consultants in the planning of the new Japanese management. With its head office in Medan, the Noyen Renggo Kai was run by a small group of Japanese and a larger staff of European advisers under the auspices of several large private Japanese concerns.

In May 1942 the estate workers were again paid and rubber plantations that had ceased operation prior to the war resumed production. Stockpiles were also built up in preparation for shipment to industrial concerns in Japan, and cultivation of oil palm (one derivative of which was used as ersatz fuel) received renewed emphasis. Several months later, however, the NRK was dissolved (presumably owing to internal disagreements among various Japanese concerns over the allocation of the estates) and estate management was transferred from military to civil authorities, with the Medan office now made a branch of the Shonan Gomu Kumiai headquarters in Singapore. Japanese "group managers" replaced European "contact men" and with this shift European personnel lost what little influence they had exerted in their advisory capacity.

By mid-1943 the situation in East Sumatra had changed dramatically. Allied attacks on Japanese ships moving within the Malacca

Straits made it increasingly infeasible to export Sumatran raw materials to Japan. With huge stockpiles of rubber on the Deli estates and in the harbors, and with rubber supplies still available to Japan from Indochina and the Moluccas, Sumatran rubber production became a low priority. In June 1943 tapping was entirely stopped and was not resumed again until after the war. The order to halt rubber production was also prompted by growing food shortages, as stocks were depleted and troops confiscated more and more village produce. The East Coast, initially partitioned administratively according to former residency boundaries, was now divided into semiautonomous units between which there was little flow of communication—or goods. For the *cultuurgebied* in particular, where land devoted to the cultivation of foodstuffs was scarcest and where the populations of local inhabitants and military troops were most concentrated, the food deficits quickly assumed acute proportions.

The solution was obvious, conversion of what were now "superfluous" estates into land for subsistence production. Thus under the aegis and order of Japanese authorities, vast tracts of plantation concessions were opened to cultivators for primary foodstuffs. On the tobacco estates 160,000 hectares were ordered released for rice, corn, and root crop cultivation. On the rubber, oil palm, and tea estates jungle was cleared, older trees were felled, and by the end of the war 52,000 hectares was turned over to food production (Pelzer 1978:123–24).

By most accounts the Javanese plantation workers were the first to take advantage of the new orders—and thus the first to be taken advantage of. Clark Cunningham writes that many

had been put out of work by the reduced activity or closing of the plantations during this period. Soon the Karo of Langkat and the local Malays moved onto the tobacco estate land. The Toba-Batak of Simelungun and Tapanuli also began to come, but not yet in great numbers, for the work had only just begun to spread. The Javanese, who had lost their jobs on the estates, were the favored group in these settlements. [1958:90]

According to several sources two distinct policies were used to encourage food production. Estate workers were initially *conscripted* to grow foodstuffs; later, short-term leases replaced conscription, especially in the tobacco area, where the food production plan was centered (van Langenberg 1976:231; Cunningham 1958:90; Aziz 1955:187). Under the latter scheme,

the land designated for food production was parcelled into lots of 0.6 hectares each for issuance to landless cultivators. The lots were registered and land-loan agreements signed, such agreements being valid for two years with a provision for their extension for an additional two years. Thousands of landless laborers formerly dependent upon the food rations which formed a part of their wages were suddenly able to grow their own food. Many left the plantation barracks, built simple houses on their newly acquired lots, and began to develop small garden plots by planting fruit trees, bushes and hedgerows. [Pelzer 1978:125]

The change from conscription to land leases, however, may not have been so pervasive as some of these sources suggest. The terms under which squatter rights were allocated seem to have differed considerably from district to district and even from estate to estate. A case in point is the Lima Puluh region of Asahan, where different systems existed on adjacent plantations. At the Kwala Gunung rubber estate, for example, tapping was suspended during the entire occupation, but workers there contend that they were forced by local Japanese authorities to grow rice on estate land throughout the occupation. They were also allocated small plots of land ostensibly for their own subsistence, but half their harvest had to be sold to estate officials. Since they were paid in nonnegotiable Japanese currency, by their account the "sale" was much the same as having a portion of their harvest simply confiscated.[4] On the other hand, at the nearby Sukamulia estate, part of the estate was kept in operation and plots of 4 rantai (2,100 m^2) were allocated to estate workers for their own food needs, in this instance without leasing agreements.

Thus there is some evidence to suggest that although many estate workers were indeed unemployed and dislocated by the dismantling of the estate economy, nevertheless a large portion had obtained squatter rights on the basis of their continued ties to the plantation complexes. Furthermore, it seems that the development, and social pattern, of the squatter settlements were ethnically distinct. Although more heterogeneous settlements grew up in the tobacco area around Medan (where the food production program was better organized and included a more diverse mix of ethnic groups), it is by no means conclusive that this was the prevailing pattern throughout the East Coast.

The point is an important one since it has been suggested that food shortages, deportations, and general dislocations during the Japanese occupation helped break down the rigid social barriers between the estate population and other ethnic groups, and in so doing facilitated creation of the united (nationalist) front after 1945 (van de Waal 1959:27). But if the estate workers, even in their participation in the squatter movement, were singled out and subject to a special policy of land allocation, this would make their continued isolation in the initial phase of the revolution more understandable. Developments during the latter part of the occupation add further weight to the argument that plantation workers remained largely quartered off as they had been in the 1930s, but now under somewhat different constraints.

What were some of these developments? For one, in April 1944 the

Japanese reinstituted a variant of the Dutch coolie ordinance stipulating once again severe punishment for those who left the estate complexes without permission (BZ, E50:Apr. 1946). This may have been an attempt to check the large exodus of the estate and nonestate population into the Langkat, Deli, and Serdang tobacco regions. Furthermore, strict control over the plantation work force allowed for rapid and efficient labor mobilization for other projects. In the beginning of 1944, thousands of workers were taken from the estates and used for infrastructural projects—railways, roads, and airstrips—in Central Sumatra, Aceh to the north, and other parts of Southeast Asia. Conscription of Indonesian laborers (romusha) took place throughout Indonesia, but in North Sumatra the toll on the estate population was disproportionately high. The majority did not return, dying from lack of food and medical care.[5]

Dutch intelligence reports based on statistics collected by the Japanese estimated that between 1942 and 1945 the number of "full consumers" (calculating a man as one full consumer, a woman as 0.8, and a child as 0.5) on the tea, rubber, and oil palm estates decreased by 24%, while those on the tobacco estates increased by 12%.[6] Despite these massive dislocations and apparent mobility evidenced in the fact that 10,000 more "full consumers" were living on the tobacco estates in 1945 than in 1942, the overwhelming majority of estate dwellers remained economically crippled and tactically immobile whether they lived within the estate boundaries or on its borders. Malaria and malnutrition were rampant among the coolie population and, according to intelligence reports from 1946, only 15–25% of the estate laborers were physically fit to work (AR).[7] By the end of the war textiles were totally unavailable and workers were clothed in hemp sacks, sheets of crude rubber, or as a last resort, banana leaves.

On the other hand, whatever bare necessities the estate workers were able to obtain were acquired on the basis of their continued ties to the estates. Wages were never raised during the occupation, but in some cases they were paid; in addition, Japanese estate managers intermittently provided workers with coconuts, palm oil, sugar, salt, and other basic commodities, which were otherwise totally unattainable to most of the rural poor (Dootjes 1948:24). The estate population, however, paid dearly for these "advantages" by having most of their own maintenance—as well as that of the Japanese forces—foisted upon them. Native Sumatran villagers were not exempt from heavy exactions but they also did not share in these crucial but meager benefits.

Thus the survival strategies of the estate population during the occupation (and after) rested on two incompatible sources: (1) payments and provisions provided by their continued attachment to the estates, and (2) whatever food they could produce on land wrested from the

estate complexes. Other landless and impoverished rural East Sumatrans had only the latter alternative; as such they were not faced with the
same ambivalent opposition to and dependence on the estate economy
during the war—and revolution.

Both the isolation of the Javanese plantation populace from the
central idiom in which nationalist sentiments were being forged and
their exclusion from other channels by which politicization and social
mobility were being encouraged were by-products of Japanese military
strategy and specifically of the particular style in which anti-Western
propaganda was being made.

From the outset of the occupation, the Netherlands Indies was administratively divided among three regions: (1) the Outer Islands, excluding Sumatra, controlled by the navy; (2) Java, which came under the
control of the Japanese 16th Army; and (3) Sumatra and Malaya, admin-
istered by the 25th Army, which altogether formed "the nuclear zone of
the Empire's plans for Southeast Asia because of their strategic importance as well as their economic value as sources of oil, rubber and tin"
(Reid 1971:22). These administrative divisions were paralleled by dis-
tinctly divergent policies toward the nationalist movements in each of
these locales. While plans for independence were given far more substance in Java, on Sumatra the nationalist movement was carefully supervised and maneuvered along a limited and specific course. In an
effort to demonstrate the "natural" communality of Sumatran and Malayan interests, the Japanese propaganda machine emphasized this
kinship, at the same time actively discouraging links between Sumatra
and Java. Communications between the two islands were already difficult; the Japanese authorities made sure that it remained so (van Langenberg 1976:180).

Thus Sumatra was not only cut off from the nationalist movement in
Java but was also encouraged to develop a form of nationalism that was
strongly Javaphobic, calling for Sumatran autonomy and promoting a
belief that Sumatra should not be subordinated to Java-based interests
(ibid. 177–81). Not surprisingly then, the Javanese estate workers on the
East Coast found themselves from the outset with several strikes against
them; not only were they alien to the ethnic idiom of Sumatran nationalism but, as always, were disdained for what native Sumatrans saw
as their direct and compliant subordination to colonial rule.

The process of politicization was ethnically distinct and class specific. This can be seen clearly in the composition of the *pemuda* (youth)
movement, whose preparation and training under the Japanese placed it
at the vanguard of the armed struggle for independence. In late 1943 as
more and more Japanese troops were sent from Sumatra and Java to the

front in the South Pacific, new defense strategies against an Allied offensive were created for the Javan and Sumatran bases of Japanese control.

Under instructions from the Japanese Southern Area Command an intensive campaign was launched to expand the local militia "with native forces inspired with national sentiments" (Reid 1979:118). Among the new units created were Heiho (indigenous auxiliary forces), incorporated into the Japanese army for "menial tasks, guard duty, and labor" (ibid. 117); and Giyugun, later known as PETA, a voluntary and local people's militia (referred to as *laskyar rakyat* in Indonesian) with native officers. Both were manned (in Sumatra there were no women recruits) by Indonesians between the ages of 17 and 25 who were given basic military training, Japanese military uniforms, and weapons (van Lagenberg 1976:200). On Sumatra's East Coast there were only about 1,500 enlistees in Heiho and Giyugun by the end of the war, the majority were from the non-Malay population, not only aggressively nationalist but strongly anti-*kerajaan* (literally antisultanate) in spirit (ibid. 212).

Recruitment for these units was vigorously supported by both moderate and radical nationalist leaders, who used the framework of these Japanese institutions to further their own plans for independence. The training programs are said to have provided the recruits with a new solidarity surmounting regional and class differences (Reid 1979:118). For Java, Ben Anderson writes, "it was the *experience* of being in an organization that pushed the elite youth out into the masses and sucked uneducated youth up towards the elite that gave the [nationalist] ideology its concrete meaning" (1972:30). In East Sumatra, however, it seems that at least one major social class, making up the largest ethnic group in the region, was grossly underrepresented, namely, *pemuda* from the vast Javanese estate laboring population.

Some reasons for this are clear. The energy and leadership provided by *pemuda* in the early years of the nationalist struggle have perhaps overshadowed the fact that its membership remained small and highly select for quite some time.[8] Most of those included in the social category of *pemuda* during the Japanese occupation were from social classes that could afford the luxury of sending their children to school rather than to work. They were the children of civil servants, teachers, government officials, or village heads and functionaries (Shirasishi 1977). Second, many of the *pemuda* who joined the various militia were urban based (though not necessarily of urban origin), living in those towns and cities where higher educational traning was available. For the most part the *pemuda* leaders were junior and high school students in native or Dutch language schools who, having had their institutions closed down, found themselves thrown upon their own resources and responsible for their own future (van Langenberg 1976:193–94). By late 1944 "a large number of *pemuda* gangs had emerged in Medan and other big towns in North Sumatra," many of whom developed both their own economic means of survival and a high degree of politicization (ibid.). In any case, this rambunctious and aggressive movement was still an urban phenomenon.

Third, the educational requirements for enlistment in Giyugun officer training programs meant that recruits from the plantation poor were excluded entirely. Primary schooling was required and in practice most recruits had either Dutch or Japanese language training. Certainly the children of most estate workers could not afford the luxury of primary schooling, much less of higher education. Enlistment in Heiho, on the other hand, stipulated no educational requirements and among those who did join were supposedly many youths from the urban poor, attracted by the prospect of material security as well as a more promising future (Reid 1979:118).

But how would those from the Javanese estate community have joined the leadership or ranks of either organization? For one, *pemuda* designated not only an age group but a social category with little relevance to the estate laboring class. The child of an estate laborer had a life trajectory that left precious little room for the hiatus of "youth." By the age of fifteen, male and female estate dwellers were employed as full-time *buruh* (manual workers) on their own account. Thus not only were they subject to the same labor demands as their elder counterparts (and the same restrictive ordinances prohibiting their absence from the estate), but more importantly they were *buruh* not *pemuda* and it was this experience that would later define their political commitment. Although the children of some Batak, Chinese, and Javanese estate clerks and head foremen may have enjoyed the privilege of an educational interlude, by the age of sixteen, the minimum age of Giyugun and Heiho recruits, most children of estate laborers already would have been working for several years as independent wage earners or as helpers to their parents. In short, the nationalist appeal to *pemuda* fell on deaf ears in the estate barracks, where the young neither had the mobility to join nor shared in that experience of dislocation which helped build a cohesive *pemuda* movement.

The fact that the plantation youth were not trained for armed struggle early on is not to suggest that they remained nonpartisan or unpoliticized. But *pemuda* visions and the anti-*kerajaan* hostility they harbored were still tangential to those whose life experience—and immediate survival—were tied to the estates. As we shall see below, their participation came in the process of defending their squatter rights and mobilizing around estate labor demands.

Revolution and the Politics of Estate Control

Proclamation of the Republic of Indonesia in August 1945 in Java received mixed reviews on Sumatra's East Coast, reflecting the disparate interests of the Japanese-appointed regional government, those adamant supporters of sultanate power and Dutch rule, and those resolute in their opposition to it. When Sumatra's participation in the Republic was finally declared two months later by (the moderate and armchair nationalist) Governor T. Muhamad Hasan, his attempts to win sultanate backing without provoking *pemuda* hostility only accelerated the polarization of these factions all the more.

The landing of British troops in September (just a few weeks after the Japanese surrender) and the concomitant organization of a "transitional" Netherlands Indies Civil Administration (NICA) by the Allied command was applauded by the pro-Dutch *kerajaan*, who welcomed this tripartite alliance. These events simply confirmed the suspicion of *pemuda* that independence would never be won through conciliatory politics. Unwilling to rely on Hasan's commitment to defending the republic against its Dutch, Allied, sultanate, and ethnic Chinese adversaries, *pemuda* bands took the task upon themselves, forming local people's militia (*laskyar rakyat*) based on the ethnically distinct organizations of which they were already a part.

In November the *pemuda*-led nationalist offensive was consolidated under an organization of Indonesian Socialist Youth (PESINDO, Pemuda Socialis Indonesia), which, according to Anthony Reid, "represented the revolutionary, 'modern,' and relatively secular left-wing in each different residency situation" (Reid 1974:80; van Langenberg 1976:328). Although unified in the same month with the official Republican army (Tentera Rakyat Keamanan, TKR), these local militias were far more widespread and violent, evinced in their frequent clashes with Allied troops in Medan and with Japanese forces in smaller towns, where the latter were charged with keeping order.

For the most part, *pemuda* activities in these early months remained urban skirmishes in which the rural majority of the East Coast was still uninvolved. By December, however, after several particularly gruesome confrontations—in one of which between 2,000 and 5,000 casualties were counted in Tebing Tinggi—the *pergerakan* (a generic term for the popular nationalist movement) forces retreated southward. They then spread into the heart of the *cultuurgebied* to build up their manpower, weapons, and supplies, rendering more accessible the social import of the nationalist struggle (van Langenberg 1976:343). For the plantation populace their entry was a mixed blessing. On the one hand, it signaled yet another period of severe economic deprivation. On the other hand, these forces brought closer the immediacy of independence and an organizational know-how that helped shape the estate labor movement.

Control over the vast plantation complexes housing immense stores of material wealth and labor power quickly became the economic and military nexus of republican resistance. Moreover, since the estates were the most palpable symbol of collaboration between traditional elites and foreign rule, their seizure became a political gesture in defiance of concessionary politics. How critical the political space of the estates actually was became more than obvious as PESINDO militia units mushroomed throughout the residency, accompanied by a profusion of radical nationalist forces and political parties that were forming and expanding with their own *laskyar* attachments.

Among these were the PKI, headed in North Sumatra by Abdul Xarim M.S., which strongly advocated a nationalist and socialist revolution *within* Indonesian society itself. Although most of the PKI's 11,000 members in February 1946 were in urban centers, its platform urging the nationalization and redistribution of estate lands supposedly earned it an early base for support among the plantation workers (Reid 1979:174). At the same time, Tan Malaka's Persatuan Perjuangan (struggle union) with its call for "100% *merdeka*" (independence) was launched with full support of the youth movement and Communist party. As Reid notes, its "demand for a people's army and people's government and for the confiscation of Dutch plantations and other property, gave clarity and legitimacy to the direction the revolution was already taking in East Sumatra" (ibid. 226).

On the labor front various attempts were made to provide a strategy from which to attack the foreign and domestic ruling elite. Most striking were the efforts of the short-lived Indonesian Labor Front (Barisan Buruh Indonesia), which called for continued and permanent worker control of plantations and other industries taken over from the Japanese at the end of the war (U.S. Dept. of Labor 1951:81). Their platform was quickly labeled "anarcho-syndicalist" (by Sukarno among others) and detrimental to the aims of the nascent state (ibid.; see also Sutter 1959:377–80). In any case, in North Sumatra, unlike in Java, the question of *workers'* control of the estates—even on a temporary basis—was never at issue since there were too many other more powerful hands waiting to seize them. In the plantation belt the Indonesia Labor Party (Partai Buruh Indonesia) was influential in another field, that is, in calling for the formation of workers' militia (*laskyar buruh*) to support the resistance effort. But even on this account, it is not clear that local, estate-based *laskyar buruh* were the outcome of this "outside" instigation or in anyway aligned with the Labor Party. It seems that *laskyar buruh* was often only a generic term used to designate the estate guard formed by whatever Republican troops were then occupying specific plantations.

As left-wing political forces were taking temporary control over the course of the revolution in East Sumatra, organization of the entire estate economy was also being remodeled along similar lines. With the departure of Japanese estate managers in December 1945, local administration of the estates was put in the hands of Indonesian clerks, who had virtually been running them through most of the occupation. Protection and sale of estate produce, on the other hand, were far too important to be left to such ad hoc measures.[9] After a brief interlude of trial strategies ERRI (Ekonomi Rakyat Republik Indonesia, People's Economy of Indonesia) was set up and given virtually single-handed command over the entire Republican economy, under an aggressive and radical direction. With the populist banner of *sama rata sama rasa* (equality and brotherhood) it controlled "plantation products and basic commodities, ostensibly at least for socialist purposes, and to prevent such supplies falling into allied hands" (Said 1973:173). Despite or because of its purported aim to finance *pemuda* brigades, the diatribes against it were fierce. Its leaders were publicly denounced for embezzlement, anarcho-syndicalism, and for contributing to the further impoverishment of the rural poor (Sutter 1959:362–64; see also Reid 1979:238). Under heavy attack from all quarters it was banned within a few months of its creation.

Despite these various attempts to channel estate materials and produce through some centralized organ, de facto control of the estates eventually fell into the hands of those on the spot to take it. This usually turned out to be the various brigades (*pasukan*) and local militia linked—often only tangentially—to the political parties whose names they bore. The ways in which estate property and produce were requisitioned for (and sometimes against) the revolution were as varied as the needs of those who occupied the complexes at any given moment. In Kisaran, for example, the Bunut rubber factory of the HAPM estate was converted into a small arms workshop, manufacturing guns from old train rails under the guidance of an ex-foreman (AR)[10] The Deli Tua and Two Rivers estates served as an arsenal for firearms seized from Japanese troops (van Langenberg 1976:363). On the Dolok Ilir plantation Japanese officers themselves allegedly helped manufacture weapons, and at the Bangun estate the factory was turned over for the production of small firearms (AR).[11]

Most of the arms for the revolution, however, came from elsewhere, obtained through an extensive barter trade in estate produce. Initially with Governor Hasan's sanction, 6,000 tons of rubber was sold in Singapore to procure weapons and supplies for the Republican army (Reid 1979:220). In 1946, however, as numerous regional "armies" and Chinese entrepreneurs learned the ropes of the smuggling network, the barter trade assumed fantastic proportions, the profits from which often did not go to supporting the Republican cause. "In the first ten months of 1946 a total of 129 million dollars worth of Sumatran goods arrived in Singapore, most of it produce and equipment from the estates of East Sumatra" (ibid.).

As the Republican brigades established themselves in Deli, Serdang, Asahan, and Labuhan Batu it was *food*, as well as boots and weapons, that they needed. Ex-plantation workers cultivating estate *ladang* (dry field plots) and those working part-time on the estates, part-time on their own squatter plots were charged with providing their own subsistence as well as that of the *laskyar* troops. Clearly this was not always feasible because in some areas malnutrition was still a serious problem and workers themselves were heavily dependent on food distributions by the government. Elsewhere though, as in Kisaran, as much as 20% of the cultivator's harvest was allocated for PESINDO and other Republican forces (AR).[12] From several perspectives then, the experience of *merdeka* (independence) from under the rubber trees and in the squatter fields may not have been an altogether liberating one.

View from the *Pondok*

The earliest intelligence reports coming into Dutch hands after the Japanese surrender repeatedly claimed that the "coolies long for the return of the Dutch" (ibid.). This might have been woefully wishful thinking, but it is not unlikely that some of the estate population did long for what they remembered as "normalcy" while still remaining strong supporters of the new Republic. Many were living on the edge of starvation while the social relations of production under which they lived and labored were not always that different from what they had known before.

Take, for example, their position within the estate hierarchy. When the Japanese surrendered in 1945 de facto management of the East Coast plantations was given over to those Toba, Mandailing, and Batak clerks who had worked as low-level clerks and foremen under the Dutch and had handled the nuts and bolts operation of the estates during the occupation. As management was transferred into Indonesian hands, it was the educated and experienced Batak personnel who were elevated to high and middle level administrative posts. Although in Java "plantations . . . were spontaneously seized by the workers employed there" (Anderson 1972:146), in North Sumatra the transfer of authority was carried out by the Japanese themselves, without prodding by armed *pemuda* forces. And since the majority of clerks and foremen were strongly nationalist, takeovers initiated by common workers gained little impetus. In short, estate management not infrequently passed into the hands of a class and ethnic group distinct from those who made up the bulk of the plantation populace.

These hierarchies were not retained in the rigidly structured sphere of estate administration alone. Not one reference in Dutch military or civil archives refers to a plantation worker in a position of authority in plantation management, local party leadership, or military (*laskyar*) command. The head of PESINDO on the Kisaran estate was a Mandailing former clerk (*krani*), and on the nearby estates clerks were usually put in charge (AR).[13] At the Aek Kanopan estate, PKI leadership was under a Malay, a former forestry employee, and at Damoeli estate, PESINDO was headed by a Batak "terrorist" (profession not stated) with second in command a Minangkabau estate clerk (AR).[14] This makeup of the rural, local-level revolutionary leadership is not surprising given the recruitment patterns of Heiho and Giyugun from which most of this leadership was drawn. But it does suggest that the practice of revolution still fell short of turning the domestic social order upside down.

In the Membang Muda district of southern Asahan, where PESINDO troops had taken charge, all estate clerks were made members and on each estate a PESINDO office was opened. An informant for the Dutch reporting on the conditions there in March 1946 wrote:

Seventy-five percent of the members of the defense corp are Javanese who were there before. The Javanese are very discontented with the fact that they, rather than the local populus, are charged with a disproportionate part of the task of defense, and are becoming less and less satisfied with the advantages of independence. [AR][15]

Such reports are difficult to assess since they were authored by pro-Dutch agents more than eager to point out popular dissatisfaction with the Republican administration. Evidence from elsewhere, however, suggests that such findings were not very far off the mark.

The gulf separating the upper and lower crusts of the plantation population showed up in a variety of more basic matters. While the new estate supervisors were reported well-clothed and well-fed, the workers remained in hemp sacks and rubber attire for several more years. Among them, beriberi, malaria, and other illnesses were pervasive and went unalleviated in subsequent months because of a shortage of medical supplies. For the same period, estate staff were invariably reported in good health. In addition, throughout the *cultuurgebied*, many workers were living, at best, on a starvation diet. Although some accounts suggest that the first year of independence in 1946 brought some easing of the food shortages (see, e.g., Reid 1974), in a number of estate districts this was certainly not the case. In fact, workers from the Asahan estates contend that the food situation rapidly deteriorated after the Japanese surrender.[16]

Even the food ration of $7\frac{1}{2}$ kg per worker (a combination of rice, corn, and cassava) reported as the average monthly allotment on several estates was far below minimum subsistence requirements. Those estate workers with no *ladang* of their own were severely underfed (AR).[17] In most districts workers divided their time, as under the Japanese, between food cultivation and estate work. Near Tebing Tinggi, for example, 70% of the workers on the Dolok Merangir (Goodyear) estate were engaged only in food production. For the others, Allied intelligence reported that

work on the estates is limited so as not to interfere with the labourers' work in their own fields. In the Tebing Tinggi area, estate labourers work only 4 hours a day on the estates and 2 hours in their own rice fields. . . . in conclusion it seems probable that by a generally competent handling of the food situation the Republican administration has done much to strengthen its hold over the people of Sumatra. [MD][18]

Despite such optimistic reports the food situation was clearly not uniform:

In the outlying estate districts where in normal times 400,000 [*sic*] coolies are employed, there is mounting misery. According to rather reliable sources, there are about 180,000 workers on the estates in a very bad state. The rest are swarming out, trying to provide themselves with sustenance by cultivating ladang or dying by the roadsides from hunger and illness. [MD][19]

On estates where rubber stockpiles could be sold to meet operating costs, the workers fared somewhat better. Daily wages commensurate with those paid under the Japanese were distributed, sometimes along with food and clothing. However, in other districts, where rice stocks had been carted off by departing Japanese troops and little *ladang* had been cleared, the incoming *laskyar* units were a heavy burden on the already depleted food supplies of the workers.

The Republican forces entering these rural areas were keenly aware of the high priority of food cultivation for themselves and the inhabitants, but this was by no means their only concern. As units moved south they "informed the workers that they were now employees of the Republican government and *enforced continuation of* [estate crop] *production*" (van Langenberg 1976:364). On many estates this required feats of veritable bricolage since much of the essential machinery and materials (such as generators, centrifuges, tools, and electrical supplies) had been moved by the Japanese to military installations elsewhere. Where estate hardware was still intact but materials were lacking (such as on the Dolok Sinumbah estate in Simalungun), ersatz cylinder oil was manufactured from low-quality coconut or palm oil, while higher quality palm oil was processed for the cooking needs of the resident workers. On the Dolok Merangir estate, rubber not destined for export was used to manufacture bicycle tires, tubes, ground sheets, sandals, and fanbelts for use on the estate itself (MD).[20]

But even on Dolok Merangir, where management was relatively efficient, owing to the food shortage only 200 of the 1,000–1,500 prewar employees could be kept on (ibid.). Elsewhere, desertion rates were very high. Damoeli, Aek Loba, and Kanopan Ulu had much diminished populations and at Londut estate the entire labor force deserted (AR).[21] Between February and March 1946 alone, Deli Tua and Marihat estates lost, respectively, 1,958 and 2,105 "full consumers." Pabatu lost 940, Binjei 792, and on other estates between 100 and 300 left in the same period (BZ).[22]

Aside from the continued responsibility for their own reproduction, additional labor was siphoned off for military defense of the estate complex. All males between the ages of 15 and 30 received training three times a week from former Heiho and Giyugun instructors with whatever weapons were available, bamboo spears or light arms. Because these sessions were obligatory, they represented a further drain on the estate laboring population, which already had a significant portion of its male youth removed by the Japanese as *romusha* elsewhere.

Limits of the "Social Revolution"

In short, the revolutionary movement in its first few months was still one in which the vast majority of the rural population was allocated only an ancillary and subordinate role. This was more than evident in early March 1946, when hostilities against the pro-Dutch *kerajaan* factions crescendoed into a brief and bloody "social revolution" (as it was then called) in which the sultans, their families, and lackeys, as well as more moderate Republican officials, were kidnapped and murdered.

While commentators disagree on the motivation behind this violent usurpation of traditional authority, there is general consensus that it was fomented by an alliance of radical Republican forces (embodied in the Persatuan Perjuangan front in which PKI, PESINDO, and PNI leaders played a dominant role).[23] Acknowledgment of this radical influence aside, there is little evidence to suggest a "widespread communist proletarian movement," as was the prevailing Dutch opinion at the time (Dootjes 1948:92). This was so not least of all because the estate populace, the largest body of East Sumatra's "proletarian" community, seems to have remained largely peripheral to it.

Aside from one reference to "several hundred Javanese plantation workers [who] had joined the *laskyar* units in raiding *kerajaan* homes" (van Langenberg 1976:434), plantation laborers were notably absent from the vanguard of the March coup. In Karoland, assaults on the *kerajaan* were carried out by ethnic Karo, in Simalungun by Toba Bataks, and elsewhere by "armed *pemuda*" without reference to ethnic origin (Reid 1979:231–32). While the situation of the estate workers was unique on several counts, their absence from the scene calls into question not only the character of the action but the extent to which it was a "social revolution" at all.

Ben Anderson, in a critical analysis of the early revolutionary movement in Java, singles out certain features that gave *pemuda* their unity and strength:

Equality was experienced in the crumbling of the existing structure of authority. In the process of disintegration officials, policemen, political leaders in established institutions, all were discovered to be without effective power. Stripped of the armature of hierarchy, law, legitimacy and guns, they were no greater than those they ruled. Men were now defined by their actions, not by their office, rank, or status. The opacity of the social order no longer exercised its hegemonic hold. . . . It was a community of shared experience, a solidarity not defined by social structure, but growing at its dissolving margins. [1972:185]

While this may capture what occurred within the *pemuda* ranks, there seems to have been a somewhat different relationship between *pemuda* and at least certain segments of the rural poor. The contrast between the above account and conditions on Sumatra's East Coast is striking. In Deli, office, rank, and status continued to demarcate critical social cleavages within the populace and between them and their leaders. Nowhere was this more evident than on the estates, where, as we have seen, the fundamental social relations of production under which workers lived and experienced the struggle remained largely intact. One could almost say that the work force retained its "coolie" status, subservient to the economic interests, military priorities, and political concerns of more powerful social groups, be they Dutch, Japanese, or Indonesian.

From the perspective of political experience rather than consequence alone, "social revolution" seems all the more a misnomer. Unlike the indigenous Sumatran population, those within the plantation enclave had never been directly subject to traditional sultanate authority. As early as 1884, the Netherlands Indies government drew a sharp administrative distinction between "immigrants" and Sumatrans with the result that the "estate villages remained permanently *Fremdkopper* [foreign bodies] in local Indonesian society" (van de Waal 1959:27). This legacy had critical consequences. Javanese immigrants were subject to Dutch law not *adat* [customary law], to European rather than sultanate subordination. In most cases the indigenous elite had neither alienated their land nor appropriated their labor.[24] As such, their experience of domination was mediated not by the demands of avaricious sultans but by the plantation hierarchy in which they lived. True, a large number of Javanese lived outside the estate borders, but for the half-million of those within its confines (and a much larger number within its purview) the antagonisms dividing *kerajaan* and Malay and Batak peasants were of only marginal concern. In 1946, then, the "real" enemy was absent, and it was not until the Dutch returned in mid-1947 to regain control of the estates by armed force that the plantation workers emerged as active agents, on a wide scale, in the resistance movement and as strong supporters of the Republican campaign.

Thus traditional authority was badly battered but not destroyed. According to Reid, "no positive restructuring of the lower levels of society took place" (1974:254). In fact, much of the independence struggle in North Sumatra not only proceeded without clear benefit to the rural poor but more importantly without their involvement (ibid.). The plantation community was not the only one relegated to the sidelines during the initial wave of "revolutionary" social practice. Peasant mobilization in late 1945 and early 1946 was confined to those regions of Aceh and Karoland with long traditions of popular resistance against the Dutch and their own indigenous elite. Reid captures the situation for elsewhere:

The revolution was in fact carried through by urban or semi-militarized youth, without opening any positive new horizons for the poor rural majority. . . . The political and military leaders who now enjoyed the houses and cars of the overthrown rulers, and in some cases amassed large bank accounts in Singapore, became contemptuously known as the "new rich" or the "new feudals." . . . By contrast the living conditions of the bulk of plantation labourers and peasants deteriorated steadily . . . accentuating their bitterness and cynicism towards leadership of any kind. [ibid. 258]

Return of the Dutch

In the months following the "social revolution" of East Sumatra, Aceh, and Java, Republican authorities reacted to what they saw as dangerous expressions of popular radicalism. These scattered and localized acts of insurgency were seen as a threat to securing international recognition of the Republic, and as a danger to state authority itself. From spring 1946 to summer 1947 a clear shift was evident in national politics as per-

juangan tactics were denounced and a more conservative domestic policy was encouraged (Anderson 1972:407).

In this atmosphere in November 1946 Sjahrir's cabinet ratified the Linggadjati agreement, which many nationalists saw as an unwarranted concession to Dutch demands. With it, the Republic was recognized on Java and Sumatra; in exchange it pledged to cooperate in establishing, along federalist lines, a sovereign United States of Indonesia (USI). Holland's pragmatic support of federalism was based on a strategy that would allow it temporarily to maintain control over, and access to, the economic resources of the Outer Islands. At the same time, by advocating a strong regionalism, it encouraged indigenous forces to counter the powerful weight of the more radical Java-based Republic within the USI as a whole.

Ostensibly because of an impasse in implementing the Linggadjati accord, and with Western capitalist concerns threatening to withdraw from Indonesia unless their property was protected, the first Dutch "police action" was launched in July 1947 to recapture most of West Java, part of Eastern Java and Madura, and a major portion of East Sumatra. The offensive was remarkably successful in that Republican troops not only far outnumbered Dutch forces but in some areas mounted strong resistance. On the East Coast, Dutch attention focused on recapture of the estates. Within a few months more than two-thirds were in Dutch hands. Republican troops were forced to retreat south of the Asahan River, west of Kaban Jahe (in the Karo highlands), and north of Tanjung Pura (van Langenberg 1976:578).

Dutch success was partly by default since a major decentralization of Republican forces had occurred in the months after the March coup. As various brigades competed for control of rural (read: estate) resources, it was not surprising that the front they represented was neither united nor effective. Disorganized and on the defensive, many units resorted to a scorched earth policy, burning estate installations, destroying stockpiles and harvests as they were pushed farther to the fringes of the East Coast. Not infrequently workers' housing, the *pondok*, was also burned, forcing the occupants to retreat along with the *laskyar* units into Republican-held areas. Many of these workers, however, joined in the battle before withdrawing. In Asahan the workers' militia organized under PESINDO at the Bunut complex of the HAPM [Uniroyal] estate "constituted the nucleus of popular resistance by sabotaging [property] and cutting down rubber trees across the planting rows so that enemy [Dutch] vehicles could not get through" (Mansyur 1978:55). According to the same source (a *laskyar buruh* leader at Bunut), the estate workers on the nearby divisions of Gurach Batu and Pulau Mandi armed themselves with spears, knives, and makeshift weapons and flanked the armed Republican units as they staged midnight assaults on power plants, railroad stations, and fuel depots (ibid. 103–04). Such guerrilla tactics prolonged the Dutch offensive but were unable to stop it. At the end of August a ceasefire was declared and the new "van Mook line" was drawn whereby all areas already held by the Dutch were entrusted to them.

Immediately a provisional non-Republican administration was set up in which Dutch nationals were given leading positions. The Malay community, for its part, embraced the change of events with unveiled delight and began negotiations to establish a Malay-dominated autonomous state within the federated USI (van Langenberg 1976:593). By December 1947 the Negara Sumatera Timur (NST, State of East Sumatra) was established with full Dutch backing—and, as might be expected, with the Javanese majority virtually unrepresented.

The NST quickly revealed itself as liegeman to the Dutch, and structurally the situation differed little from prewar Deli. The Malays were again the ensconced elite, the Dutch and other Europeans returned as the planter aristocracy, and the estate workers remained underpaid peons of this reconstituted Dutch-Malay "joint-venture"—the critical difference being that a large bulk of the estate population had no intention of accepting a Deli restoration.

For estate workers and poor farmers this experience was a politicizing one. For both those who lost their homesteads by having to retreat into Republican territory, as well as for those who remained on the estates to see their plots tractored down to make way for new rubber and tobacco crops, the reentry of the Dutch represented a direct assault on their lives. The "enemy" was in person, the battle was over their own homesteads, and the terrain of struggle was on the familiar ground of the estates themselves.

Although Republican territory was severely diminished, the Republican *cause* was taken up more strongly than ever by the rural population. Over the next two years the NST was to become a prime symbol of collaboration with the Dutch, and the most striking proof that federalism would do little but sell out the rural poor. Among the estate workers in particular but throughout Indonesia, the independence struggle consolidated and spread across a wider social and political spectrum than it had ever done before.

Deli Restored: 1948–49

As the companies, following in the wake of the Federalist troops, gained control of the estates (by February 1948, 173 estates were recovered by their owners, totaling almost 300,000 ha), they found themselves in possession of plantations bearing little resemblance to the ones they had left behind. The damage was extensive, as "the farewell fire of the Laskyars destroyed perhaps twice as many factories as were recovered in running condition" (Maas 1948:2). On the tea estates one-third of the area had been stubbed and only one factory was left standing. On the rubber estates 8 factories were dismantled but the fields fared somewhat better since mainly old strands had been uprooted for food crop production. On the tobacco estates, 13 fermenting sheds and other installations had been destroyed (Prillwitz 1947:139).

Aside from demolished factories and damaged plants, more than 10% of the land was held by squatters, seized during either the occupation or immediately after the "social revolution," when such actions were encouraged as patriotic and considered fair reward. Within the Dutch-held territories only 72,500 workers were still resident, slightly more than one-third the prewar figure, making labor shortage one of the most serious problems faced by the returning companies. Compounding this was the emergence of an organized and widespread estate labor movement sprouting beneath the stubble of the old order and unrecognized by the returning planters for sometime.

Despite these obstacles the recovery of Deli's export economy was very rapid—and to some, along frighteningly familiar lines. In November 1947 one optimistic Dutch observer wrote (in English):

The Deli Railway runs again as regularly as of yore. The roads are being diligently repaired. Numerous old estates could be taken over, and many of them are at work to supply their first products to the world market. . . . Magnificent factories were burnt down, but small, sometimes very small, groups of men who do not envisage defeat, have returned to the estates, sometimes under the most primitive conditions, and they are working day and night. The outcome of their labours, including those of thousands of workers, is not by any means negligible. There is a pleasant atmosphere pervading the East Coast Province of Sumatra, and it looks as if an effort is being made to catch up with the time lost in purposeless waiting. [Anonymous 1947:181]

Planters interviewed about their experiences during these early postwar years all expressed a similar sentiment, namely, that the colony was secure—even if life in it was somewhat dangerous. Those who had been in Japanese concentration camps for several years were in large part oblivious to the popular political movement building around them and to the fact that most Indonesians would not have used the word *pleasant* to describe the atmosphere. One former Dutch estate manager recalled:

We went back to Sumatra in 1947. . . . the factories were running again. . . . we had to rehabilitate the estates under difficult conditions, but we had a wonderful time, it was a wonderful time. We were welcomed by the old people, they didn't have any clothes and we brought clothes with us. Every day more people came back. . . . first there were only two workers and then there was a whole gang again.[25]

And from another Dutch estate staff member speaking of the same period:

We just resumed our normal life in Indonesia again with all the difficulties of living on an estate, but the whole philosophy was still, well—this is not Indonesia, this was the Netherlands Indies.[26]

On the other hand, when questioned about the strength of anti-Dutch sentiment and the immediate threat of violence, the same man and his wife recounted different memories:

Mrs. X: It was you [addressing her husband] who was walking around with a Sten gun.
Mr. X: OK, yah, but for me, we were back in our own land.
Mrs. X: But it was not normal. . . .
Mr. X: No, it was not normal, because I remember I always went to check the estate divisions accompanied by two armed guards, and on paydays I took my own Sten gun with me.[27]

Such contradictory images of the late 1940s were not uncommon, reflecting an ambiguous reality of normalcy and siege. Although Dutch employees resumed their former positions, the estates were by no means impervious to resistance, from within or outside their borders. That an estate could not be reopened in 1947 without two permanent managerial staff members accompanied by at least 30 armed guards suggests that not everyone was welcoming the returning Europeans with open arms (Anonymous 1947:460).

A former estate administrator with whom I spoke in the Netherlands vigorously denied any physical threat to European personnel and then added:

Of course I did have a bullet right through my lungs in 1949. I was shot by some people who wanted to revenge themselves on a certain assistant who usually used a blue jeep, and since I was using a blue jeep that day I got it. They [the assaulters] were two Bataks, office clerks. A few months later we lost two people who were carrying money on payday, so in this case it was simply a robber. And a year later 3 of our assistants were killed in the same way. These were robbers, that's all. People were shot because of these robbers.[28]

Assaults on higher personnel and pilferage of estate produce were not unfamiliar problems to management. But even the presence now of unions did little to shake the European community out of its colonial lethargy. Although the communist-oriented SARBUPRI (Sarekat Buruh Perkebunan Republik Indonesia, Union of Indonesian Plantation Workers) already claimed a large number of North Sumatran workers in its ranks, the estate labor force was still not reckoned as a political force in its own right. As such the incidents described above were rarely linked (as in the prewar period) to political motive but were neutralized as personal vendettas or the acts of nonpartisan thieves.

It is conceivable that this was partly true. Given the number of military units that had been living off sale of latex and palm oil, it is not unreasonable to suppose that some resorted to highway robbery in the name of the revolution. Similarly, it is not unlikely that many workers were relieved to have the Dutch return, if only to alleviate the deprivation they had experienced over the last five years. Since alternative income sources were few, by implementing a comprehensive distribution program for food and clothing, the companies were able to draw back to the estates a large number of workers who contend that they otherwise would not have been so inclined.

The Dutch were not the only ones to deny the political import of the Javanese plantation community. Within the indigenous NST elite, Javanese participation was conspicuously absent. Langenberg explains:

This was not only because the size of the Javanese population posed an obvious threat to *orang asli* [native Malay] interests but also because of the attitudes that the NST leaders held toward the Javanese community in general. They viewed the mass of the Javanese population as coolies, indentured laborers, who up to now had been pawns in the hands of the Republican leaders in Java and of "communists" and "extremists" in Sumatra. Regarding the Javanese as uneducated, politically naive, and hence, easily controlled by whoever controlled the political system as a whole, they saw little need for anything more than token gestures. [van Langenberg 1976:640]

This turned out to be an unfortunate misappraisal on the NST's part since its success rested on solving two related problems, in both of which the plantation population was inextricably involved. One was an extensive and expanding squatter movement onto estate lands and the other a serious labor shortage. Both had the potential to effectively block rehabilitation of the industry and therefore to jeopardize foreign confidence in the efficacy of federalism. As such they became central political issues, played on by the Republican opposition and dividing the domestic and foreign elite.

The Squatter Movement

Although various radical Republican political organizations and their farmers' and workers' affiliates and/or branches were officially banned in the wake of the mid-1947 Dutch offensive, many continued to operate and gain much wider support in the NST-administered areas. Largely this was due to the NST leadership's decision to take direct action to stop the seizure of estate land and to forcibly retake control of land already under squatter cultivation. Ethnic conflicts were further exacerbated by the NST's advocation of (restored) *jaluran* (rotational access to tobacco lands) rights for Malay farmers to the exclusion of other non-Malay groups. As the NST's hard line against squatters became more evident, its opponents were quick to capitalize on the underlying conflict of interest between the mass of peasants and estate workers versus the prevailing Malay elite.

Significantly, the first estate strike of the postwar years received the active support of both squatter and workers' organizations.[29] In May 1948, 180 workers from the Batang Koewis estate in Lubuk Pakam called a work stoppage. In sympathy one of the recently established farmers' unions urged its members "to stop [estate] work and not give up their squatter plots" (BZ).[30] The following month NST authorities responded by issuing an ordinance threatening to punish severely anyone illegally occupying either public or estate land (Pelzer 1957:157). Bulldozers cleared out the settlements and leveled squatter fields but the ordinance had little effect against those obstinate enough to return and resume cultivation (van Langenberg 1976:655).

In 1948 and 1949 squatter rights and further occupation of estate area were central components of the local Republican campaign. The companies for their part wavered between two distinct approaches to the problem. In some areas they simply wrested the land from squatters by armed force. In other areas, where the food deficit and labor shortage were especially severe, temporary plots were issued to workers in exchange for labor on the estates—with the condition that these plots would be returned when the food shortage was alleviated. Although many workers accepted these allocations, not all were willing to resume estate work, and an even larger number were later unwilling to relinquish the land. In May 1950, several months after the transfer of sovereignty, another attempt was made to curb the movement. Like its predecessor this (standfast) order merely encouraged squatter militance and turned more of the population toward those farmers' organizations claiming squatter rights as their fair reward.

The Politics of the Labor Shortage

The severe labor shortage in the industry was only partially due to the large number of workers now engaged in subsistence cultivation on plantation lands. Many former workers had fled into the Republican areas, while the labor force remaining in the Dutch territories tended to be weak and malnourished, plunging labor productivity to levels far below the prewar years. In addition the estate population was made up of a disproportionate number of older men, while the tasks of clearing and reconstructing the plantation complexes demanded young male laborers and a greater number of them. In early 1948 HVA estates were operating with only 50% of their former labor force. On the Gohor Lama estate, 1,000 hectares lay dormant because of a shortage of tappers. And on the Harrison and Crosfield estates, production was only one-third of its potential for the same reason.[31]

Many companies tried to lure their workers back with far more attractive wage packages than they had offered before, but total cash and in-kind payments still remained below what even Dutch authorities calculated as a bare minimum. In 1948 male wages (0.70 guilder per day) were less than the labor inspectorate deemed necessary to support a single male worker, let alone his wife and children.[32] The question of family support had become particularly pressing since much of the initial work of cutting and clearing out the damaged crops and rebuilding estate infrastructure involved jobs supposedly done only by men.

In the meantime, employment opportunities for women were few, and thus according to one observer, "the whole economic structure of the coolie families was warped" by the fact that female labor was temporarily in low demand. From table 4.1 we can see that in 1948 more than twice as many men as women were in estate employment. As an interim measure designed to encourage the return of male workers the labor inspectorate called for wage payments on a family basis. Some companies complied and attracted more workers. But the caloric value of wages still remained 2,200 calories below the minimum calculated for a family of four. Other companies refused to make even this concession, convinced that a family wage would be hard to revoke once introduced.

Preferring to avoid wage increases, the AVROS and DPV planters' associations turned their attention to renewed recruitment from Java. The strongly Malay-oriented NST leaders, however, were firmly opposed to more immigration, especially of Javanese, contending that land pressure was already serious and that demographic increase would only make the (political) situation worse. The companies, for their part, estimated a labor shortage on the rubber estates alone of 30,000 to 40,000 workers, and in 1948 they actively campaigned for the recruitment of 3,000 families from central Java, a request repeatedly denied by the NST.[33] By the time it agreed to the planters' demand, conditions in Java had become so difficult that few families could be induced to come.

As an alternative proposition, and one that AVROS thought was sure to placate NST officials, the earlier request was replaced with one asking permission to import 3,000 *female workers* rather than families.

Table 4.1. Plantation labor force in Negara Sumatera Timur, 1942–49

Date	No. of estates	Male workers	Female workers	Total
1942	196	133,800	75,000	208,800
1948				
Jan.	128	54,700	17,000	71,700
Feb.		67,926	21,997	89,923
Mar.		74,927	26,304	101,231
Apr.		78,874	31,508	110,382
May	185	84,423	38,431	122,824
June		87,565	41,923	129,488
July		91,050	42,570	133,620
Aug.		94,872	45,558	140,430
Sept.		106,398	51,248	157,646
Oct.		108,682	52,195	160,877
Dec.		108,267	52,388	160,655
1949				
Jan.		98,412	48,832	147,244
Feb.		105,380	54,560	159,940
Mar.		107,321	58,835	166,156
Apr.		107,241	60,727	167,968
May		105,841	61,498	167,389
June		107,220	58,944	166,164
July		106,287	55,704	161,991
Aug.		106,807	58,794	165,601
Sept.		108,271	59,917	161,188

Sources: BZ, MR 325/x/48: monthly reports filed at Ministry of Interior Affairs (BZ), Jan.
1948–Sept. 1949.

For the companies this had the advantage of reducing labor costs since family allowances need not be granted. Also female recruits would presumably return to Java at the end of their contracts or marry men already resident on the East Coast. Although the NST could make no claim that this would add to the land shortage and squatter problem, the proposal was flatly rejected on several grounds. In a series of classified position papers passed among AVROS, NST authorities, and Dutch representatives of the crown, the underlying strategies of each was made clear.[34]

In short, the NST argued that there was no evidence of a local labor shortage. From the 60,000 nonworking wives in the Javanese estate community surely 3,000 individuals could be mustered to work for the estates if wages were raised to a reasonable level. AVROS refuted the claim, contending that these married women felt no economic necessity for wage employment (as many of them were cultivating squatter fields) and often deserted their jobs soon after they were hired. The NST again countered, holding that if wages were made more attractive, many women currently working squatter plots would be drawn to the estates.

AVROS continued to identify the problem in other terms, maintaining that male wages were too high (not that female wages were too low) and only by decreasing male wages could women be induced back to estate work. As it turned out, this particular plan was never carried through. But the basis on which it was contested and the conflict of interests it revealed between foreign capital and local politicians foreshadowed themes that recurred long after the transfer of sovereignty a year later.

While the NST remained obstinate in its refusal to allow further Javanese immigration, the companies resorted to other measures to meet the labor shortage. Many companies began hiring contractors (aannemer) to procure workers on a temporary basis from surrounding villages and squatter settlements. In other cases, when the estate complexes were under attack by armed gangs or Republican brigades, entire planting divisions were simply sublet to contractors who were responsible both for recruiting labor and for maintaining and harvesting the crops. Among these aannemer competition for contracts was fierce. Although AVROS condemned the common aannemer practice of "stealing" workers from neighboring estates, in fact the contract system became more prevalent as additional estates were brought back into operation and the labor shortage continued unabated.[35]

While this shortage did not cause estate wages to increase, it did force the companies to accept for employment a broader cross-section of individuals than they were wont to before the war. From management's perspective many of those hired during this period were decidedly "bad elements." First came newcomers from the Republican-held territories. Then, after the second Dutch "police action" in December 1948, when the remaining outer fringes of the cultuurgebied were brought under NST (and thus Dutch) control, they accepted many former laskyar members as well as squatters. As this more politicized population joined the ranks of the estate community, the labor movement gained new momentum, prompting renewed government efforts to counter its strength.

Proliferation of union activities on the estates and guerrilla activities on their borders once again refocused attention on estate security. One sign of the change in times particularly disturbing to those in power was the expression of Republican sympathies even within the NST territories. In 1949 an increasing number of estate guards, stationed to protect foreign properties, "defected" to the Republican camp, carrying off supplies and arms with them. In July 1949 at least 45 watchmen (most of whom were Javanese) disappeared from five different estates with 30 weapons and a jeep (BZ).[36] On the Marjanji tea plantation in Simalungun a Dutch manager was killed by one of his own watchmen (ibid.). On the Marbau estate an administrator was kidnapped and an assistant killed (BZ),[37] and elsewhere a planter was carted off by a *laskyar* unit in broad daylight. Planters surrounded themselves with bodyguards and whenever possible traveled only in convoy (ibid.).

Hostility toward the NST and the Dutch manifested itself on the estates in other forms. In one incident, when 500 workers were assembled to listen to the speech of an NST official making a district tour, the workers staged a walkout, leaving only 40 people listening to the speaker. Sentiments were not always this peacefully expressed or in the open. On the Tanah Hitam Ulu estate a secret organization of workers allegedly had been formed to "sow hate against the Dutch." And on the Tanah Gambus and Kisaran estates in northern Asahan, the Republican nationalist front was given active support. Even in the heart of the NST-controlled area, far from the border regions, pro-Republican pamphlets were dispersed and pictures of Tan Malaka and Musso, two of the most prominent and radical left-wing nationalist leaders, were found in workers' quarters (BZ).[38]

The Estate Labor Unions

Along with harboring Republican sympathizers and troops, plantation workers were being organized and organizing on their own behalf in North Sumatra as throughout Indonesia. Soon after independence was proclaimed in August 1945, the Java-based Indonesian Labor Front (BBI, Barisan Buruh Indonesia) was formed, and a year later, after repeated reorganization and internal splits, the United Federation of Labor Unions (SOBSI, Sentral Organisasi Buruh Seluruh Indonesia) emerged to represent a socially progressive, anti-imperialist labor movement—with unequivocal support for the Republican cause.[39] In the same year SARBUPRI was created and quickly became the largest union affiliate in the SOBSI federation. By mid-1947 SOBSI included 29 affiliated trade and craft unions with a reported total of 1.2 million members. Of these, 1 million were supposedly estate workers, making SARBUPRI overwhemingly the largest union in Indonesia (Wolf 1948:69).

While changes in the leadership, programs, and organizational structure of the labor movement during these early years are fairly well-documented, the course of events in East Sumatra is far less clear, not least of all because the planters' associations were often unaware of what was going on. For example, one AVROS report cites December 1949 as the date of the first public announcement of plans to establish a union of agricultural estate workers in the NST,[40] but other sources suggest that SARBUPRI had begun organizing on estates two years earlier. By 1947 Sumatran trade union membership was estimated at 500,000, but figures are unavailable for the number of estate workers included in this count (U.S. Dept. of Labor 1951:85).

In any case, labor actions in the form of strikes and work stoppages were not yet on the agenda. The SBP (Sarekat Buruh Perkebunan, Union of Plantation Workers), later merged with SARBUPRI, confined its efforts to building up workers' militia and supporting squatter rights (van Langenberg 1976:571),[41] both as part of an all-out campaign against NST-Dutch control. SBP/SARBUPRI did not monopolize the labor scene. As we shall see in the next chapter its predominance was repeatedly challenged by rival unions and anticommunist federations. By 1949 North Sumatran labor unions were "mushrooming like toadstools" appearing all over the *cultuurgebied*, with nearly 50 new unions established in the space of six months (Dootjes 1950:119).

The readiness of the workers themselves to mobilize only partially accounts for the labor movement's initial success. Plantation complexes, and those of the East Coast in particular, were linked and structured in a way that rendered their work forces eminently organizable. With estate borders adjacent and railroad and other transport facilities reaching to the remotest estates, a ready-made network was available for easy access and coordinated action. Moreover, the residential patterns of the workers were conducive to mass meetings and an easy and a quick flow of information since most workers lived in concentrated clusters of estate housing or in nearby villages on the periphery. In addition, organizers were often drawn from, or carefully placed in, low supervisory positions (e.g., as foremen). From this vantage point they enjoyed some degree of authority over workers without necessarily being considered on the side of management. These were people to whom workers were most responsible for their jobs, and on whom they were dependent for their welfare. In this dense, hothouse environment union members were quickly recruited, carefully nurtured, and on their own account became actively engaged.

Although North Sumatra's labor movement might have been a step behind that of Java, Deli's plantation workers soon earned the reputation of being among the most organized and militant in Indonesia. Their leading role in a series of mass strikes in 1950 at once created and confirmed that reputation. Demanding wage increases at a time when the price of consumer goods in Medan had risen more than 40% in three months (from 15 January to 15 April 1950), more than 80,000 plantation workers from 35 tobacco and 17 rubber estates led a strike, massively supported by railroad and telephone employees and truck drivers (AVROS, 11 Aug. 1950; van Langenberg 1976:871). From 21 August to 10 September, 700,000 plantation workers in Java and Sumatra refused to work. Eventually the strikes were brought to a halt by the intervention of two Republican leaders from Java who negotiated pay increases for railway and estate employees on the East Coast. The second action in August was settled before an arbitration board in the workers' favor. The first method reportedly went far to weaken the NST's status, displaying its inability to solve local problems. The outcome of the second action drew attention to the political power behind the labor unions.

Looking back over the period 1942–49, there is some evidence to indicate that popular participation in the revolution was neither as pervasive nor as wholehearted as some have suggested. For the plantation poor in Deli, the years immediately after the Japanese surrender were only partially liberating since much of the social and economic structure in which colonial capitalism had operated remained intact. This is not to downplay the importance of the squatter movement and the new opportunities that it made available. But it is clear that in these initial years of *increasing* hardship, seizure of estate land was an act of survival more than political committment. Politicization came later with attempts to gain recognition for squatter rights, not in the early seizures themselves.

While other classes in North Sumatran society were experiencing a radical realignment of political-economic authority, such was not the case for the bulk of the Javanese estate population. During the occupation the estate labor force was charged with feeding the Japanese army, and in later years the Republican forces as well. The strategic importance of the estates in the independence struggle ensured that whoever won, estate management would be kept out of workers' control and that estate laborers would continue to produce goods either to fill Dutch coffers or to finance the Republican effort. Much as women have traditionally been assigned to the "revolutionary kitchens," there is good reason to believe that Deli's coolies were assigned a role in the early years of the revolution not all that different from the one they had occupied before.[42]

Thus, virtually by definition, the interests of the social revolution in 1946—and the idiom in which they were expressed—were marginal to the estate workers' experience of domination, and marginalized them temporarily from one critical sphere in which the old order might have been overturned. Conversely, as the focus of the independence movement shifted to a more familiar context, that is, as the issues became centered at the site of estate production and at the nexus of management–labor relations, the plantation population became far more engaged.

Occupation of this politically and economically crucial terrain both hampered and facilitated their cause. As a primary symbol of economic imperialism and as a vital source of national revenue, the estates continued to remain the battleground of national politics, and a place where the contradictory tendencies of foreign policy and economic development were often most apparent. By one shift in the disposition of power, estate workers were pushed to the wings of at least one phase of the revolution. By yet another shift in the 1950s, they were to earn a spotlight—as it turned out a rather harsh one—in the next round of the contest for power.

5
Ambivalent Radicalism: The Estate Labor Movement, 1950–1965

The Indonesian labor movement's rapid ascendancy at a time of intense political and armed struggle against Dutch supremacy indelibly shaped its future course. Backed by a government mandate sanctioning the rights of assembly, association, and strike, in 1950 Indonesian workers were quick to avail themselves of these newly won freedoms and to lay claim to their revolutionary rewards. Particularly on the estates, where political and economic domination by North Atlantic capital was most direct, the proliferation of unions and the mobilization of their membership were rapid and widespread. Workers' militias (*laskyar buruh*), formed in 1946 and 1947 as auxiliary units to regular Republican forces, were transformed into active union locals as popular demand shifted from issues of political sovereignty to those of social and economic reform. With the initial support of the Republican government and a radical union leadership the labor movement seemed strong enough to express and even shape the new expectations of the rural poor.

In 1950 more than 700,000 working days were "lost" due to labor actions in Indonesia (Feith 1962:84). Work stoppages and slowdowns in North Sumatra—with its dense concentration of foreign firms—accounted for nearly half of all labor demonstrations in subsequent years (Biro Pusat Statistik 1957–61). Support of the 1961 workers' movements was strongly represented in the national parliament and regional councils. And at a popular level, literally hundreds of thousands of workers throughout Indonesia took part in mass demonstrations that both asserted and gave concrete expression to their democratic rights. In North Sumatra estate workers remember this period well and savor their memories. Many say it was the only time they felt *berani* ("brave") enough to make demands and *kuat* ("strong") enough to have them met. Both women and men recount stories of their own actions that would certainly be grounds for severe reprimand, dismissal, or even imprisonment today.

The 1950s was a period of apparent triumph for labor, yet in several critical respects, as this chapter will show, such an evaluation is misleading. First, the intensity of labor protest from 1950 to 1965 fluctuated enormously in a pattern that indicates a sharp decline after the mid-1950s. Second, as a vanguard of progressive social change, the labor movement had only partial and diminishing success. Ameliorating some of the more oppressive features of estate life, it never challenged the basic relations of production on which exploitation was based or the class structure in which those relations were reproduced. For reasons internal and external to the labor unions radical social change became an infeasible aspiration.

On the one hand, the means by which some of labor's victories were won, and the repression triggered by this apparent surge of popular protest and politicization increasingly constrained the labor movement's ability to promote the interests of its constituency. At the same time, a shift in the ideology and praxis of the PKI and the estate labor union most closely associated with it, SARBUPRI, from confrontation to compromise and from class-based to nationalist priorities, limited the possibilities for action and the politicization of the estate population.

In North Sumatra, the discrepancy between the strength of organized labor and the ability of its constituency to actively contest the conditions under which it lived and worked provide the focus of the present chapter. The barrage of statistics attesting to vast union membership, new labor legislation, huge losses for foreign enterprises, and an unparalleled number of labor actions in the 1950s should not overshadow the fact of an underlying and persistent opposition to popular forms of protest nurtured along with independence itself.

In tracing the rise and demise of the estate labor movement I will focus on (1) a set of basic contradictions evident in the changing mechanisms and agents of labor control, and (2) a multiplicity of constraints imposed by management, unions, political parties, and not least of all, by intervention of a growing state and military apparatus that operated against the formation of a popularly led (and inspired) workers' movement.

The fifteen years are treated here as two distinct phases of the post-independence years (1950–57, 1958–65), divided by the transition from "constitutional" to "guided democracy," by the nationalization of Dutch-owned enterprises, and by the emergence of a new class of bureaucratic elite in the estate industry—changes that all directly affected the lives of the plantation populace and the direction taken by the labor movement.

Labor in Action

The display of labor militancy that shook the political and economic life of Indonesia during the 1950s was of a magnitude meriting headline copy in the national and international press. In North Sumatra alone several foreign estate firms were forced to close and labor unrest was directly or indirectly responsible for an annual loss of millions of guilder. Production costs rose astronomically from 1940 to 1952, estate wages alone in East Sumatra increasing by 3,000 to 3,500%(De Javasche Bank 1952: 156).

These assaults on corporate capitalism were not without success. The SARBUPRI-led strike of August/September 1950 won a marked rise in the minimum wage for estate workers, and the strike of September 1953 resulted in a 30% wage increase at a time of *stable* prices (Hindley 1964: 148). In 1951 a labor code was ratified in which the companies agreed to a seven-hour day and a forty-hour week (Hawkins 1963: 263). Each year an increasing number of in-kind (*natura*) payments were provided to North Sumatra estate workers as protection against the effects of high inflation and scarce goods on the open market. In addition, various forms of protective legislation were passed and enforced to limit child labor and to ensure that women workers were granted menstrual and maternity leave.

On Sumatra's East Coast campaigns were launched by SARBUPRI to do away with the last vestiges of barrack housing and to demand that workers be allotted materials and time (during paid working hours) to keep their dwellings in repair. On issues of internal management SARBUPRI was particularly effective in ousting undesirable foremen and replacing them with those more sympathetic to the workers' cause.[1] On a more everyday level, cases of low-quality rice rations or sexual abuse of female workers by their superiors were regularly—and effectively—protested with what one foreign manager referred to as "unnerving persistence."[2]

In short, conditions that formerly had been tolerated as an inevitable part of colonial estate society became the nuts and bolts of contestation, issues on which SARBUPRI focused its efforts to alleviate the more excessive signs of oppression, if not exploitation. SARBUPRI'S success in attracting nearly 100,000 estate workers in North Sumatra, and 1 million throughout Indonesia,[3] was the result of attention to just such issues, the seemingly banal but nonetheless grating vexations of a working day: "running a kind of claims bureau in each locality in which the personal problems and needs of its members are met, SOBSI probably reaches more individual Indonesians than any other organization in the country."[4]

Just how much labor unrest disrupted business as usual on the estates obviously cannot be measured in workdays lost and guilder alone. Disruption was much more widespread than union-stage actions indicate and some of it was only marginally in their control. Company, shareholder, and AVROS reports provide some insight, not only into the strategies of organized labor, but more importantly, into the "spontaneous" and union-independent response of workers to the tactical mobility they were now experiencing.

Labor actions in the early 1950s were extremely varied in size, form, and content. In some a small group of estate laborers refused to work until a delayed shipment of rice rations arrived, in others thousands of workers throughout the *cultuurgebied* struck in unison for wage increases. Strikes were called by local union branches to demand dismissal, transfer, or reinstatement of personnel. Many of the local strikes were short, lasting a few hours or a single day, whereas other larger, coordinated actions often went on for weeks.

Foreign concerns were quick to disparage the "unprofessional nature" of union leadership and the unsophisticated and "blind trust" the uneducated rank and file had in them. Nonetheless, these early forms of protest were undeniably extremely effective and often ingeniously staged. Some of this success was due to the fact that union strategies were carefully tailored to the peculiarities of the agricultural industry and to the precarious security of the labor force tied to it. As such, certain actions in the repertoire of traditional labor union tactics were more popular than others.[5]

For example, because union dues were difficult to collect and strike funds almost nonexistent, SARBUPRI invariably demanded full wage payment, or at least the continued payment of subsidized food provisions, during legal strikes. This often entailed a bitter battle in which the unions were not always victorious. For this reason, sit-down strikes, for which the companies could easily calculate wage deductions, were less frequently used than go-slow or slow-down actions, for which this was not the case. In the latter the workers would be on their jobs, "working" full-time, though producing one-third to one-half their "normal" output—and still demanding a full-day's pay. These actions were the bane of the companies. It was difficult to assess losses and fix blame. And as a concerted, often undeclared action, slow-downs represented a form of silent sabotage outside the legal framework of government strike regulations.

Selectively directed go-slow actions had a similar effect. In these cases, only workers in key positions would be involved, while the rest of the labor force would be on the job and supposedly prepared to work. If strategic groups of workers, such as machine operators, refused to run the coagulators just as the rubber was ready for processing, the entire estate production process was forced to a halt. In addition the companies clearly had no legal grounds on which to dock the pay of the majority of passive participants.

Assaults on the estate industry were not confined to the labor unions. In some cases workers and squatters staged actions in synchrony, making it virtually impossible for management and estate security guards to deal with or constrain either group. After the transfer of sovereignty in late 1949, the squatter movement continued to escalate despite repeated government injunctions against it. In 1954, 80,000 hectares of estate concession was illegally occupied and by late 1959 the number was well above 130,000 ha in North Sumatra alone.[6]

While it is true that union tactics were somewhat limited by having to accommodate the specific features of the estate labor force, it is also true that the actions that were staged caused the companies far greater financial damages than could be estimated from losses incurred on strike days alone. Hundreds of thousands of working days taken up in agricultural work stoppages are hardly comparable to the same number in a manufacturing concern. In tobacco, which is by far the most labor intensive estate crop and the most sensitive to changes in labor inputs, millions of American dollars were written off, in part because pest control was halted for a two-week strike, during which tobacco leaves were ravaged by insects. Oil palm, which needs to be harvested at a precise moment of ripeness, fell sharply in quality, sometimes below the standard required for export. And rubber trees, subject to frequent illegal and unskilled tapping during strike actions, suffered incalculable long-term damage.[7]

Management paid heavily for labor's defiance in other ways. Aside from the actual strike actions, one of the most common company grievances during these years was the low labor performance of the work force in general. AVROS strongly protested the increased provision of in-kind payments, arguing that this was "pyschologically very unfavorable" to increased labor productivity; as workers became more secure in subsistence needs and independent of market fluctuations in basic goods, labor output reportedly dropped significantly.[8] The question, of course, is whether laborers were actually less productive during working hours, or whether high absenteeism lowered average labor output.

The companies claimed that both were true since a growing number of estate laborers were squatter farmers (which entailed arduous labor) and less willing to exert themselves during estate working hours in hopes of being able to "save their labor for their own fields." Second, many workers cum squatters refused to work overtime (which the unions had only just partially succeeded in making a matter of choice), preferring to spend this extra-time on their own plots, regardless of high wage rates paid for the additional hours (see n. 7). It does seem likely that as these other income-earning opportunities multiplied, many workers took full advantage of the leeway that union support offered them, by distancing themselves more than ever from the estate labor sphere. This was certainly the case during the early 1950s for women, many of whom withdrew all together from plantation labor and became the family "farmers" in estate laboring households.

Refusal to work overtime, absenteeism, and "saving one's labor power" were all disruptions to the labor process intimately tied to the acceleration of the squatter movement. This is a significant point for several reasons. First, it illustrates one of the basic contradictions between the labor and squatter movements; the gains labor was making on the estates were allowing more workers to *disengage* themselves from their status as the heads or members of full-fledged rural proletarian households. Second, as these actions took their toll on company profits, it became increasingly difficult for the companies both to meet wage increases and other union demands and to financially justify continued investment in Indonesia. In short, union "success" entailed placing more of the labor force outside the social and economic arena of labor action. Indirectly it forced the companies to drastically reorganize—or fold completely. Of course this is assuming that they were under some obligation to continue earning the extraordinary profits to which they had—so to speak—grown accustomed.

There were other alternatives, as the PKI was quick to note, such as the immediate nationalization of the estate industry or severe wage cuts for foreign employees and consultants. But given the importance of foreign investment in Indonesia (government revenues at the time were still largely dependent on it), these were not yet considered viable options. Instead, the government usually opted to protect foreign interests, concurrently advocating openly anti-imperialist and nationalist development plans. This fence-sitting (by just about everyone involved) had its toll on the labor and squatter movements, a subject we will return to in a later section. In the meantime the companies held tight to their fortunes and launched a comprehensive strategy of defense.

The Companies' Defense

> The estate laboring population in the NST [is] not yet ripe for labor unions.
> [AVROS, 5 Oct. 1948]

> Probably nowhere in the world have there been so many strikes in 1950 as in East Sumatra.
> [AVROS, 10 Oct. 1951]

That such discrepancies could mark assessment of the labor situation in 1948 and the realities of the situation three years later reflects a sanguine self-delusion on the planters' part that became increasingly difficult to maintain. As late as 1949, AVROS remained convinced that it could avert the invasion of labor unionism by employing measures that were embarrassingly anachronistic to everyone but AVROS. In 1948 the prewar institution of *vertrouwensmannen* was reestablished on each of the recaptured estates to provide company-sponsored "liaison men" between management and labor. While the companies claimed that this institution would render a "greater service to the workers than modern unions," the estate workers were less convinced and showed little enthusiasm for it, preferring to deal with their grievances either through direct confrontation, or by appointing a delegation of their own choosing to talk with management.

In one heated meeting in 1949 between the president of AVROS and various representatives from the Department of Social Affairs in Jakarta and Medan, the planters' intransigence provoked this response from an Indonesian participant:

AVROS's plan, which would replace better living conditions, social security and other stipulations vital to labor relations with the provision of cooking utensils, movie shows, and other trinkets, displays an alarming lack of awareness for anyone living in the midst of a progressive world and Indonesia's development. Moreover, the AVROS *vertrouwensmannen* organization is in direct conflict with all contemporary social views and trends.[9]

In all fairness, not all those concerned with protecting estate interests were so shortsighted. In fact, some of the more pragmatic members of the planters' circles saw the *vertrouwensmannen* organization not so much as a substitute for labor unionism but as a way of controlling its course:

We see in the institution of *vertrouwensmannen* a possibility to avert the formation of politically oriented labor unions. We see [it] as a forerunner to a real union without a political bent. I am convinced that this labor unionism will be upon us quickly. And now there only remains the question; by what means can we jointly steer this emerging unionism on a proper course without mishap?[10]

Table 5.1. Plantation labor unions in East Sumatra, 1952–56

Labor union	Members			Percentage of total		
	1952	1954	1956	1952	1954	1956
SARBUPRI	96,417	91,206	87,154	56	55	51
PERBUPRI	31,069	27,112	23,113	18	17	14
OBPI	13,856	20,931	18,726	8	13	11
KBKI	—	125	11,267	—	—	7
SBII	1,668	2,863	8,810	1	2	5
OBSI	—	4,758	4,924	—	3	3
SBP	11,027	5,845	4,502	6	4	3
Others	1,466	3,562	3,593	1	2	2
Nonunion	16,143	8,659	8,100	10	5	5
Total	171,646	165,061	169,547	100	100	100

Source: Adapted from an AVROS list compiled in 1956, BKSPPS.

As it turned out, *vertrouwensmannen* were not of much use in countering the tide of labor activism. By 1950 reports were coming in from several estates that these "trusted men" (which is what *vertrouwensmannen* literally means) were not as trustworthy as some had hoped. In fact they often acted on behalf of the unions, championing their cause rather than management's.[11]

Conceding to the times, AVROS changed its tack, if not its intention, and concentrated on supporting "good" (read: noncommunist) labor organizations. Thus, the companies watched the internal splits in SARBUPRI with great interest, being especially attentive to the formation in 1949–50 of PERBUPRI (Persatuan Buruh Perkebunan Republik Indonesia, Union of Indonesian Plantation Workers) which had the strong support of the Indonesian Socialist Party (Partizi Sosialis Indonesia, PSI) and other conservative, pro-Dutch factions. Under the leadership of a lawyer, Humula Silitonga, PERBUPRI remained the primary opponent to SARBUPRI and radical unionism in general (see fig. 5.1).[12] Unlike SARBUPRI, PERBUPRI was confined solely to North Sumatra. Thus, although it had political support from the PSI, it never had the organizational network and financial backing that SARBUPRI enjoyed. Moreover, it was a union whose loyal membership was drawn more from estate office clerks (*krani*) than common laborers (*buruh*). Although membership lists published by AVROS (see table 5.1) and the Ministry of Labor seem to indicate that PERBUPRI and its later offshoots (OBPI and OBSI) made some significant inroads into SARBUPRI's numerical strength, these statistics were manifestly fictitious.[13] In North Sumatra,

Figure 5.1. Developmental links among estate labor unions, 1949–72.
(This chart, although doubtlessly inaccurate, provides the
broad outline of interunion links. Source: AVROS files,
Perjanjian untuk melakukan pekerjaan ditinjau dari segi
pekerja dan pengusaha perkebunan sebagai pikah-2,
S. Wiratma, 1973.)

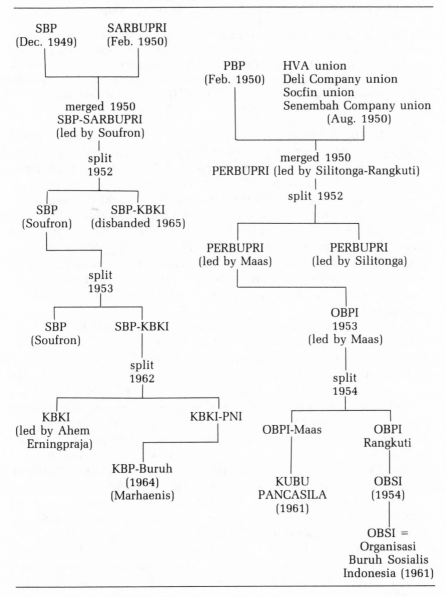

SARBUPRI firmly retained its predominance since no other union was as attentive to, and supportive of, the estate workers' demands.

The companies were not alone in their effort to counter the overwhelming supremacy of SARBUPRI on the estates and SOBSI in the labor movement in general. According to a U.S. Department of Labor report from 1951, PERBUPRI attempted to strengthen its base on the East Coast by presenting a more compliant face to the companies:

While the communist unions were fighting among themselves, the non-communist PERBUPRI sent a circular letter to employers expressing "hope for good cooperation" and asking the companies not to work against it and its activities. Although this was not expressly stated, the latter implied that the employers could expect more cooperation from PERBUPRI than other unions because it was free from communist ties. [U.S. Dept. of Labor 1951: 113]

In fact, PERBUPRI tended to side with SARBUPRI on certain issues and to oppose it on others, as in the the strike of August 1950, when PERBUPRI reached a separate agreement and withdrew from the strike on the East Coast before all SARBUPRI's demands had been met (ibid.).[14]

The estate industry's effort to discredit SARBUPRI was evident in the familiar but newly adapted lexicon of company jargon. Subscribing to the AVROS definition of a *bonafide labor union* as one that "does not concern itself with political issues" (AVROS, 11 Aug. 1950) would have meant, in practice, denying the authenticity of most Indonesian labor organizations, since a nonpartisan union without political party affiliation—or at least association—was, in this historical context, a contradiction in terms.

The criteria by which certain unions, such as SARBUPRI, were designated as "political" and others were not, were largely contingent on the extent to which their activities were amenable to those in power. In this connection AVROS was willing to classify as "modern" only those unions that were unequivocally "right wing"—of which PERBUPRI was certainly one.[15] "Political unionism" thus was a somewhat arbitrary epithet hurled against those labor and farmers' groups whose aims and actions were inimical to those supporting the prevailing social and economic order. As in the 1920s, any economic demand by labor seen as "excessive" was labeled "political" and considered outside of, and inappropriate to, the sphere of estate labor relations.

This is not to deny that political parties were intimately involved with the labor movement, often using the language of class struggle and invoking the interests of labor to further their own power.[16] To what extent this weakened the credibility of many labor organizations will be discussed below. This was, however, an issue distinct from AVROS's notion of what was "political," equated most often with those forces that might threaten the continued presence of foreign capital in Indonesia.

SARBUPRI's candidacy as the "political" union was assured on several counts: for repeatedly denoucing imperialist actions elsewhere in the Third World, for exposing the "politics" of labor control in the estate industry and beyond, in questioning the "politics" of allowing foreign companies to remain on Indonesian soil, and for exposing some of those company practices clearly designed to weaken the indigenous labor movement.

On the other hand, SARBUPRI should not be given credit for initiating all labor protest against such practices. Often it merely lent support to, and brought into the open, objections that workers themselves had long harbored and that the companies had long supressed. Demands for increased wages, social security, improved housing, shorter working hours, vacations, and better medical facilities cut sharply into the very basis of the industry's profitability. Essentially, they challenged the companies' rights to policies that rendered these foreign enterprises responsible for only part of the costs of reproducing the labor power of the active and reserve plantation work force. In the end the enforcement of these changes was more than agribusiness could bare. The state, the companies, and even the unions themselves worked in their own ways to check the audacity of labor, and thus to enforce new and renewed methods of labor control.

One of the first steps taken by the companies to defend themselves against encroachments into their profits, power, and property was to bring the two planters' associations of AVROS and DPV (the former representing perennial crop estates, the latter tobacco concerns) under a single, consolidated organization. In previous years DPV and AVROS had worked together on some policy decisions, but because of differences in the nature of tobacco and perennial crop production and marketing, they had always maintained their own wage policies and guidelines for labor–management relations. Now with the membership of some unions spanning both types of estates, the division between AVROS and DPV was no longer feasible. If the unions were going to maintain a united front in strike actions, the companies had to do the same. In 1951 the two organizations were merged, with AVROS becoming the management representative in negotiations with regional and national union agents.

In addition, in 1951 the government sponsored an arbitration committee, P4P (Panitia Penjelesaian Perselisihan Perburuhan) which functioned at the national and regional levels and which "lumped together cases of a similar character—for example, all those of the estate unions on the East Coast of Sumatra—and handed down one general ruling" (Hawkins 1963: 264). This appeal to compulsory arbitration meant that labor policies tended to be fixed at a level far removed from the management–labor interface on the estates proper, since local union members

Table 5.2. Workers per hectare
in perennial estate
crops, 1941 and 1950

	1940	1951
Rubber	0.35	0.69
Oil Palm	0.40	0.87
Sisal	0.90	1.85
Tea	0.85	2.06

had virtually no say in the P4P decisions. Thus many of the small-scale and short-lived labor actions occurring during these years were confined to disputes over the implementation of labor agreements, without contesting the decisions themselves (AVROS, 9 Jan. 1952).

Scab Recruits and the Labor Shortage

The merger of AVROS and DPV was only one of the measures taken by the companies to offset the effects of strong labor unions. The labor shortage experienced by the newly reopened estates in the late 1940s went unalleviated as the squatter movement expanded and labor deficits caused by high rates of attrition, absenteeism, and labor actions increased. Despite the high costs of interisland recruitment, AVROS undertook a renewed campaign, now under much stricter government regulation, to deal with this situation. In 1951 and 1952 almost 25,000 workers were brought from Java, along with 41,000 of their dependents, for whom repatriation was also guaranteed (McNicoll 1968: 71).

This flooding of the estate labor market with more Javanese immigrants at a time when, according to SARBUPRI reports, layoffs of local plantation workers were frequent, had ambiguous results. While AVROS might have hoped that these new scab recruits would prove more docile than established union workers, one company executive assured me that almost all those brought from Java entered the ranks of SARBUPRI. Still, new contract laborers were preferable to none at all. Labor productivity had fallen far below the prewar levels and between 1940 and 1951 the number of workers per hectare for some estate crops (see table 5.2) had increased by more than 100% (AR).[17]

Some of this increase was due to the massive labor inputs required for rehabilitation (such as in tea, whole divisions of which had been demolished during the war and revolution), to the decreased number of working days per year, and to the introduction of the seven-hour day and forty-hour week. Many companies contended that workers were simply not working as hard as they had before the war.

Recruitment of new workers from Java was calculated to provide some relief to this problem. According to management these newcomers would not be squatter farming but solely dependent on the estates for their livelihood and, having signed three-year contracts, would be less likely to involve themselves in labor actions since *all* new workers had families in tow. As a further safeguard, some stringent measures were implemented to avoid the costly expenses of repatriation. Many estates "adopted a policy of not rehiring any estate workers who applied for long leave to go back to Java, since if all legal conditions were fulfilled, this required a considerable payment on the part of the estate. . . . This policy tended to hold a number of Javanese in Sumatra somewhat against their will because they did not want to lose their jobs—a sort of forced committment" (Hawkins 1963: 222). Despite this policy some estimates indicate that the proportion of returnees to Java was as high as 90% (McNicoll 1968: 70). In any case, by 1953 interisland recruitment had dropped to a few thousand per year. Whatever shortages still existed were now met through local recruitment of temporary labor.

The Issue of Temporary Workers

The use of temporary estate workers in the early 1950s combined motives of economic and political expediency. Temporary workers (*buruh lepas*) and teams of outside workers (*borongan*) under the supervision of a labor contractor had been used before World War II for a limited number of relatively short-term tasks demanding skill and/or large labor inputs. Such work included land clearing, building construction, and large-scale replanting schemes, for which local Malays and Bataks as well as Javanese were recruited. This kind of recruitment had rarely been used for crop maintenance or harvesting as in the Java-based tobacco and sugar industry. Now, however, the companies, still complaining of a labor shortage, began employing an increasing number of temporary workers to tap rubber and harvest oil palm—tasks that had always been considered the domain of semiskilled permanent employees. Because temporary workers were accorded virtually no protection under government labor legislation, the companies were able to relinquish all responsibility for social security, housing, and other benefits stipulated for a permanent work force, thus offsetting some of the mounting costs incurred by union demands.[18]

The introduction of temporary workers during the height of North Sumatran labor activism was carefully conceived, since "casual labor

[was] not organized in unions and [was] not in a position to use the strike weapon" (Blake 1962: 117). The fact that this did not become the prevalent mode of labor recruitment on the East Coast was due primarily to the fierce SARBUPRI campaign waged against it. One estate administrator stated it this way: "We would have preferred to bring in casual labor because this would have undermined the strength of SARBUPRI. Casual laborers couldn't belong to SARBUPRI and this would have smashed the movement by splitting it; but SARBUPRI was strong enough to enforce the SKU [terms for permanent workers] at this time."[19] Not all of management was in accord on this issue. The HVA company, for example, opposed the use of temporary workers precisely because a large number of "undesirable elements" were unwittingly recruited on this basis.[20]

From SARBUPRI's perspective, this policy of divide and rule not only weakened the labor front but threatened to wipe out those very benefits for which the unions had fought. As such the abolition of temporary labor became SARBUPRI's cause célèbre, typifying the strategies of the "monopoly-capital, imperialist" camp. In vehement protest, one SARBUPRI branch wrote to the governor of North Sumatra: "With this system foreign management can easily make use of the labor of Indonesian workers without taking any responsibility for their fate."[21] AVROS responded to these accusations in much the same tone it used 18 years later when questioned on the same issue. In a letter to the governor, AVROS strongly denied that there was any such thing as *buruh lepas* with the following explanation:

SARBUPRI is referring to workers that work under the direction of a contractor. These workers do not work *for* the estate, but for a contractor who carries out specific work *at* the estate. Therefore, the estate is totally free of any work agreements between the contractor and those who choose to work for him.[22] [emphasis added]

Such semantic subtleties doubtless did little to appease SARBUPRI or the workers who saw their livelihoods threatened. In some parts of the East Coast, union branches appealed for the abolishment of temporary work status altogether. Elsewhere, they demanded that permanent and temporary workers receive equal protection and wage benefits. Although this was never achieved, the Ministry of Labor did take up the workers' case. All *aannemer* workers had to be registered, and, theoretically, those who worked more than 20 days per month were entitled to some of the advantages of their permanently employed counterparts. During these years SARBUPRI's recalcitrance did check the expansion of this type of recruitment. When the issue came up again in the early 1960s, the unions were unable to block it.

The introduction of temporary labor has been presented as a unilateral and largely political decision imposed by management. But for some of the rural poor whose squatter fields were insufficient to provide their entire subsistence needs, this work was a convenient and an essential source of cash income. For others, it was a welcome supplement. In political and economic terms, this group living on the estate periphery had removed itself from both the sphere of management and union control. For many who remained with one foot in the *kebun* (plantation) and one in the *sawah* (rice field), their ties to organized labor and their commitment to its struggle were sharply attenuated.

"Taylorism" in Agribusiness

As labor became more adept at wielding its weapons, the companies in turn perfected their own. The new political and social context of postindependence Indonesia rendered many of the traditional methods of labor control obsolete. Confronted with rising labor costs and a labile work force, the companies turned their attention within, to organizational features of the production process, to management-efficiency, cost-benefit analysis of variable to fixed capital, and to measures for increasing the productivity of individual workers as unobtrusively as possible. The methods used were perhaps not worthy of Taylorism's modern descendants but certainly well within that tradition. Rubber tapping schedules were modified, time-motion studies were carried out on certain factory operations, and bottlenecks were eliminated by reshuffling the number of workers assigned to different estate tasks (see nn. 6, 7).

In principle, this attempt to increase labor productivity was not inimical to the economic policies of the majority of national cabinets that followed one another in quick succession in the 1950s. Government slogans often urged that the continuing struggle for Indonesian independence could be attained only by augmenting the gross national product, and increased labor productivity was an essential component of this effort. SARBUPRI's position vis-à-vis this issue frequently wavered between outright support and opposition, voicing the latter sentiment more often during the reign of those anti-PKI cabinets whose support of labor's interests was not as strong.

In 1954 SARBUPRI accused the "foreign monopoly capitalists [of] forcing the workers to work harder, faster and longer for ever diminishing wage payments."[23] Again in 1956 it claimed that the new catch phrase *labor productivity* was simply a modern euphemism for "hard labor."[24] Its objections to these new methods of exploitation, however, were often inconsistent and ambiguous as it became increasingly dangerous to support workers on issues that could be construed to hamper the course of national development. In 1958, when the minister of labor set up an institute of labor productivity to continue the research of foreign estate companies, SARBUPRI gave its unqualified endorsement.

The companies for their part avoided provoking the unions and many of the changes in the production process were carried out with little opposition. For instance, on tobacco estates, where labor accounted for more than 70% of production costs, mechanization was introduced. This included the use of small aircraft for spraying insecticides, mechanized transport facilities, and new agricultural machinery for land clearing (AR).[25] On some rubber and oil palm estates, weeding costs were reduced one-third by reorganizing the division of work among the gangs of women workers. The production line for sorting rubber sheets was accelerated 25% by concentrating more skilled and higher paid workers in the final operations and allocating the less demanding tasks to unskilled and lower paid workers (AR).[26]

Not all methods of rationalizing the industry were so innocuous. Throughout Java and Sumatra various plantation companies closed down unprofitable factories and threatened more of the same if labor unrest continued at the same level. While SARBUPRI reported an increasing number of dismissals of union activists, some estates simply cut back on replacing workers lost through normal attrition rather than firing those already employed. Since the attrition rate was particularly high during these years (especially for women), this "passive" policy could quickly and significantly reduce the total work force.

The real bête noire for SARBUPRI, however, was the introduction of a new rubber tapping method, referred to as the "univers-system," which increased the piecework of a tapper from 350 to as many as 450 to 600 trees per day.[27] A division previously using 32 workers now needed only 24. New incentive bonus payments were offered to oil palm harvesters and rubber tappers, and severe penalties were imposed for under-production. Although there were repeated wage increases in the 1950s, the real value of wages was continually eroded by inflation, which encouraged more and more workers (especially those without squatter plots) to seek overtime bonuses.

On oil palm estates task work was raised from 800 to as much as 1,150 kg of harvested fruit per day. Here again, workers were fined for low yields and rewarded for high ones. On sisal estates, the weeding allotment was reduced from 3 to 1 worker per hectare. These reductions in production costs affected both the common workers and the Indonesian supervisory personnel. Division clerks were replaced by apprenticing clerks paid the wages of common laborers. Frequently a foreman charged with the functions of a superior would receive a salary conforming to his former position rather than the function he now performed. According to SARBUPRI the bonus system was particularly insidious in that it provoked new rivalries and competition among co-workers (see n. 26).

Some estates also changed over to a system in which two groups of laborers worked for shifts of 15 days, thereby doing away with Sunday as a paid day off for either group. Other estates reduced costs by cutting back on transport facilities (unlike the tobacco estates mentioned above), making the workers themselves carry their produce to the processing centers (*Warta Sarbupri*, 1954). It is difficult to fix the scope of many of these practices, whether they were pervasive throughout the *cultuurgebied* or limited to only a few estates. The fact that they are regularly reported not only by the unions, as examples of increased foreign exploitation, but also by management, as examples of increased efficiency, suggests that they were common and important enough to be carefully noted by both parties.

In conclusion it should be stated that these efforts of foreign owned companies to protect their capital investment in Indonesia were accompanied by long-term schemes for investment elsewhere in the Third World. Although nationalization of Dutch estates did not occur until 1958, such companies as HVA had seen the writing on the wall long before. Many of the Dutch firms were ventures with holdings in Africa, South America, and other parts of Southeast Asia. In the 1950s, in greater or lesser degree, they shifted their holdings to more secure and profitable terrain.

As early as 1951, for example, HVA had established a vast agroindustry for sugar cultivation and processing in Ethiopia that was to include two factories and more than 7,000 hectares (see Brand 1979: 77). RCMA, another major Dutch estate consortium whose preparations were somewhat later and less extensive, had similarly begun small cacao, kapok, and sisal estates in Tanganyika in the mid-1950s. By 1962 it had rubber holdings in Liberia, sugar in Ghana, oil palm in Panama, Colombia, and Surinam, and sisal in Tanganyika and Mozambique.[28] The tobacco companies, whose fortunes were dependent on the rich volcanic soil of Deli, fared much worse and were liquidated with nationalization.

State Intervention in the Labor Movement

The picture presented thus far of estate labor relations in the 1950s has been incomplete. It has focused primarily on the frequency and facility with which the unions used the strike weapon and on management's defense against the consequences of these actions. Foreign firms were not fighting union activism alone—nor was the confrontation between labor and management unmediated. Although the absence of the Netherlands Indies legal and administrative apparatus severely limited the companies' ability to enforce authority, on many issues they had a powerful, albeit unpredictable, ally in the Indonesian government itself. State intervention in estate labor relations became increasingly evident, at times eclipsing management as an agent of labor control.

As early as 1950, after the first outbreak of SOBSI-led strikes on Java and Sumatra, regional military commanders began issuing orders prohibiting work stoppages in the areas for which they were responsible. In February 1951 the Ministry of Defense superseded these regional ordinances with a national strike ban in all "vital" industries.[29] Although plantations were not specifically listed in this category, some reports reveal that they were included in the strike ban as well (see n. 29 source). During the next few months numerous strikes broke out in defiance of the ban, especially among SOBSI-affiliated unions against whom the prohibition was most clearly directed. In August of that year an anticommunist campaign was started in the "interests of national security" with "arrests and large movements of tanks and armored cars in East Sumatra." Throughout Java and Sumatra communist literature was confiscated, "security sweeps" were carried out in towns, and in total 15,000 were arrested (Feith 1962: 188–89). But those rounded up during the razzia included many non-PKI supporters; in fact, they were drawn from a much larger base covering political activists expressing even vague sympathy with the labor movement.[30]

In September 1951, Emergency Law no. 16 was passed (by cabinet decree instead of parliamentary approval) designating a three-week "cooling off" period between the time that a union could declare its intention to strike and the actual strike itself. In addition, this law established a system of compulsory arbitration whereby all labor disputes would be processed through the P4P national and regional disputes committee, whose members were appointed by the Ministry of Labor. Although lip service was paid to a system of direct labor/management negotiations, in fact, "whichever side lost the argument at the bargaining table was bound to appeal to the government board," and thus final decisions were usually the result of compulsory arbitration, not collective bargaining (Hawkins 1963: 264).

Despite opposition from SOBSI and its affiliates the 1951 Emergency Law remained in effect until 1957, when it was superseded by a ruling leaving most of the former system firmly intact. This included compulsory arbitration and certain restrictions on the right to strike; only the three-week waiting period was abolished (Tejasukmama 1958: 115). Coming as it did in 1957, it was a meaningless concession since in connection with political events external to the estates a state of emergency and nationwide strike ban were declared in the same year.[31]

In North Sumatra the situation was worse. Martial law had been decreed the year before during the initial phase of a regional Sumatran-based rebellion against the central government. In the years following, new edicts were repeatedly issued reinforcing the "state of emergency" ostensibly in connection with continued disturbances in the countryside, the Irian Jaya action (1957), and the seizure of Dutch enterprises (1957–58). This state of affairs "under which the military assumed many of the powers of the civilian government" officially prevailed in North Sumatra until May 1963—and beyond (Liddle 1970: 73). Liddle writes that in the district of Simalungun, "army officers were placed on the plantations to ensure uninterrupted production, political party activity in the villages was restricted, and the military attempted to exercise control over party-affiliated labor, farmer, youth, and women's organizations through the establishment of bodies for cooperation between the army and labor, the army and women and so on." (ibid. 73–74)

In 1962 and 1963 the state of emergency was affirmed with new vigor after a short-lived increase in labor actions in the preceding year. And finally in 1965, the military coup and massacre of hundreds of thousands of purported communists annihilated whatever was left of the labor movement. This grossly abbreviated summary of state restrictions on union activities is presented here only to give some sense of the conditions under which union strategies had to be formulated during these years. The indirect consequences of state intervention are discussed in more detail below.

Class Issues and *Realpolitik*

Repression of, and control over, the labor movement's potential radicalism was not carried out by state and military authorities alone. From within the ranks of the PKI and SARBUPRI, it seems that the direction of popular protest and political activism was carefully steered away from those volatile issues that might call into question Indonesian class structure itself.

Although the PKI had, from its beginning, adhered to a platform at once both stridently anti-imperialist and committed to class struggle, it was invariably on foreign domination rather than capitalism per se that emphasis lay. Analysis of indigenous class cleavages was assiduously avoided, evoked in some cadre educational sessions, but rarely permeating the practical ideology and actions of popular organizations.[32] After the strikes in 1951 the party had "resolved to moderate its class policies in favor of nationalist slogans and campaigns (Mortimer 1974: 62). By 1954, the PKI had made some strategic choices. The primacy of class struggle in ideology and practice had been subsumed by pragmatic solutions to pressing problems. To gain political leverage, the PKI increasingly conceded to strategies of coalition, alliance, and the necessity for a united national front.

This is not to suggest that the PKI sold out its constituency or abandoned the interests of mass social welfare. But there is some evidence that the party's alliance with Sukarno sharply colored the left's strategies for social change.[33] Economic and political imperialism re-emerged as the archenemy, and class issues became "intertwined with a more populist theme" (Mortimer 1974: 160). In Sukarno's hands, class no longer designated socioeconomic categories, but a simple ideological and political division between those who were "for" or "against" the rakyat (the common people).

In the early 1960s this dichotomy was clearly formulated in terms of foreign imperialism: "all who supported the government's foreign policies and the Nasakom concept formed part of the people. Just as the Masjumi [Islamic Party], and PSI [Socialist Party] were identified with foreign interests, so too were the landlords frequently labeled 'un-patriotic' and the bureaucratic capitalist accused of acting on behalf of imperialist masters."[34] In placing class beneath national interests, the party program did not do away with the class-specific concerns of the rural poor but they were seriously circumscribed. In spite of this, as late as 1964–65, the PKI did support a militant manifestation of popular protest in rural Java that had all the earmarks of a class-based conflict. Although there is some disagreement as to whether this campaign was pressed on the party from below or represented a conscious strategy of the leadership to gain power,[35] the fact remains that the focus of protest touched on the tensions of rural class structure on Java if not elsewhere.

Quiescence on the Deli Estates

Such militancy would have been quite inconceivable during the same years on North Sumatran estates.[36] Here the subservience of class to national (and regional) interests was reinforced by a series of events that kaleidoscoped in succession after 1955, producing a very different set of conditions and constraints on popular protest. Aside from a brief swell of labor actions in 1961, the quiescence of the infamously outspoken Deli plantation workers was striking. After 1955 much of the initial vigor of the North Sumatran estate labor movement was clearly gone. Why should this have been so? If activism was undermined by strategic errors internal to the movement, one might ask what this militancy consisted of in the first place? If, on the other hand, it did not simply dissolve but was forcibly squashed, one might expect to find evidence of clandestine and unorganized forms of resistance between the interstices of organized action. Or possibly activism was the child of deprivation and now that

Figure 5.2. Labor actions in North Sumatra, 1952–62.

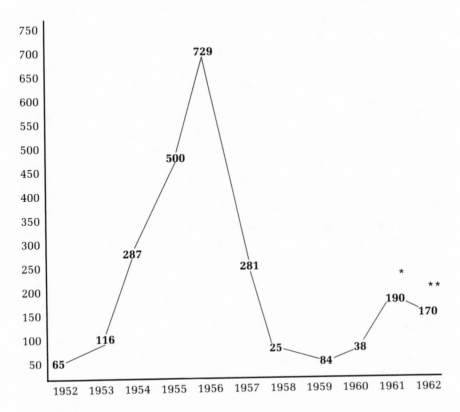

*KABIR.
**All foreign.
Source: AVROS, Medan.

estate conditions were appreciably improved, such tactics no longer had a place.

As for the pattern of strike actions in North Sumatra (see fig. 5.2)[37] during the years 1952 to 1962 the contrast between the period before and after 1956 is striking. In that year there were more than 700 work stoppages and by 1960 fewer than 50. Some of this must surely be accounted for by the state of emergency that lasted for nearly eight years. On the other hand, SARBUPRI had repeatedly ignored military decrees and government prohibitions throughout the early 1950s in protest against these restrictions on the workers' right to strike. Moreover, the squatter movement was actually gaining momentum in the late 1950s despite injunctions against the illegal occupation of estate lands. Repression was certainly one factor limiting the labor movement but it was insufficient to actually halt it. Other factors internal to the structure of labor relations were involved.

For one, the process of settling estate labor disputes underwent important modification in 1956. In that year the Central Committee for Labor Disputes (P4P), whose decisions were binding, made legal provisions for general estate working conditions,[38] which specified, among other things, wages, social security, holiday payments, and obligations of labor and management. This alone took some of the urgency out of estate labor actions since decisions regarding labor were becoming more contingent on the political lobbying of union leaders than on the mobilization of mass support. It also tended, as noted earlier, to confine union activities on the estates proper largely to the implementation of the P4P decision and its subsequent amendments (Sayuti 1968: 224). Disputes over implementation were local matters handled by union branch representatives and individual estate managers. They were not issues around which large numbers of workers needed to—or could—mobilize.

Unions and Labor Control

As the PKI gained more power through its alliance with Sukarno in the late 1950s, it was also accorded new responsibilities, one of the gravest of which was foisted on its associate unions, that is, control over the labor force that they represented. SARBUPRI's ability to control its constituency, as well as represent it, thus became a primary prerequisite for its acceptance as a spokesman for estate labor and its continued eligibility for political support from the PKI.

The structural properties of labor unions that make them obvious and effective vehicles of labor control are certainly not specific to their Indonesian variants. Stanley Aronowitz, describing the development of U.S. trade unionism, writes:

If the trade union remains an elementary organ of struggle, it has also evolved into a force for integrating the workers into the corporate capitalist system. Inherent in the modern labor contract is the means both to insure some benefit to the workers and to provide a stable, disciplined labor force to the employer. [1973: 218]

In Indonesia this function became all the more prominent with the nationalization of Dutch enterprises in 1958, after which the state came to share with "foreign imperialists" status as a major employer in the plantation industry.

Whether or not we accept the somewhat glib proposition that PKI-affiliated leaders had "their revolutionary ardor cooled by occupying positions of high status," there is some indication that the inclusion of SARBUPRI leaders in Sukarno's inner power circle in the late 1950s and early 1960s compromised their ability to negotiate as agents of labor against a management that now often represented the state. One former SARBUPRI high official described this transformation:

There was an important change in the leadership from the early 1950s to early 1960s. During the earlier period if we had negotiations we would tell our representative not to mix with those people who were representing management, not to sleep in the same hotel, not to go on the same plane, not to go in the same jeep to the estate. Not only would they be influenced by this contact, but what would the workers think if they saw their SARBUPRI leaders rubbing shoulders with the enemy. . . . in later years things changed a lot . . . for me as well. . . . it was something that I took part in too. We were easily seduced in the late 1950s and early 1960s. If we were invited to eat with management we did so, we began to see them as our friends, rather than as the enemy. They [management] were afraid of SARBUPRI, and befriended us. It's hard to fight in negotiations against someone who just fed you, and this was precisely their intention.[39]

There are several issues here. "Rubbing shoulders" does not necessarily result in cooptation. In this case it is almost certainly a symptom of other changes and contradictions in SARBUPRI's status, not a cause. Especially among workers on the newly nationalized estates, it became injudicious to support much less provoke labor activism. One might even contend that SARBUPRI leaders were forced to be the new *vertrouwensmannen*, in this case not directly beholden to the companies but to the state.

Nationalization and Labor Protest

The series of events—starting in 1956 with abrogation of the Round Table Agreement protecting privileged Dutch proprietary rights in Indonesia and ending three years later with the takeover and nationalization of all Dutch enterprises—developed out of a succession of internal and international political intrigues in which the plantation population played only a marginal role (Thomas and Glassburner 1965: 158–79). The *consequences* of these events for the industry and labor relations within it, however, were profound, reaching far beyond the borders of the individual estates involved.

During the process of takeover, more than 2,300 Dutch nationals departed from the East Coast, and by early 1960s, 101 of the 217 estates in North Sumatra were brought under government ownership and control (Withington 1964; Mackie 1962). The impact of this transfer of wealth and management into select Indonesian hands affected union activities in a number of ways. SARBUPRI's support of workers' rights in the 1950s had been predicated on an aggressive anti-imperialist program, legitimized in part because it fell within what could be construed as democratic and nationalist goals. The "enemy" as it was identified up to this time remained foreign capitalist exploitation, not exploitation as engendered and supported by any indigenous class.

By the time of takeover, when a new Indonesian managerial elite emerged on the estates, class issues had long since ceased to be a feasible priority in the PKI's party program. Thus it is not surprising that from this time on, the cases in which government-run estates were the targets of labor protest stand out as exceptions in both Java and North Sumatra. Although SARBUPRI kept up a stream of minor complaints and demands on the new PPN (Pusat Perkebunan Negara, Government Estates General) plantations, the general tenor of labor relations was, for the moment, circumspect—even conciliatory—not least of all because the process of takeover had brought with it a vast influx of military personnel into all levels of estate administration.

Starting at least as early as military supervision during seizures of the estates (Thomas and Glassburner 1965: 169) and continuing through the formal nationalization process itself, army officers were invariably included either on the boards of the new PPN or in some other high supervisory capacity. In 1957, Defense Minister General Nasution established BUMIL (Buruh-Militer, Labor-Military), a cooperative body between army and labor whose purported purpose was to "advise the military on matters in the labor field and see that workers did their duty in firms taken over from the Dutch, that no sabotage took place, and that the plants were kept in good running condition" (Hawkins 1963: 268).[40] In fact, its purpose seems to have been more specific; it allowed military commanders to intervene in labor policy, union activity, and labor disputes (van der Kroef 1965: 210). Thus, despite the fact that few army people actually managed estates in North Sumatra, their unequivocal predominance in decision-making would certainly have deterred radical labor actions against the state-run companies.

More generally, the new managerial elite held a novel combination of political power and responsibility for production, two spheres that had been separated in the years before takeover, as was noted by Mackie at the time (1962: 340). In 1961 he could still write: "there is no indication that they [Indonesian managers] [were] able to influence wider government policy in its all pervasive ideological and political manifestations" (ibid. 354). Ten years later this is precisely what PPN executive bodies were able to do. In the early 1960s these "indispensable technicians with wealth-producing property in their charge" were still feeling out their terrain and solidifying alliances with other regional elites of "similar social status and background" (ibid.). In the late 1970s

the executive boards of the large government estate corporations included some of the most influential men in the region, among the
wealthiest in Indonesia.

Constraints on the Labor Movement: Further Consequences

Some observers have contended that the lack of strikes in the years
following nationalization reflected the workers' self-abnegating role and
support for the government during a period of national economic
stress;[41] but evidence of increased army presence on the estates and in
the political life of the residency suggests that this was not wholly a
matter of choice.

From 1951 to 1964, real wages of North Sumatran estate workers fell
dramatically, from an index of 100 in 1953 to 34 ten years later. [42]
Between 1951 and 1957, during the height of union activity, the real
wage index remained between 62 and 100; in the years after the strike
ban the index fell to well under half the 1953 level. Although estate
workers fared somewhat better than other wage earners not graced with
such extensive in-kind payments, it is clear that after 1957 restriction on
civil liberties seriously weakened their bargaining position as well.

With diminished ability to contest the deteriorating conditions of
permanent estate work in the early 1960s, at a time of exorbitant inflation, many more of these workers abandoned the estates altogether,
joining the ranks of the expanding squatter movement (Sayuti 1962: 31).
This coincided with the disruptions in interisland transport (accompanying the nationalization of Dutch companies) that had temporarily
halted labor recruitment from Java. Thus in 1958 the companies were
once again complaining of a critical labor shortage (ibid.; see also Thalib
1962). Matters were made worse by the fact that most of the workers still
nominally employed full-time were devoting an increasing amount of
their working days to their own plots. The response of both foreign and
national companies was to employ more temporary workers to do regular estate jobs, a move that met with little or no resistance from organized labor. According to an ILO report from 1960 the Indonesian palm
oil industry (all of which was in North Sumatra) had a temporary labor
force nearly half the size of its permanent one (International Labour
Office 1966: 60). No flood of SARBUPRI protests accompanied this development. Cash wages for borongan workers were high and a growing
number of Javanese and even Batak squatters were willing to accept
these terms whether the unions agreed to them or not.

A Popular Perspective on Regional Rebellion

By focusing on the ramifications of nationalization, we have bypassed
one of the factors that most critically constrained SARBUPRI's activities

during the late 1950s: an episode in North Sumatran history that has been viewed largely in terms of power politics rather than its consequences for the laboring poor.

Between December 1956 and July 1958, two major attempts were made by regional military commanders to wrest civil and military control of Sumatra from Sukarno and the central government and to check the tide of communist influence. According to the received account, this action was mostly confined to two limited, and essentialy intramilitary, intrigues. The first was, despite large-scale military maneuvers, reportedly "bloodless" and resolved in late 1957 (Feith 1962: 531; Smail 1968: 173). The second phase, manifested by the declaration of the Revolutionary Republic of Indonesia (Pemerintah Revolusioner Republik Indonesia, PRRI) in Padang, West Sumatra in February 1958, was ended by the central government within a few months.

Emphasis on these two events alone misrepresents the social implications of these actions. Not only did guerilla resistance continue for another three years, but repeated incidences of arson, sabotage, rape, murder, kidnapping, extortion, and theft against the estate companies, and the *estate workers* themselves, accounted for as many casualties as there were in the "bloody social revolution" of 1946.[43] The military politics of the rebellion have been analyzed and only the briefest summary is offered here because the popular history with which we are concerned starts after the drama of elite politics had long since ended.

In December 1956 Colonel Maludin Simbolon, a fervent anticommunist Toba Batak, severed ties with the central government and declared a state of war and siege in North Sumatra pending the appointment of a new national cabinet.[44] Sukarno responded by immediately divesting Simbolon of his position and ordering his subordinate Lt. Djamin Gintings, a Karo Batak, to assume control. It was stipulated that in the event that the latter could not do so, Lt. Col. Abdul Wahad Makmour, an officer with strong communist support, was then to assume command. As Feith points out, this was a clever tactical move on the part of the Jakarta government, since if Gintings showed any hesitation to act against his superior, any move by Makmour to take control would undoubtedly prod the anticommunist military leadership in North Sumatra to force Gintings into action. And in fact as soon as Makmour began to arm his civilian supporters, many of whom were men from SARBUPRI, SOBSI, and the PKI, Gintings and those of his followers who were more strongly opposed to communism than to Sukarno, quickly took action and forced Simbolon to retreat into the Tapanuli highlands.

In early 1957 Makmour was forced to relinquish his claim to North Sumatra's command, and by October of that year most of the village and estate-based armed civilian groups, the OPD (Organisasi Pengawal

Desa), established by Makmour, surrendered their weapons. According to Smail's account there were more than 17,000 OPD members in East Sumatra, although it is not certain how many were from SARBUPRI and how many were actually armed. From Simbolon's perspective, and that of his rebel militia, however, there was good reason why the estates and the populations on them should have been made the primary target of guerrilla operations.

For one, the estate population both was Javanese and housed the most concentrated loci of communist support, two attributes that characterized plantation workers as the "natural" enemy of the rebel groups. Second, destruction of foreign estate property was a gambit meant to discredit further the central government in the eyes of Western powers, who would then presumably throw their support behind the rebellion.[45] Third, by disrupting government PPN estates the rebels were directly attacking a primary source of national revenue. Finally, as always, the estates were repositories of the largest source of ready cash, food, and other material provisions on which the rebels' ability to subsist indefinitely depended.

Simbolon's troops were pushed back into Tapanuli temporarily; soon afterward they moved eastward through Simalungun, Asahan, and south into Labuhan Batu, leaving their mark on most of the estates in their path. During 1958, 1959, and 1960, the number of rebel attacks on the estates in the southern region of the *cultuurgebied* reached staggering, although almost unheralded, proportions. For example, Harrison and Crosfield's Normark plantation was forced to close when factory installations were burned and workers, under rebel attack, had to evacuate their homes. At Laut Tador estate, owned by the same company, rebels posted signs warning workers that if they continued to stay on the job they would be killed. At the Gunung Melaju plantations, a rebel gang destroyed the power plant of the palm oil factory with repeated fire of heavy arms, and at Goodyear's Wingfoot estate, "bazooka and automatic arms did extensive damage to the estate power house, telephone exchanges, and [the rebels] almost completely wrecked the estate manager's office by firing a bazooka shell through it."[46]

On plantation after plantation godowns were stripped of their stock, while tons of rice, huge numbers of poultry, and mounds of clothing were "collected" from workers' homes. Gangs remaining in an area for some length of time levied taxes on workers in the name of the PRRI and extorted hundreds of thousands of *rupiah* from the companies on a monthly basis. Not infrequently estate personnel were kidnapped and held for ransom, estate women raped, and Europeans who dared to travel between Rantau Prapat and Medan risked losing their possessions—and their lives.

Hundreds of workers' houses were burned or stoned and then ransacked. From among those families that had not already fled, men were conscripted to carry the stolen supplies for the rebel militia. Jeeps were confiscated and trucks carrying produce were set afire. These illustrations are not isolated incidents, carefully chosen for their vividness, but a fairly representative sample of occurrences that was reported almost daily between 1957 and 1960 for Labuhan Batu and even central Asahan to the north.[47]

Although these events seem marked by a degree of *arbitrary* violence, there is evidence to suggest that SARBUPRI and its members were specifically singled out for special "attention." In one case when a SARBUPRI office was burned to the ground, all other estate buildings were left standing. When news arrived at the Maligas estate that the rebels were coming, SARBUPRI ripped down the sign outside its headquarters, while that of the Muslim Party's associate union, the SBII (which enjoyed the rebel's favor), was left in full view. At Wingfoot estate in July 1958 a group of armed men entered the compound demanding to see the SBII union identification of the foremen and to know the whereabouts of the "communists." Although all Wingfoot's workers were SARBUPRI members, when asked, no one would volunteer the information. In 1959 and 1960 the estates which were foreign controlled were also ones where SARBUPRI retained its strongest support, so it is difficult to know by what criteria certain estates were marked for harassment and destruction rather than others. In any case it is certain that SARBUPRI strongholds rarely went unscathed.

One side effect of this general chaos was that others, outside the rebel *gerombolan* (gangs), partook in the free-for-all. Management seldom could identify its assailants or distinguish between different military garb. In a few cases, managers wondered aloud whether they were being attacked by rebels or their own workers in disguise, but cases where local villagers or workers were caught red-handed were rare. It is probable that many workers, forced by rebel attacks to leave their homes and work, sought other means to support themselves; some tapped estate rubber illicitly, and where food shortages had become particularly severe because of rebel levies, workers too broke into company storehouses. Foreigners living in this battle zone found themselves in a singularly hostile environment. Under constant assault from outside, their only "allies" were their own workers, who under "normal" conditions would themselves have been carrying on their own brand of anticompany sabotage.

This episode of power politics and guerrilla action affected the *cultuurgebied* unevenly; in those areas where rebel activities were incessant and fierce, the estate industry along with the labor movement was ravaged. Although Smail suggested that the OPD civil guard, with its large left-wing popular base, comprised a social movement in its own right, daily reports from individual estates suggest that the bulk of the estate laboring population was more victimized than radicalized by these events—certainly not in an offensive position vis-à-vis the companies or the rebels. On the other hand, in the aftermath of the rebellion, labor's support for Sukarno was stronger than ever. Even in safer estate districts, virtually untouched by the rebellion, the choice between Guided Democracy, whatever its restrictions, and Simbolon was not a difficult one to make. Once again the necessity of alliance with the central state apparatus helped protect and constrain the workers' cause.

The Squatter Movement

The fate of the labor unions in the late 1950s contrasts sharply with that of the squatter movement with which it was so ambiguously tied; as the former faded in militancy, the latter accelerated with unprecedented vigor. The differences between these two are worth looking at in some detail, both because their communalities have sometimes been over-emphasized and because they point to such distinct bases of popular support.

Some of the reasons that the labor movement was constrained from within and without have been related above to the pragmatics of political leverage and to the decision-making hierarchies within the unions themselves. For the squatter movement such leadership-based mechanisms for control were much more difficult to apply.

First, those who participated in the illegal occupation of estate land were, in a practical sense, not part of a unified movement at all. They were Javanese ex-estate workers, land-poor Bataks from the Tapanuli highlands, refugees from the rebel regions of Aceh, ex-military men now thrown on their own resources (with the end of armed struggle), and Malay villagers "reclaiming" their hereditary rights (see Cunningham 1958 and Pelzer 1957). Also dispersed among these various ethnic groups were a large number of land speculators, buying and selling squatter rights before these rights were legally recognized.

This does not mean that there were no farmers' organizations actively supporting squatter rights and encouraging land occupation;[48] among them, the Barisan Tani Indonesia (or BTI, Indonesian Farmers' Front), associated with the PKI, was one of the largest and most aggressive. But, of the half-million people who were squatters in North Sumatra in 1957, there were probably as many outside these organizations as there were those within. Although much of the squatting was indeed the result of veritable invasions orchestrated by the BTI in which hundreds of men, women, and children acted in concert in night raids on estate land, squatting was also carried out on a much more modest scale. It was not uncommon for a family or a small group of households to quietly, and surreptitiously, start cultivating small plots of unused land on the estate peripheries. Fields would gradually be cleared, thatch houses built, and in a matter of days, before estate guards were even aware of their presence, a *kampung* (hamlet) would have appeared.

On estates of 2,000 m² it was nearly impossible to patrol the entire circumference. The guerrilla tactics of squatters made the patrols largely ineffectual, as large-scale, coordinated invasions were well planned and because, in more haphazard seizures, the participants were often relentless. Squatters ordered off the land often complied and simply returned again the following night. If tractors were brought in by the companies to level squatter fields, women and children would place themselves in front of the vehicles and refuse to budge; drivers confronted with such a situation chose to be fired rather than carry out their orders—and the squatters remained. Such resistance tactics were not taught to squatters by a professional leadership; they were learned through the experience of continual confrontation and became the intuitive, "natural" responses of those whose livelihoods rested on no other conceivable option.[49]

Thus what distinguishes these squatter actions so clearly from work stoppages is that they were not strategic *gestures* of resistance or a means to an end but actions that *embodied the end in itself.* Work stoppages, on the other hand, were weapons used to win other concessions, provocations to force the company's hand. As such, there was no iconographic resemblance between a strike action and its hoped-for result. This is a crucial distinction because it meant that most labor actions were bracketed arenas of resistance, lasting as long as a particular dispute, and quickly discharged when a settlement was reached or promised.

In the case of the squatter actions, nothing short of the right to remain on the land was acceptable, and this meant the recognition of the right for *everyone* who had participated. Under such conditions there were no partial compromises or appeasement for those who were "tractored" off. Moreover, there was no way in which one could be represented by another at a squatter action; either one took—and defended—land oneself, or one got no land. Leadership hierarchies, the basis of collective bargaining, simply made no sense in the squatter context because negotiations, at this level, played little part in the process.

There were, of course, many attempts by both government and company authorities to inhibit this encroachment on the material assets of foreign firms. By 1951 it had become evident that the standfast order issued the year before to freeze further squatting had no restraining effect. The tobacco companies thus agreed to return 130,000 of their 250,000 hectares to the public domain in exchange for the right to a new thirty-year lease on the remaining land (Pelzer 1957: 157). On the face of it this seemed to be a generous concession on the part of the companies until it became clear what land they had chosen to give up. A report by a committee on land reform showed that 40,000 hectares of this was un-cultivable mountain land, another 40,000 hectares was forest and swamps, and 20,000 hectares comprised long-standing village settle-ments; this left 30,000 hectares, most of which had already been claimed by squatters before the war.[50] Not surprisingly, this agreement did little to alleviate the problem, instead it turned more farmers' organizations against the iniquitous companies.

For several years this government/tobacco estate pact remained on paper only. When an attempt was made in 1953 to put it into effect by forcibly evicting occupants from an area designated for return to the Tanjung Morawa tobacco estate, the ensuing clash between police and squatters (who tried to disarm the police) resulted in the shooting of four Chinese and one Javanese and a large number of arrests. This was no local affair. The Wilopo cabinet's support of the eviction, and its un-equivocal siding with foreign capital, made this notorious Tanjung Mor-awa affair an immediate and a principal cause of that cabinet's fall (see Feith 1958).

In 1954 Emergency Order no. 8 was issued conferring legal status on those people already occupying land and calling for the removal of those who seized land after the law went into effect (Pelzer 1957; Gautama and Harsono 1972: 113). The order also had little impact, particularly after the Round Table Agreement was abrogated in 1956. A wave of new squatters took to the estates in the same year and so paralyzed the tobac-co concerns that they threatened to close down unless the government took immediate action. In 1956, still another emergency order was issu-ed imposing even more stringent penalties but it too was largely ignored. By the late 1950s the squatter problem had become more serious, outside the control of even the most powerful farmers' organizations.

The movement was continuing to expand in a way that presented new problems. Early squatters had used their fields for dry crops, and after one, or at the most a couple of years, the soil could no longer bear this kind of cultivation without losing its fertility altogether. Many squatter groups thus began constructing irrigation channels, diverting water from small rivers into estate land, in the process destroying vast numbers of palm and rubber trees that required well-regulated drainage. Estate seedbeds and new planting areas were often inundated and roads were eroded by intersecting aqueducts. Ditchdigging teams did their work by moonlight, and estate guards were prevented from filling in the channels by women and children lying in them. When ditches were filled in, they were simply dug out by the squatters the following night.

The squatter invasion continued to escalate until 1960, when it was effectively halted by a new law, strictly enforced by military authorities. This law no. 51 provided an ordinary legislative prohibition against squatting, in place of the earlier emergency orders. Superseding all previous rulings, it decreed that a squatter could be evicted without court order. In addition to imposing severe penalties on the squatters themselves, it stipulated that anyone who "instructs, orders, induces, or proposes orally or in writing" others to perform such acts would also be legally culpable (Gautama and Harsono 1972: 13–14). The combination of this curb on farmers' unions with much more energetic military participation in enforcement of the ruling meant that the amount of land under illegal occupation fell sharply and large numbers of squatters were *ditraktorkan* (tractored) off their plots.

Very basically, the squatter movement embodied a unique combination of militant popular action, far-reaching political consequence, and intrinsically conservative individual motivation. Many of those who participated did so with a commitment and tenacity unparalleled in other contemporary popular movements. For foreign capital the squatters posed a more serious threat than the labor movement: this was no bid for equity within the system but was an attempt—conscious or not— at destroying the system itself, inasmuch as appropriating estate lands entailed the destruction of the industry.

For many of the Javanese rural poor, however, their engagement in these activities was animated by a goal not unfamiliar to contract coolies twenty-five years before or Javanese in Sumatra today, namely, the desire for a small, independent, and individually owned homestead. The 1950s' scenario offered only a slight modification from the earlier one. Instead of returning to Java with enough savings to buy a small plot, the dream was now transposed to Sumatran soil—and squatter cultivation was a cheaper, more convenient and realistic fulfillment of it.

Older people in the villages on the estate periphery today, when recollecting their own part in the squatter invasion in the 1950s, say it was the first time they could give concrete expression to their distaste for estate work—and act on that sentiment. Some believed at the time that squatting would allow them to break their ties altogether with the companies. The phrase often repeated *ora gilem direh* ("I didn't like being ordered about"), expressed a sentiment that drove many Javanese to abandon their meager pensions and bet totally on a livelihood from farming alone. At the time this was not a far-fetched expectation; despite the legal insecurity of their claims, the political climate of the 1950s made many feel they were taking a reasonable risk.

Viewed from the perspective of the 1980s, however, this concurrence between homesteading and the estate labor movement backfired on the participants as few households could subsist from farming alone. Drawn back to the estates later, as temporary workers, the squatters themselves became that labor reserve which the planters had tried to create so many years earlier. As an even larger percentage of the labor force was drawn off the estates, the companies in their turn were relieved of much of the burden of their reproduction. Land occupation seemed to offer a way out, but a contradictory one since it went far to weaken any fundamental commitment to labor activism in its plantation form.

Labor in Protest: A Revival of the 1960s

The short-lived resurgence of SARBUPRI's plantation-based activities in the early 1960s was precipitated by increased army intervention in labor relations, and specifically by Sukarno's unsuccessful attempt in 1960 to do away entirely with plural unionism (by establishing the OPPI [Organisasi Persatuan Perburuhan Indonesia], a united labor federation for all Indonesia). Such an action would have effectively terminated SOBSI's control of the labor movement. Nevertheless, labor put its faith and numbers behind Sukarno, and scrupulously avoided any attack on him during those actions that were mounted in the early 1960s.

The most vivid example of this in North Sumatra came in 1961, when a strike had been called demanding wage increases and protesting military mismanagement. Lasting several weeks, the strike was interrupted only once, for a 24-hour moratorium called during Sukarno's one-day stopover in Medan.[51] After his departure the strike was resumed, leaving no doubt as to the significance of this gesture.

SOBSI's response to OPPI and to military interference in labor issues was to mobilize workers—even though strikes were still forbidden—on political issues that were undeniably within what were defined as national interests. One of these was a campaign launched against Belgian companies in Indonesia in reprisal for "Belgian imperialism" in the Congo. In March 1961 SARBUPRI occupied the Belgian estates in Labuhan Batu and Asahan (Van der Kroef 1965: 244). Although the estates were not actually expropriated by the workers but put under government (military) control, the fact that the action was lauded from a nationalist perspective successfully diverted attention from the fact that SOBSI itself was temporarily banned.

One student of Indonesian labor history has suggested that this focus on external political issues, in particular imperialist forays by foreign countries with holdings in Indonesia, was used by SOBSI as a legitimate excuse for mobilization at strategic moments, even after the army and state had otherwise paralyzed the movement (LeClerc, personal commun.). In North Sumatra union actions alternated between attacks on foreign imperialism and the military in a series of successive, sustained disturbances. As political statements they were clear, but it is doubtful that they allowed for any significant improvement in the working conditions of the estate population.

Between 1960 and 1961 the number of strikes in North Sumatra rose from 38 to 197, all of which were "spontaneous," that is, unannounced and therefore illegal, and many of which were on government estates. Charging military mismanagement, SARBUPRI here first applied the label *bureaucratic capitalist* (KABIR) to describe estate managers in North Sumatra (Mortimer 1974: 258). In July and August 1961 a cluster of such wildcat strikes broke out over wage issues and in protest against the deteriorating living conditions on the estates (Van der Kroef 1965: 244).

Some observers have questioned SARBUPRI's claim that these were indeed "spontaneous" forms of protest rather than demonstrations engineered from its Jakarta headquarters (Mintz 1965: 11; Van der Kroef 1965: 244). A former Jakarta-based SARBUPRI organizer contends that there were elements of both. He had been sent to Medan to help organize a mass strike from Siantar. By his account, the initiative for the strikes and the desire to keep them going *berapa lama saja* ("as long as necessary") came clearly from the local union representatives. It was they, he contends, who said *harus mogok* ("we must strike"); the fact that strike plans were communicated in secret code among a limited number of branch leaders does seem to indicate that the work stoppages in the summer of 1961 were probably not spontaneous, but they were not necessarily engineered from afar. The army's reaction was to arrest many local union leaders and subsequently to fire hundreds of workers.[52] As PKI, SOBSI, and SARBUPRI had kept a low profile in the local actions, these organizations were never officially implicated.

Work stoppages continued in 1962 but followed a different tack. Of all the actions taking place between January and October of that year, totaling 141 strike days, only 2 one-day strikes occurred on government estates, while the majority were directed against American concerns. The claim that SARBUPRI stepped up its campaign against the army and KABIR with a "new aggressiveness" (Van der Kroef 1965: 243) contradicts what is known of the situation in North Sumatra, where most of the strikes were called on Goodyear and Uniroyal estates over delayed deliveries of rice.[53] On the other hand, this apparently nuts and bolts issue was not as straightforward as might at first appear. Rice deliveries were not under the control of foreign companies where the strikes took place but were managed by a government board in Medan, a fact that company reports repeatedly emphasized. Thus with scanty camouflage, these protests reflected on, and were directed at, military mismanagement of estate and more general regional affairs.

SARBUPRI's diminished ability to mobilize workers on government estates was exacerbated by the formation in 1962 of an army-sponsored workers' organization embracing all state employees, vertically integrated and dominated by management.[54] SOKSI (the Central Organization of Indonesian Socialist Workers) was one of several attempts at dismantling the conceptual and practical basis of the SOBSI-led labor movement. In North Sumatra, SOKSI fared rather poorly, succeeding only on some government estates where the military was most well entrenched. Its very existence, however, significantly thwarted SARBUPRI's organizing capacities among these plantation workers.

Accompanying this military foray into mass organization was the use, initiated by SOKSI, of an entirely new social vocabulary. The most striking example of this was the substitution of the word *karyawan* for *buruh* (workers), the former applying indiscriminately to all employees from top management down, connoting undifferentiated service and duty to the state. As such these *karyawan* organizations not only attempted to undermine the structural autonomy of the workers' unions but conceptually challenged the basis for them by, in one fell blow, obliterating—at least lexically—the necessity for class struggle.[55]

SARBUPRI's campaign directed against the military KABIR proved untenable and between 1963 and 1965 its energies and tactics for mobilization once again turned against foreign imperialism. This attempt to radicalize politics by focusing more attention on British and particularly American "neoimperialism" resulted in the takeover of British firms in 1963 and American enterprises in early 1965. The first case was precipitated by confrontation with Malaya over the establishment of a Malayan federation under British aegis, and the second by growing fear of a political conservatism and economic dependence that many felt would inevitably accompany Indonesia's imminent acceptance of U.S. foreign aid. American intervention in the Gulf of Tonkin in late 1964 added credibility to the PKI's warnings against ties with the United States, and in the ensuing months American cultural, political, and economic installations were boycotted across the board (see Mortimer 1974: 203–46; Van der Kroef 1965: 280–84).

While both these actions, in which the labor unions played a major role, were indisputably victories for the left, the fact remains that they had little on-the-ground import for the mass of plantation workers. Although control of these estates passed from European hands to Indonesian military personnel, the change was literally only skin deep since the structure of labor relations remained virtually unaltered. In many ways it was a Pyrrhic victory for SARBUPRI because more direct military control meant more direct pressure on workers to join SOKSI, or at the very least not to participate in SARBUPRI-sponsored actions.

From the same sources that provided such a plethora of detail concerning labor protest and union activities during the period 1950 to 1962, for the final three years before the 1965 coup, there is a disturbing lack of data. Sporadic reports of combined labor-squatter actions on the Uniroyal estates in 1965 exist, but such entries are few and far between. This in part was simply due to the fact that during this period the planters' association was in complete disarray; the systematic intelligence network that had been AVROS's hallmark until the mid-1950s had already begun breaking down with nationalization. Nonetheless, summary lists of labor unrest continued to be prepared, which suggests that if there had been many incidents between 1963 and 1965, traces of them would show up somewhere in the AVROS files.

Some of the constraints on union activity during this period have already been alluded to: the KABIR had become a formidable foe and one whose vested interests obviously increased as their power grew. Second, between 1963 and 1965, recruitment of contract labor from Java had increased twofold to more than 55,000 new workers in this three-year period (McNicoll 1968: 71). Not only have recruits never been among the most militant workers, but this influx of new labor power left many former temporary estate workers unemployed; certainly labor surpluses have never strengthened the bargaining position of labor with management. Third, much of SOBSI's energies were now focused on political jockeying for national power, on the radicalization of national level politics, a strategy that ultimately might have benefited workers, but in the shortrun left them—and their interests—unattended. Finally, despite otherwise deteriorating living conditions on the estates, the plantation population, compared to other wageworkers, was relatively well protected from runaway inflation by a wage packet made up almost entirely of in-kind payments.

The quiescence of local organized labor actions during these years does not mean that the Javanese rural poor in Sumatra were passively accepting their fate. Between the interstices of organized action, estate workers, with or without backing, were pursuing their own strategies of survival and protest. Their efforts to "reconstitute" as a peasantry certainly qualify as one mode of resistance, a line of defense. The experience of the previous fifteen years had taught them how far they could go to improve their own terms of existence, and what options were available to them despite military, state, and union constraints. Squatter tactics were more refined and the continued encroachment onto estate lands, both foreign and national, during 1964 and 1965 attests to the fact that many were still prepared to take major risks. Similarly, theft of estate produce continued unabated, as did high rates of absenteeism and low rates of productivity, and this despite the fact that both the ILO and SARBUPRI now supported the goal of increased production as critical to national independence.

But these strategies of individualized resistance were of ambiguous import, as much adaptations to the prevailing economic order as a serious assault on it. The signs of popular protest that do emerge at a time when the official union apparatus is most constrained are of a particular kind. They are not the tactics of offense but acts of disengagement, signs of retreat onto the political and economic periphery of the estates—and the labor movement.

6

The Contemporary Contours of
Labor Control, 1965–1979

Part I: Political Economy in the *Cultuurgebied* after 1965

Régis Debray has said that political time accelerates in periods of crisis and stagnates in periods of reflux (1970: 1940). The military takeover of Indonesia in 1965 represented one such instance of dense political acceleration—in this case, in recoil, in a wave of violent reaction against the preceding decades of left-wing ascendance. On September 30, 1965, six high-command generals were murdered, allegedly as part of an attempted coup planned and executed by the PKI. Although communist involvement in the action is relatively certain, much of the evidence suggests that the PKI was a pawn, not the mastermind behind this bid for power.[1]

Whatever obscurities remain surrounding the September 30th movement its catastrophic aftermath was gruesomely evident. The military took it as a long-sought warrant to wrest power from the PKI. It led almost immediately to the eclipse of Sukarno by Suharto, and to the wholesale massacre, under the military's aegis, of hundreds of thousands of Indonesians allegedly members of, or sympathetic to, the PKI and its affiliates.

Within a few months the largest communist party in Asia outside China and the USSR was virtually extirpated, its leadership and membership were killed, imprisoned, or dispersed. Within a few months the left-wing labor movement, which had largely set the tenor of postindependence Indonesia, was outlawed and destroyed. Within weeks of the coup, squatters who had tilled as their own former estate land since the 1940s found themselves ousted from their homes and divested of their livelihoods. In short, what had seemed to be the assured realities of

162

much of Indonesian political life built up over the preceding fifteen years, were in a matter of weeks obliterated.

The mix of power politics, foreign (especially U.S.) involvement, and social tensions that gave rise to this grisly scenario are outside the purview of my discussion here. Rather, this chapter is an attempt to examine the critical economic and political changes brought about by this disjuncture, and their translation into the lives of those working in the charged arena of North Sumatra's plantation belt. Part I deals with the broad domestic and foreign policy changes that dramatically altered corporate strategies of labor recruitment, retrenchment, and control. Part II examines the changing class composition on Sumatra's rural East Coast. And part III questions how these policies have affected the domestic and community organization of several estate laboring populations in the Asahan district of North Sumatra today.

Toward an Account of the Unaccounted

While estimates of the number actually killed during the six months succeeding the coup vary enormously, most accounts agree that somewhere between 250,000 and 1 million Indonesians were killed by army personnel, right-wing Muslims, or other civilians given license and encouragement by the military to help wipe out "communists and their sympathizers."[2] According to figures reported by a team of Indonesian researchers in 1966, the victims included 800,000 in Java, 100,000 in Bali, and "almost as many in Sumatra" (Hughes 1967: 184).

Most of the killings in Sumatra were centered on the East Coast, and more specifically on the estates where card-holding left-wing labor union members were concentrated. According to one of the few foreign journalists reporting on North Sumatra during this period, the army reported killing "twenty-percent of the rubber plantation workers in the Medan area" (ibid. 142). The statement, however, is either misleading, misquoted, or false since Medan itself is immediately surrounded by estates of tobacco, not rubber. Either Hughes confused the crops or, and more likely, the statement refers to a much larger radius, including a significant portion of the Deli–Serdang region extending to the north and south.

If the estimate is at all representative of the casualties suffered by the estate labor force as a whole, it would mean that more than 56,000 workers were killed in late 1965. There is no direct evidence to substantiate this claim. All we do know is that on the eve of the coup, the total estate work force numbered nearly 283,000.[3] A year later that number had been reduced by 47,000, or by 16%.[4] What proportion of these casualties were killed—as opposed to imprisoned, fired, or missing (having fled)—is unknown. It is the case, however, that very few of the SARBUPRI union leaders, branch heads, or estate division representatives are known to be alive today.

Estate workers from the Asahan district say that the nearby rivers were clogged with the bodies of their co-workers, that sons whose fathers were SARBUPRI ketua (local leaders) were forced to watch their executions, lest they and their families be subject to the same fate. The silence and fear that still reign concerning the massacre are broken only by government officials who voluntarily boast of their successful campaigns to weed out all sisa-sisa PKI ("communist remnants"). They too are silent about the number killed, preferring to talk about the "large numbers of PKI" before 1965 and the small number of TAPOL (an abbreviation for tahanan politik, i.e., political prisoners) resident in their districts now.

For those not killed, the stigma of having belonged to SARBUPRI seriously changed their lives. Under Suharto's new order, all left-leaning labor unions and other organizations were outlawed, and in some estate regions SARBUPRI members were summarily fired and blacklisted from permanent estate work. This practice, however, was not always efficacious or uniformly the case; on some estates, where as much as 90% of the work force belonged to that union, such large-scale firings were infeasible and SARBUPRI workers were allowed to remain temporarily on the job. In conjunction with new estate policies designed to rationalize production and reduce labor costs, as late as 1976—eleven years after the coup—a large number of workers were fired ostensibly "because of their former PKI affiliation." To see just how effectively this ruse was employed, we need to look more closely at some of the elements entailed in the new government's program for economic "stablization."

Foreign Aid to the Estate Industry

One of the first steps taken by Suharto's new administration was to reaffirm old ties and make new ones with foreign investors and funding agencies. Of the latter, among the quickest to reappear on the scene was the World Bank. A Bank reconnaisance report from 1954 deemed Indonesia's political and economic climate "unstable," rendering it an undesirable risk and thus ineligible for loans. In August 1965 Sukarno withdrew altogether from the Bank and other international agencies. Under the New Order membership was renewed in April 1967 and a year later Indonesia joined the International Development Agency (Thompson and Manning 1974).

In a development lending program designed to expedite a rapid increase in foreign exchange earnings, rehabilitation and rationalization of the estate industry were given top priority. Out of a total of $1.334 billion allocated for various projects between 1968 and 1974, the single largest ($59 million) loan (excluding a project for road construction) went to the government estates. There were obvious reasons for this; for IDA and the Bank, these loans represented eminently "bankable" investments. The payoff would be quick and foreign export earnings could reasonably be expected to increase more rapidly than those of other sectors. To ensure this, the Bank advised funding the most prosperous government estate complexes, keeping within a well-honed tradition of "betting on the strong" (that is, on those estates that least needed the loans) on the putative assumption that the beneficial effect of these projects would trickle down to smallholders and boost the rural economy as a whole.[5]

Such arguments, however, were flimsy rationales for projects that not only ignored the pervasive problem of unemployment in North Sumatra but also directly contributed to it. This is not to suggest that all the new labor policies adopted by the estates were implemented on the advice of the World Bank alone. Even before its first project was started, estates throughout the East Coast had already begun a concerted effort to reduce their permanent labor force, this time with the government's assent and no viable unions to protest. As noted in one Bank report from 1972 *consolidation* was the "watchword" of the times; between 1965 and 1968 the estate labor force had already been whittled down by 34% (World Bank 1972: 5). The report states:

Recruitment of estate labor slowed down considerably after 1966, and the last few years show that returning laborers [to Java] exceed the number of new recruits. . . . While this outflow [from North Sumatra] is not important in comparison with the total number of unskilled permanent labor in Sumatra it may well become so, if the present drive to increase labor productivity in the government estates is translated into a labor force reduction rather than output increases. For several years to come, this may indeed be the case. In the estates visited, the watchword was consolidation, with little or no addition to the labor force. [ibid.]

In fact increased labor productivity was already in large part conceived in terms of a "labor force reduction," and Bank projects from 1969 already included this assumption in their project cost estimates. In one such 100-page document only two brief statements alluded to this issue: "Most estates employ more labor than is required; consequently no increase is needed in the labor force to implement the project" (IBRD 1969: 6). And elsewhere a footnote reads: "It has been assumed that [the] wages will rise continuously at 3% per annum cumulatively throughout the project life, compared to the general level of other costs. For the

Table 6.1. Permanent estate workers and their dependents in North
        Sumatra, 1965–78

	Total no. workers	Men	Women	Nonworking women	Dependent children
1965	282,804	218,521	64,283	118,617	467,429
1966	235,559	174,003	61,556	115,706	n.a.
1968	186,350	130,750	55,600	100,142	443,567
1969	175,500	127,800	47,700	98,990	452,710
1970	158,187	111,090	47,097	85,538	432,956
1971	151,176	106,926	44,250	81,992	429,994
1972	132,987	95,480	37,498	75,975	399,371
1973	126,222	91,923	34,299	74,682	384,781
1974	123,785	90,637	33,148	71,226	363,808
1975	121,485	89,281	32,204	71,190	345,832
1976	119,125	87,818	31,307	71,080	341,008
1977	119,006	88,176	30,830	72,939	339,097
1978	119,738	89,299	30,439	73,431	332,606

Source: BKSPPS, Medan.

investment period, however, *it has also been assumed that an annual
retrenchment of labor at a rate of 3% would be achieved with improved
management practices.*" (ibid. 15).

As it turned out, labor force reductions averaged not 3% but 6% per
year (ranging from 2 to 12%) between 1969 and 1974, bringing the total
permanent labor force in 1974 to just a little more than *half* what it was
nine years earlier (see table 6.1). First, we should immediately dispel
any notion that this reduction reflected adverse economic conditions
experienced by the estate industry as a whole. During the same period,
production increased enormously, especially for palm oil, and the total
area under production was expanded through vast replanting schemes
to replace old rubber trees and through conversion of rubber to oil palm.[6]

Both production increases (of 44% in rubber alone) and decreases in
the number of permanent workers per hectare were in part the result of
technological innovations and reorganization of the labor process.
Among the most important of these have been the introduction of high-
yielding rubber and palm clones, the application of stimulants to increase the latex flow in old as well as young trees, the introduction of
chemical spraying to replace hand weeding, extensive and increased use
of chemical fertilizer, conversion from rubber to oil palm, rehabilitation
of old factories and construction of new and more efficient processing

plants, and new tapping methods and schedules that increase the number of trees tapped by each worker per day.[7]

Obviously not all these methods have been used by all companies to the same extent or with the same effect. Few companies, for example, paralleled the advanced labor-saving schemes introduced by the Belgian-Indonesian joint venture, SOCFINDO, over the last ten years. Whereas some companies have steered clear of chemical weeding because of its high capital costs, SOCFINDO has used spray chemicals to replace hand weeding across the board. Between 1967 and 1977 it was able to reduce the number of workers per hectare on some estates by as much as 60%; that is, from 0.49 workers/hectare to 0.19 workers/hectare. Elsewhere labor retrenchment has been less dramatic, but the fact remains that for the North Sumatran estate industry as a whole, the trend often has been to do away (where possible) with those operations, and the cultivation of those crops, that are more labor intensive.[8]

The two most striking examples of this are witnessed in the region-wide shift from rubber to oil palm culivation, and in the replacement of permanent by temporary laborers. A report from the Indonesian Department of Agriculture showed that between 1972 and 1976, although the area allotted to oil palm increased by only 25% (with a concomitant decrease in rubber), its production increased by 250% (see Departemen Pertanian 1979: 110, 118–19). Several important factors have contributed to the move away from rubber and to this new emphasis on palm oil. For one, the world demand for oil palm products as well as their world market prices has risen sharply and this trend is expected to continue. Rubber prices, on the other hand, declined in the late 1960s and continued to do so throughout the 1970s. Second, oil palm represents a more profitable undertaking per unit of land and offers a much quicker return on investment. Its maturation period is only three years, as opposed to that of rubber, which is nearly seven. Third, its labor demands are far less rigorous than those of rubber. Of all the nonextractive commodities produced in Indonesia, oil palm has the lowest labor intensity of any crop (Paauw 1978: 453). Not only is it much less labor intensive than rubber, tea, or tobacco, but its harvesting operations are simpler and less dependent on skilled workers. Consequently—and very importantly—it allows the use of more temporary rather than permanent labor. Finally, as many estate managers explained, oil palm products are far more difficult to steal than latex, the theft of which is a well-practiced tradition on the East Coast. (Actually palm products have not proved as "theft-proof" as some managers hoped; they are much more subject to in-house, large-scale acts of plunder and speculation, as opposed to the series of frequently but pettier thefts by individual workers associated with rubber. This issue will be discussed in more detail below.)

Indonesia has not been alone in its switch to this more lucrative industrial crop. In fact, Malaysia's conversion programs have been far more extensive, but without the same consequence. In North Sumatra just the fact of this conversion certainly has added to the unemployment problem. But more significantly this shift has been accompanied by various other labor cost-cutting devices that have compounded the problem all the more—the most serious being the replacement of permanent by "temporary" laborers.

The Rise of "Temporary" Estate Labor

As described in chapter 5, the use of temporary workers has long been a vigorously contested issue, resisted by estate labor unions of all political persuasions throughout the 1950s. SARBUPRI and PERBURPI in particular led a joint campaign calling alternately for government controls or outright abolition. Soon after the 1965 coup, however, the companies again turned to temporary workers, this time with no holds barred. According to the official government count, from 1973 to 1976, temporary workers increased from 10% to 29% of the total work force on the government estates. (Departemen Pertanian 1979: 109). This is a highly conservative estimate. On many of the private foreign and national estates, as well as on some of those that are government owned, temporary workers (referred to as either *buruh lepas* or *buruh borong*) make up more than 50% of the labor force and are employed at wages far below what they would earn for doing the *same* tasks as permanent employees.[9]

Other estates have reduced their labor costs for some operations by as much as 70% by using this lower paid, outside labor source drawn from villages surrounding the estates and from the estate compounds themselves. For the companies there is an obvious advantage: these workers are recruited and managed by a labor contractor (*pemborong*), who pays their wages and to whom they are responsible. No social security, housing, family rice allowances, or other social benefits are accorded them. In addition the companies may easily feign ignorance of the abuses to which this growing segment of the work force is subject. Widespread use of child labor and wage payments below the official minimum are ostensibly outside their control, ken, and concern.

Aside from the obvious benefits accruing to the companies from this form of recruitment, many estate managers contended that they were *forced* to employ temporary workers because of a rural labor shortage in the late 1960s.[10] The questions are obvious: How could this have been the case when the World Bank reported a *surfeit* of estate workers and planned to continue a policy of further retrenchment for the same years? How could this possibly have been the case when thousands of squatters lost their plots during the late 1960s and early 1970s and were thrown back on the estates for much of their livelihood?

Even with the evidence presented thus far, it is clear that a potential work force made up of those who had lost their squatter land, who were fired for political reasons, and who were dismissed for economic ones was far larger than the estates had use for at the time. The fact that the companies were unwilling to hire these workers meant only that there was a "shortage" that was gender specific and politically contingent; that is, they refused to hire on a permanent basis anyone with previous involvement in SARBUPRI or, in many cases, women. But these two categories aside, how could one speak of a labor shortage when tens of thousands of Javanese adults and children avidly sought out temporary estate jobs despite the low remuneration and insecurity offered by this type of work?

There is one respect in which this "shortage" of permanent workers may not have been all together fictive. From 1965 to 1968 the permanent estate labor force was reduced by 96,550 workers, or 34.1% . Most of the large-scale replanting schemes were begun just after this period as foreign funds were again channeled to the estates. Many companies were just embarking on huge projects demanding high and concentrated inputs of labor for cutting and clearing old trees, for intensive weeding in the initial years of replanting, for dispersing chemical fertilizers and for other operations tied to this extraordinary period of high capital investment. While replanting schemes are obviously cyclical and occur throughout the life of an estate, they are rarely done on such a large scale in such a short period of time. Thus the high labor demands of the early 1970s were, in a sense, artifically inflated. Having reduced the permanent labor force as much as they had, few companies were willing to take on more permanent workers simply for these transitory operations, although for several years they were definitely in need of them. An ILO report from 1967 indicated that oil palm estates employed fewer than half the workers they actually needed (McNicoll 1968: 70). No wonder then that this estate-imposed restriction on hiring permanent workers generated the need for a massive number of temporary ones. Still this is a far cry from arguing that the estate industry had "difficulty in attracting workers" (Pasaribu and Sitorus 1976: 35), which implies that there was a surfeit of jobs and not enough people to fill them.

Female and Child Labor in the Temporary Labor Market

Changes in estate policy have not been confined to a reorganization of the labor process but have been accompanied by a major shift in the age and sexual composition of the work force employed to fill these new positions. This change is most apparent in the increased gender specificity of estate employment. On many estates in the prewar period, and even up until the 1960s, both men and women were employed as rubber tappers; now there are no women tappers in North Sumatra. Weeding, replanting, and pest control were also traditionally done by permanent women workers; now, almost all these tasks are performed by women, adolescents, and children on a temporary basis. Oil palm harvesting, for which young male labor is preferred and relatively high paid, is totally closed to women workers. And there are almost no women in the estate factories on the East Coast.

During the last ten years the number of female estate workers has been reduced by as much as 50% on some estates, compared to only 30% for men. Many women who voluntarily quit their *dinas* (permanent) jobs to tend squatter fields in the 1950s, or those who were "released" from their jobs for unspecified reasons, have moved into the labor market, but now as temporary workers. Estate officials contend that women prefer the "flexibility" of temporary jobs and suggest that most women ceased to work *dinas* on their own accord. Whether or not this is true, the fact remains that the choice is no longer their own. Estate officials readily admit that the costs of permanent women workers are simply too high; since none of the government-stipulated regulations concerning pregnancy and menstruation leave applies to temporary workers, the relegation of women to this type of work represents a significant reduction in estate labor costs.

The introduction of temporary workers on the present scale has also been accompanied by an increase in the use of child labor, adolescents below the minimum age of 18 stipulated for permanent work, as well as elementary school-aged children, as young as 9 years old. The lack of official statistics on these members of the work force and the reluctance of estate personnel to collect them reflect a general attitude on the part of the companies and the state. Most estate managers disclaim any knowledge of this increase while others say very simply, "We prefer not to know." And for good reason; this "ignorance" has allowed some companies to continue employment practices that were made illegal 65 years ago.

The facts, however, have become more difficult to deny. As many teachers and village officials pointed out to me in 1977–78, the sharp decline in school attendance after second grade (elsewhere after first) offers strong evidence that children are being drawn into estate work at an early age. This professed ignorance on the part of estate personnel in early 1978 seemed all the more unnecessary when only a few months later a series of exposé articles appeared in the national press focusing specifically on the use of child labor on the North Sumatran estates (see *Tempo*, 4 Nov. 1978). One such article in *Tempo* (Indonesia's equivalent of *Time*) detailed the labor practices of the American Uniroyal Company in Asahan, where children of ages 7 to 12 were being employed directly by contractors or indirectly as "helpers" to their parents. A somewhat perfunctory "clean-up campaign" by government officials followed. Many children did stop work for the duration of the inspections—only to return to their jobs again after the campaign and the press's interest in the issue passed.

Thus far, we have looked at some of those changes in labor recruitment practices that possibly could be construed to have been adopted as "emergency" measures in the initial years of estate rehabilitation. They allowed the companies to increase labor productivity and decrease the total labor time necessary for specific tasks at a time when the new government and its creditors saw themselves in need of increased export earnings at any cost. But the adverse consequences for the estate laboring population neither have been transitory nor have they abated. In one of the final IBRD appraisal reports evaluating the success of its North Sumatra estates project, the possibility was noted "that wages may have not only failed to increase, but given the additional hours worked on the estate by the average laborer on overtime, that his hourly real wage has declined."[11]

While the IBRD report was wary to draw this conclusion too hastily, there are other factors supporting this claim, the most important being the abolishment of all eleven commodities (supposedly converted into cash equivalents), except family rice subsidies, included as in-kind (*natura*) wage payments. Given that the present cash wage is a mere fraction of what it now would take to buy these same goods, the real value of wages has fallen drastically. Second, we are now talking about an estate labor force whose composition differs sharply from that of ten years earlier. If we were to calculate the changes in average real wages of *all* estate workers—including those employed on a temporary basis—it is clear that the real value of wages has decreased far more than most official calculations admit since an ever increasing percentage of the total labor force (anywhere from 25 to 60%) is made up of temporary workers.

Labor retrenchment has been gender specific. It has also been highly selective in another sense; between 1970 and 1978 the number of "married" male workers (read: those with dependents) was decreased by 32%. The number of "unmarried" males *increased* by 22.4% for the same years. Or, seen from a somewhat more striking perspective, between 1965 and 1978 the estate industry rid itself of the costs of providing for the more than 130,000 dependent children eligible for rice subsidies.[12]

None of this, of course, means that there are fewer people dependent on the industry than there were fifteen years ago. If anything, there are more living in the company's shadow, on income sources very loosely defined as legitimate.

Part II: Class Structure and the Corporate Hierarchy

The shift in Indonesian national politics has recast the economic prospects of the estate industry as well as that of certain select social groups whose livelihoods are now directly or indirectly dependent on it. In giving a new tenor to management–labor relations, this shift has also crystallized an indigenous class structure already nascent in the post independence years, particularly after the 1957 nationalization of Dutch enterprises.

On the one hand, the estate corporate hierarchy has a new set of Indonesian agents filling old positions. In this respect the formal structure of the hierarchy retains much of its colonial facade. There remain, as under Dutch rule, a head estate administrator (ADM), several assistant managers (Asisten Kepala, ASKEP), supervisory assistants charged with specific planting divisions, office clerks (krani), technicians, foremen (mandor) responsible for specific blocks within these divisions, and the bulk of ordinary workers responsible to these foremen. In some respects corporate and class structure parallel each other but they are by no means isomorphic. What has significantly changed are the new political and economic uses to which these positions are put, and the kinds of wealth and investment generated by them.

In turn, new positions have been created by the restructuring of the industry as a whole. These are not new classes but fractions thereof that have emerged as by-products of the industry's frequent reorganizations. We can begin by looking briefly at the apex of the corporate hierarchy and then at certain segments of rural society.

The government-owned estates (formerly Dutch owned and nationalized) were organized in 1968 into 28 independent management units, clustered generally according to crop and geographical location. Each of these units or PNP (Perusahaan Negara Perkebunan, Government Estate Enterprises) has its headquarters in Medan or on one of its centrally located estates and controls a total of anywhere between 13,000 and 44,000 hectares of crop area. Each unit is headed by a board of directors, appointed by and responsible to the Ministry of Agriculture (or in the case of the new PTPs—government estates with somewhat more financial autonomy—to the Ministry of Finance).

Members of these boards comprise the upper crust of the industry, and few have worked themselves from the bottom up. They are well-educated, cosmopolitan, politically well-placed, and by either national or international standards, men of great wealth. Their children are often schooled abroad, their vactions are spent in Europe, and most own luxurious second homes in Medan or Jakarta in addition to their estate residences provided by the companies. They are, in short, one of several groups at the top of the bureaucratic capitalist elite, who derive their wealth and power not so much from their high-salaried jobs as from their strategic positions in the flow of goods, services, and contracts that come under their ostensible control.[13]

Within the corporate hierarchy, it is the group below these men, the estate managers and their small circle of administrative assistants, who are the immediate and local representatives of state and/or corporate authority. Although budgets and general guidelines for production on the government estates are determined by the Ministry of Agriculture and the PNP directors, estate managers are given relatively free rein in matters concerning the hiring and firing of personnel, the use of temporary workers, and negotiations with labor contractors.

Not surprisingly, it is they, far more than their corporate superiors, who have donned colonial garb, whose life-styles are vividly reminiscent of their European predecessors of decades earlier. Some of the resemblance is circumstanial; most managers live in the manorial houses built by planters in the flush of Deli's fluorescence. Often surrounded by manicured gardens, these fortresses were usually built on slightly higher ground, near head offices, overlooking—but always distant from—the workers' compounds. Estate managers and certainly their wives were and are rarely seen on foot; the ADM (pronounced "ah-day-em") and each member of his top staff has a jeep and driver at his official and personal disposal. Their homes are equipped de rigueur with expensive, albeit plastic, furniture, color television sets, refrigerators, a bevy of domestic servants, and other necessary accoutrements marking their middle-class status and urban sensibilities.

It is they who patronize the Chinese luxury stores in the towns, which once served the foreign planter aristocracy. They are not, and do not consider themselves, part of rural society and go to great lengths to make sure that their high status is well-marked and always apparent. Their children are sent off to schools in Medan, their wives mix socially only with other locally residing staff members of more or less equivalent rank. Although there are those managers who do "descend" to the *lapangan* (the estate fields) a number do not. The majority of administrators with whom I talked on visits to more than 20 North Sumatran plantations did not know the names of any of the villages surrounding their estates, much less the particular ones from which the bulk of their workers were drawn. Most had never set foot in the villages at all.

In all fairness, I should note that this isolation was not entirely of their own making. As one merchant put it, "Mereka tidak boleh campur" ("They're not allowed to mix"). As in the colonial period, but perhaps even more so now, job transfers among higher level personnel are frequent and obligatory. A manager rarely stays at the same plantation for more than three or four years. In addition, promotions almost always entail a transfer elsewhere. Thus, it is easily understandable that many staff members are neither on familiar terms with their subordinates nor knowledgeable about their local surroundings. On the other hand, some have profited well from their combined estate functions and rural residence, mainly through land speculation and other investments. This "participation" in the rural economy is a relatively recent development and seems to have followed quickly after the government's crackdown on squatter rights in the late 1960s. Many estate squatter villages were razed. In some cases the occupants were simply tractored off the land; in other cases they were compensated with nominal cash reimbursements or other (smaller) plots.

We can look at an instance of one such scheme from 1977, which brings out some of the new social dimensions of these relocations:

In one district of Asahan a foreign company relocated an entire squatter community from an estate division where the majority of occupants had lived since the war. According to Indonesian agrarian law, squatters who occupied estate lands before 1954 were supposedly protected from having their land alienated, but in some circumstances they could be moved "with full compensation." For the instance in question, this particular stretch of squatter land had been an issue of contention throughout the 1950s, and at the time the left-wing farmers' organization, Barisan Tani Indonesia, had strongly supported the squatters' rights to remain.

After 1965 such squatter settlements were singled out as hotbeds of alleged PKI sympathy and were the first to be broken up. Although the squatters themselves often knew their rights, they did nothing to defend them, fearing that they might be labeled "sisa PKI." Many people in the area felt the eviction was singularly unjust. Even one local government official readily admitted that the majority of squatters were simply "korban politik" ("victims of the political situation").

In any case, some of the squatters who had been farming as much as 10 rantai (nearly .5 hectare) were "compensated" with plots of 1.5 rantai (600 m²) of marginal, unirrigable land within the estate concession. Within two months of being moved onto the new plots, more than 10 rantai of the area had found its way into the hands of three Indonesian staff members of the foreign firm concerned: a head factory assistant, an estate inspector, and the estate manager himself. Several months later, they sold the entire 10 rantai for 1 million Rupiah (about $2,500) to a staff member from a neighboring government estate. And shortly after, 10 more *rantai* from the same area was sold to an important local official.

In the meantime, the value of the small bits of roadfront property allocated to the ex-squatters soared, and merchants from the nearby town and staff personnel from surrounding estates quickly bought them up. Within six months after the relocation scheme had begun, most of the compensated, squatter households had sold a good part of their holdings, leaving themselves with no more than 200 to 400m² as homelots for their makeshift dwellings. Those who witnessed these rapid-fire transactions first hand say that such practices are not uncommon. Almost any villager can recall several such accounts in exacting detail. In the case at hand, the situation was aggravated by the fact that the estate staff member who bought up the property was bringing in workers from his own estate to clear and fence it. The fact that the villagers themselves were not employed to do the work provoked heated discussion and plans for retaliation. One group of village men even plotted to pull out the fence stakes at night in protest but the plan was never carried out.

Land speculation is only one of several new lucrative income sources for the estate supervisory personnel. There are others following closely on changes in the labor process. *Pungli* ("corruption") is endemic in Indonesia, but many people (from workers to government officials) say that its spread into the estate sector is reaching unprecedented proportions. The most prevalent form of graft seems to be related to negotiations between estate management and various *pemborong* (contractors) called in for specific construction and cultivation jobs.

As noted above, in the new and "stable" political climate of the 1970s, most estates, whether government or privately owned, embarked on massive rehabilitation projects for improving their infrastructure, processing plants, and cultivation systems. These projects were carried out largely by outside contractors, chosen, in principle, through competitive bidding. In practice the contracts were and are rarely decided in this fashion. Between management and contractor a full-fledged exchange network of goods and services has developed, the details of which even common estate workers are fully aware.

The following is a common scenario, one of many variations on the same theme recounted by contractors themselves and corroborated by other estate personnel not directly involved:

An estate administrator or assistant will file a contract estimate at, say Rp. 500,000, far above its actual cost. A contractor with whom he is already in silent "partnership" receives the tender. The ADM then borrows Rp. 300,000 from the contractor with the unstated agreement that the loan will never be repaid. The contractor pockets Rp. 100,000, the ADM Rp. 300,000, and Rp. 100,000 is set aside for paying the workers one-half to one-fourth the amount of the daily wage calculated in the original estimate. According to other variants about two-thirds of labor contract budgets fall into the hands of management and *pemborong*. I found independent confirmation of these practices in examining labor contract estimates; in many cases the average daily wage was calculated at Rp. 450/day/worker, when in fact temporary estate workers were receiving no more than Rp. 125–150/day. Such practices represent one type of arrangement in a varied network of backscratching ties.

One sign of the closeness of these alliances between estate managers and particular contractors is the fact that these relationships often endure longer than, and are independent of, a manager's three- to four-year tenure on a particular estate. One contractor whom I knew well consistently won contract bids on each of the four estates to which his "patron" manager was transferred over an eight-year period. Presumably the other contractors followed their "patron" managers elsewhere. According to many informed sources, contractors are willing to pay dearly to maintain such "good will." Gifts ranging from televisions to cartons of Johnnie Walker Black Label, to bicycles for a manager's children, and to call girls on demand are only a few of the concrete tokens of a relationship, secure and bound.

Company directors do not seem to be fully aware of these dealings. In fact, the owner of one private (*swasta*) national estate said he was forced to fire an assistant and do away with the use of *pemborong* altogether because their work was inferior and because huge sums were being siphoned off company profits by methods that directly implicated his trusted staff as well as the contractor. On other estates, however, some assistant managers charged with arranging contract work have bypassed the contractors, often unbeknownst to the directors. Rather than pay a *pemborong*, the assistants pay their foremen and clerks to recruit outside labor and pocket the contracting costs themselves.

In addition to bribes and embezzlements, in-house theft of estate produce also pads the pockets of many personnel, commonly referred to by workers as *wereng*, or "parasites," a particularly graphic description; these rice pests bore from the *inside* out, destroying the plant. Such theft is supposedly rampant, especially on the oil palm estates, where processing machinery can be easily reset to allow a large percentage of the oil-bearing kernels to be "discarded." By this method, tons of "waste" material are sold to private processing factories for profits that never enter the company records.

Obviously not all of estate management is participating in, or benefiting from, such practices. If compared to the oil scandals plastered across headlines of the international press, these forms of *pungli* are trivial. But they are not inconsequential in analyzing the contemporary trajectory of rural class relations, or why certain groups have a vested interest in its present course. Many of the dealings are directly at the expense of workers' wages; and they are arrangements grounded in the fact that there is a large temporary work force, and that it should remain. Moreover, the power that supervisory personnel wield over their underlings should not be underestimated. Many estate staff members loanshark to ordinary workers, while some assistant managers call on their division workers to perform personal odd jobs with no recompense. And as in an earlier period, there is little a person can do, save quit, if a female relative catches the fancy of one of the managerial staff.

Labor Contractors: Rural Hustlers

Plantation staff members sometimes use their estate positions to participate in illicit and semilegal ventures. Labor contractors, on the other hand, are using their positions in the estate labor system as a base for investment in a far wider range of rural enterprises. As middlemen between the estates and the laboring populations on their peripheries, they make up the newest class of rural entrepreneurs, combining business connections in the estate and urban economy with a commanding position in the flow of rural wealth. Socially, they straddle—and deftly maneuver—the vast social distance between management and labor, rubbing white-starched shoulders with the one, lounging easily in the bamboo-thatched homes of the other. They are characterized by a wide range of wealth and ethnic origin and some have a fair amount of political clout.

In southern Asahan, for example, the majority of estate contractors are ethnic Chinese, from families who have long been merchants serving the plantation companies. Some own as many as 14 trucks for transporting their workers to estates dispersed throughout the area. Others supplement their incomes as estate owners (of plantations as large as 5,000 hectares) in their own right. In northern Asahan the *pemborong* operate on a somewhat smaller scale. They are ethnically mixed, including a larger number of Batak, Indian, and even Javanese origin. And such work often runs in the family. As "good connections" with estate managers are deeply coveted, "good will" is carefully transferred between siblings and inherited from father to son.

Of the eight to ten contractors whom I knew well, all were engaged in various capital-intensive investment projects in addition to their work on the estates. Some owned large tracts of land in southern Asahan; others owned hulling machines that they themselves operated or rented out; some built restaurants on heavily trafficked thoroughfares to Medan. One had installed a generator and electricity lines in several hamlets from which he recruited most of his temporary estate labor. After several months he had the lines torn out, claiming that villagers were not keeping up their payments. Several weeks later the generator showed up in a neighboring village to power a rice-huller.

Unlike the income-earning activities of estate management, nearly all these investments combine an intimate knowledge of the region *and* its population; one needs to know where village unemployment is especially high, where rice land is abundant or scarce, where the harvests have failed and when the harvests will take place. Second, most of these ventures make use of the patronage-like ties between the contractors and their temporary estate-laboring recruits. For example, since agricultural wages are higher in the south, many contractors transport their estate workers for short periods of planting or harvesting to their land in these districts. Contractors often help out their "regulars" by advancing them cheaper rice or, in cases of illness, they may even foot some of the costs. For those workers who have lost access to permanent estate work and the social security it offers, these are strong incentives to accept the attendant demands and obligations such a relationship implies.

Some contractors simultaneously run several large operations and thus employ a number of assistants to do their labor recruiting, but many of the smaller *pemborong* take care of the "public relations department" themselves, weaving on their Hondas through the estates and villages surrounding them, hailing a worker by name here, stopping briefly for a cup of tea there. Other contractors expend more of their time securing management connections, especially where the labor supply is abundant and secure.

As people who work *buruh lepas* are the first to say, there are no hard and fast rules governing these relationships. Some contractors are considered stingy, unreliable, and—when possible—they are avoided. Others are more "agreeable," flexible, and thus preferred. But, for the most part, these relations are still formative, negotiable, and varied. While there are some enduring ties between contractors and their regulars, for most workers the relationships are ephemeral and brittle. If a contractor, for example, does not keep his wages up to the going rate, even regulars will quit at the next payday and go elsewhere until he has raised them. But such situations rarely occur. Among themselves, the contractors have created an informal labor monopoly; they tend not to trespass on one another's domain, stake out certain hamlets as their own, and set wages at the lowest level the workers will bear. Some of the reasons why villagers are forced to accept these conditions should already be clear. Their alternatives are discussed in the section below.

Itinerant Trade and Rural Merchants

Other groups have also profited from the reorganization of the estate industry and its labor force. From the earliest years of the *cultuurge-*

bied's expansion at the turn of the century, Medan, Siantar, Kisaran, and other small cities and large towns supported a large class of traders and middlemen, who provided goods and services to the managers of Deli's estates. In the prewar years this sector was the monopoly of Chinese merchants. After independence, when the labor unions successfully pressed to establish an extensive wage packet of in-kind payments, these basic commodities (rice, kerosene, cooking oil, cloth, and other dry goods) continued to be supplied by ethnic Chinese traders. At the same time, an active itinerant group of Batak traders worked out a barter system with plantation workers, exchanging estate-supplied goods for those not included in the workers' wage packet. Many of the commodities were simply recycled over and over again, with the traders selling back to the estates, for example, cloth they had received in exchange from the workers.

In the late 1960s, as labor policies were revamped, the provision of in-kind wages was gradually phased out and by the early 1970s abolished. Estate wages are now paid in cash with a rice subsidy. Also, since the war, the number of Javanese living off the estates has grown enormously. With these two developments, the rural economic landscape has been sharply transformed. Small towns, formerly mere crossroads between the estate concessions, have mushroomed into important trading centers, providing a rapidly expanding rural population with markets in which to sell their produce and buy other goods.

Well-stocked dry goods stores in the large market centers still tend to be owned by those of Chinese descent, but in small district centers Batak merchants are far more prevalent. The latter continue to dominate itinerant trade, bringing to the villagers and the estate *pondok* such diverse goods as cloth, cooking utensils, and furniture. Almost all this trade is negotiated on a credit basis at prices far above the current market value. Despite the fact that villagers may ultimately be charged twice as much as they would were they to pay on the spot, with little ready cash at their disposal few have any choice.

Dry goods stalls in nearby market towns are far more stringent with credit terms, and many villagers have had to pawn, and eventually have lost, their land, bicycles, or other assets to urban merchants. Absentee landownership in surrounding villages by this trading class is becoming increasingly common. The owners tend to invest in dry land, planting low-maturing but high-yielding clove orchards, requiring large initial capital inputs but little labor for maintenance. Like the labor contractors, many own land in Asahan (which they also have tended with workers from the more densely populated north), hulling machines, and personal luxury items (such as motorcycles and electrical appliances), which set them far apart from the rural poor.

The groups outlined above in no way represent an exhaustive inventory of the rural social spectrum; they have been singled out here because they hold strategic positions—socially and economically—vis-à-vis the Javanese estate laboring communities. Although there are some Javanese in their ranks, the majority are of other ethnic groups. They control access to the critical economic resources of land, capital, and labor opportunities (not necessarily in that order) and they are the groups with which the Javanese workers come into the most frequent and direct contact.

Like corporate and class structure, ethnic and class divisions are not isomorphic, but they almost always coincide. If we add to our list the preponderance of Bataks (and the absence of Javanese) among schoolteachers, local government officials, agricultural extension workers, midwives, and proprietors of almost every rural manufacturing enterprise, class and ethnicity nearly converge along the same lines. As we shall see in the following section, this convergence is critical for understanding the social reality in which rural Javanese in North Sumatra live, and their representations of that reality in social practice.

Part III: Javanese Communities on the Plantation Periphery

Parts I and II of this chapter have attended to policy changes in the estate industry over the last fifteen years, and to some of the features of rural class composition accentuated and transformed by them. This section takes as its focus the social and economic structure of several contemporary Javanese estate-laboring communities, with attention to those conditions that have altered the life trajectories of its members as well as the prevailing social relations of production and exchange.

Although Javanese villages surrounding the large plantations of North Sumatra are by no means homogeneous, they do share certain common characteristics, defined by the distinct social space in which their members live and the dominant economic constraints to which they are subject. Perhaps the most striking feature is the palpable sense in which they are Javanese. Physically, one almost leaves Sumatra and its wide open spaces; houses are constructed in Javanese fashion, near to the ground, unlike Malay and Batak homes, which tend to be raised on thick stilts. As in Java, the houses are surrounded by clean-swept houseyards with an abundance of fruit trees and vegetable crops intermixed some distance from the house itself. Crowded in large clustered formations, Javanese communities are enveloped by fields of dry crops and wet rice; one rarely find a Javanese home isolated or distant from its neighbors. A village should be *ramai* (literally "noisy" and "bustling") connotating a secure density, offering protection from outside dangers.

Simpang Lima is one such community, which we will look at in some detail. Located in the heartland of the *cultuurgebied* about 50 km equidistant from the cities of Siantar and Tebing Tinggi, and the town of Kisaran, it lies 150 km due south of Medan. On three sides it is surrounded by foreign- and government-owned plantations with only its far eastern border adjacent to another village. Like many of its counterparts, it was carved by squatters out of estate land in the late 1940s and early 1950s. Only a small portion of the earliest inhabitants still remain, but Simpang Lima has been fortunate enough to hold on to its original area up to the present day. As late as 1972, two companies were still lobbying to reappropriate their holdings, and it has only been in the last few years that villagers have received government certificates of legal ownership, assuring the rest that the land will not be confiscated.

To speak of Simpang Lima as a social entity is to refer to two distinct aspects of its identity. On the one hand, it is quintessentially Javanese in its cycle of ceremonial events, in its physical layout of clustered households, and in the forms of social and economic interaction among them. On the other hand, contained within it are about 100 households, nearly all made up of descendants of former "contract coolies," whose trajectories between Java and Sumatra have often followed a similar course. That is, Simpang Lima is a community defined as much by its specific relation to the surrounding estates as by its ethnic link to Java. While officially it belongs to a larger village administrative unit divided into named and numbered hamlets, the terms applying to these official sections are rarely employed by inhabitants or outsiders. Instead, they still refer to the constituent parts as Block X—the designation for a planting division used by estates when the land was under their control more than twenty-five years ago.

Social space and social time share this bifurcation. Although ceremonial events for childbirth, circumcision, marriage, and death closely adhere to a specifically Javanese pattern, in practice the temporal rhythms of work and leisure are tuned to, and dominated by, the cadence of the estate industry. It is not that Javanese have given up their *slametan* (ceremonial feasts), they have simply altered the criteria by which they decide when to have them—according to estate paydays rather than any divinational calendar. Otherwise most guests would be hard pressed to find the obligatory cash contributions that accompany any feast. Payday, which comes twice a month, is when itinerant traders descend on the community to sell their wares; it is when people restock their food supplies in the town market, when investments are made and loans are paid off or extended. Current events are not dated by weeks but where they fall in relationship to the payday just passed or the one that is about to come.

None of this would be particularly surprising if it were not for the fact that such communities as Simpang Lima appear—and take themselves—to be clearly divorced from their estate origin. Although the majority of its inhabitants refer to themselves as "farmers" (tani), more than half the households have no cultivation or ownership rights to rice land, and among those that do, only a small fraction actually support themselves from farming incomes. In the village administrative unit (of which Simpang Lima makes up two hamlets) average landholdings between 1957 and 1978 fell from 0.40 to 0.13 ha per capita. This was due primarily to the stream of estate workers and former plantation employees who moved into the community in the 1950s, but also to an increase within the community itself as mature children established their own homes and parental holdings were divided among them.

The large-scale retrenchment of tens of thousands of plantation workers in the late 1960s and early 1970s exacerbated population pressure in such communities all the more. Not only have fired workers been forced to find living space outside the estate compounds, but since few of their children have found permanent jobs, they too have been denied access to estate housing and have been foisted on the plantation periphery. Simpang Lima has not suffered as seriously as other squatter settlements. Many of these, formerly surrounded by dry and wet rice fields, have completely lost their agricultural base and now remain only as rural residential complexes, housing a dense reserve of unskilled labor. Almost all their inhabitants, children as well as adults, work as buruh lepas under labor contractors for the estates.

From the companies' perspective, these newly fashioned labor settlements may seem to combine the best of all possible worlds. In any case they bear close resemblance to what Deli's foreign planters envisioned as ideal labor communities some fifty years ago, namely, ones housing an abundant labor reserve in close proximity to the estates but outside the latters' responsibility. In fact the arrangement has been far from ideal for either party. It is not only the companies that have taken to raiding the villages for labor but estate workers and other villagers who have resorted to raiding the estates for sustenance. What has developed in Simpang Lima and neighboring communities is a subterranean economy, an ad hoc, shifting set of income-earning strategies derived from inefficiencies in the estates' supervisory system and production process.

Changing Income Sources in Simpang Lima

Wedged between the estate industry and these rural classes indirectly profiting from it, Javanese on the estate periphery have found that there are few income sources open to them that do not entail both selling their labor power (they say *jual tenaga*, literally "to sell one's [labor] power") and selling it cheap. Wheras two decades ago only a few of Simpang Lima's members were *buruh lepas*, now 80% of the households have at least one member, and often more, dependent on this work as their major employment.

The *buruh lepas* ranks have been swelled by almost every age and sex grouping. First, many women who quit or were fired from permanent estate work in earlier years have returned to it again on this temporary basis. Second, in those households with former SARBUPRI members fired on political grounds after 1965, usually husband, wife, and children now all work in this capacity. Third, Simpang Lima has an unusually large number of older men and women in "semiretirement"; many are still young enough to work but considered too old to remain as permanent employees by the estates. And finally, there are a growing number of children and adolescents (either too young to be eligible for permanent estate jobs or unable to get them when they are of age) who have taken on this work, in some cases to assert their financial independence but more often by necessity.

Many of the estates on which village residents work are within a 2- to 10-km radius, but younger people usually prefer jobs that take them as far as 25 km from their homes. Piled in flatbed trucks they are carted off at five or six in the morning. While the maintenance tasks of weeding, grasscutting, and hoeing last from four to six hours, the workers rarely return before early evening since the trucks make a round of stops to let laborers from other villages off first.

The estate-working young are often unavailable to do the household tasks usually expected of children their age, and they are not subject to the same parental supervision they would certainly receive working at home. Older residents, in particular, look with some disapproval upon the often flirtatious and unreserved behavior of adolescents squashed together in the lorries. In the morning shadows, groups of young girls slip to the main road adorned with bright-colored scarves, skirts, and makeup in what old people reprovingly contend looks much like a nuptial procession. Only their long pants worn under their skirts to protect them from the nettles—and their hoes—belie that they are members of a work gang.

If young people can come to terms with low wages and tedious work because of the freedom they feel it offers, older people do so by simply denying that their livelihoods are significantly dependent on doing such work at all. When one speaks in Simpang Lima of doing estate work (*kerja kebun*), one refers only to permanent (*dinas*) employment. Temporary workers use the verb *merantau*, that is "to temporarily migrate" to one estate or another. That one invariably *merantaus* to a plantation is implicit, irrelevant, assumed in the term in its local usage. That one invariably *merantaus* year around is rarely discussed. Most women say they prefer to *merantau* because they are free (*bebas*) to choose when and if they want to go. Invocation of this "freedom," however, must be sharply limited since many labor contractors will fire those who show up less than a minimum of 25 days per month.

In total there are about 13 estates which draw on labor from Simpang Lima, although most *buruh lepas* take jobs within walking distance of the village and under those contractors offering relatively steady employment. Some adults prefer more distant estates, specifically those where the supervision is nominal and where they are not, as they say, under "constant control." Among the women, working strategies are debated and shared. Experienced hands often chide the youngsters, not for working inefficiently, but for letting the foremen catch them at it. As one woman said:

I tell them [the youngsters] remember, you're selling your labor and the one who buys it wants to *see* that he gets something for it, so work when he's around, then you can relax when he goes away, but make sure you always *look like* you're working when the inspectors are there. [speaker's emphasis]

Many women are especially skilled at keeping up such appearances. They say one should never work quickly (as some of the young boys do), which might give the contractor reason to increase the load. The work is already tiring enough. One must work steadily, carefully, and always "very slow."

Permanent Estate Employees

Although *buruh lepas* work is the most widespread form of wage labor in the community, Simpang Lima's residents do not live by it alone. Nearly 20% of the adult men between 15 and 59 have permanent (*dinas*) estate jobs. Most of the middle-aged men are rubber tappers, with oil palm harvesting jobs allocated almost exclusively to younger men. There is only one village woman who still holds a *dinas* job. Many of the men with large families are bitter about the new labor recruitment policies (which select principally for bachelors or young men with few children) and are incensed by the direct and subtler methods the companies have used to get rid of them.

One *dinas* worker, for example, who had been employed by a private national estate for more than ten years, was told on short notice that he was to be transferred to another company-controlled complex in the far south of Asahan.[14] Because the firm would not underwrite the moving costs, he argued that he was virtually fired since he was unwilling and financially unable to pick up and move at his own expense. Other workers dismissed in recent years have been told that they had too many dependents or were no longer "fit" to keep up with the current work load. In an earlier period these dismissals would have been contested, but today no one is willing to take the risk of being labeled a "communist troublemaker."

Oil palm harvesting is one of the highest paid field jobs in the estate industry. It entails some degree of skill and strength but mostly endurance to work long, irregular hours—relatively well-rewarded with large bonuses. Estate production per hectare of oil palm has increased so much in the last decade (with the use of new clones and more fertilizers) that it is now almost impossible for a worker to fulfill daily production quotas on his own. Some estates have introduced a new harvesting system, whereby the *dinas* worker himself, rather than the estate, hires two helpers. One, the *tukang pikul*, carries the heavy palm bunches to the loading points; the other, the *tukang brondolan*, collects the ripened kernels that have fallen to the ground. And the bonus is shared among all three.

This rationalization of harvesting has brought with it several important changes. First, the tasks done by these two helpers are no longer performed by *dinas* workers. The estates have been able to increase significantly their production output without augmenting the permanent labor force, for whom they would have to provide family rice subsidies, pensions, and other social benefits. Second, the job of *brondolan* is almost always performed by small children, who are paid wages commensurate with those of *buruh lepas*. Although this additional labor appears in estate calculations as increased labor productivity, it could also be analyzed as an increase in the total labor time allocated to harvesting, and a *decrease* in productivity per unit of labor. It is also another sector in which child labor has become more common, but absent from official labor reports.

Other Estate-Related Income Sources

What is most striking about the economic activities of Simpang Lima's residents is the frequency and fluidity with which they change. Aside from the permanent estate employees, three schoolteachers, a *dalang* (shadow-play puppeteer), one tailor, a handful of full-time farmers, and a few pensioned old people whose income sources are relatively fixed, the bulk of the population is continuously moving from one job to another, as new opportunities open and others close down. Underemployed young men call this *mocok-mocok* (a term emphasizing the varied nature of "odd-jobbing") when referring to the wide range of activities one does in the absence of steady work.

In comparing the employment profiles of older and younger men at any given age, between 20 and 30 years old for example, one finds that the members of the younger group will have changed their work as many as ten times in the space of a few years, while their elders often remained at the same jobs, on the same estates, for decades. Employment patterns for older and younger people today, however, are much the same since both are subject to similar constraints.

The most obvious difference between work patterns of 20 years ago and today is that the majority of women and men are now not regularly employed. This does not mean that people work less. Take for instance the case of women. Before 1965, when many more women were employed in *dinas* work, they were given pregnancy leaves of 40 days. As *buruh lepas*, most of them now take no more than 15 to 20 days, that is, one-third to one-half the time they previously did when the estates paid them during their confinement.[15] The companies have freed themselves of these costs and now have these women workers available for a larger number of total working days on the estates.

Present-day work patterns for men and women also reflect the fact that neither the companies nor the communities are generating sufficient employment opportunities to absorb the growing Javanese population. In the early 1950s those who chose to sever their ties with the estates and who took control of as much as half a hectare of still relatively rich and virgin land could live off their farming incomes. Today this option is available only to a select and very small fraction of Simpang Lima's residents.

More stringent estate policies in the last 10 years have also curtailed some of the income-producing activities now seen as a threat to both the security and the quality of estate crops. Animal husbandry, for example, once an important income source for villagers on the periphery as well as for those households living within the estate borders, has all but disappeared after new company regulations forbade the keeping or grazing of livestock on plantation grounds. Most companies tolerated animal grazing in temporarily unplanted areas (i.e., those fields in which old trees had been felled but replanting had not yet begun), but as the replanting pace has quickened, the official ban is now more strictly enforced. Children still collect animal fodder within the concession, but not all estates allow even this.[16]

Whereas some income sources have become less profitable or been supressed, others have replaced them. One of these, started in the last few years, was initiated by several estate managers and part-time traders. When new oil palms are planted, the area surrounding the seedling is planted with a low-growing ground cover (*kacangan*), which both fertilizes the soil and prevents weeds and erosion. After an initial period, this ground cover is thinned out and its seedlings in turn can be used for replanting elsewhere. Rather than directly hiring workers to do this time-consuming task, the administration has opted for another method; women and children are encouraged to come onto the estates and scour the dense cover of *kacangan* for new sprouts. They then return to their villages for the business of sorting their harvest and afterward sell the seeds to an *agen* (agent), who in turn resells them to the estates. Most companies officially forbid this practice, but the plantations around Simpang Lima countenance it with a silent sanction.

Scam number two: (also related to the conversion from rubber to oil palm) on many estates where daily production quotas for oil palm harvesting are high, the *dinas* workers (even with the help of their crews) often leave a large percentage of the fallen kernels on the ground. Although this produce is legally estate property and outsiders are not allowed to collect it, many villagers are doing just that. They search the palm groves after hours for the kernels, pound off the outer husks at home, and sell them to agents, who again resell them either to private cooking oil factories or back to the estates. A variation on this entails scavenging the huge "waste" piles of kernels that have passed through the hulling machines. For these too, the husks are pounded and the kernels are sold to outside agents.

Daily income from both activities is about the same as for temporary estate work but with the distinct advantage that most of the work can be done at home, without conflicting with the daytime hours devoted to other work. Most of the scavenging and pounding is done by women, but the children of a household also take part in the work. Although many women say they prefer this vaguely illicit pursuit to any form of direct estate employment, the income from it is minimally regular. At least one government-owned estate felt that the situation had gotten out of hand in 1979 and forbade this scavenging altogether: harvesters had begun leaving more and more kernels on the ground and speeding up their work, knowing that throngs of women and children would clean up after them.

Other income-earning activities related tangentially to the estates include the sale of prepared food and snacks, sold on payday where the *buruh lepas* wages are distributed or on the estates. These too tend to be sporadic operations. Women take on such work only when they have some cash available to buy raw materials and the time to prepare them; only a very few with established food stalls (*warung*) do this regularly throughout the year.

Labor Migration

Despite these local income sources, there are still a large number of Simpang Lima's residents who cannot be absorbed by the estates, and certainly not by the community itself. A constant flow of people moving from the village for a short time, and back again, is an essential aspect of village life. Young girls, for example, often become waitresses in what used to be called roadhouses in the United States, or become house servants in Medan or nearby urban centers. Young men go off for months, and even years, at a time to become wageworkers for well-off truck farmers in Karoland, servants for middle-class urban Chinese, nightwatchmen and agricultural laborers for Toba (Batak) farmers. Others join road crews under contractors, or fishing crews on Malay trawlers. Some take on month-long jobs on forestry clearing projects or work in rural coconut or charcoal factories within the region. Both men and women follow the rich rice harvest to the south for weeks at a time but usually this demands prior connections.

While the earnings for almost all these jobs are higher than the wages paid to *buruh lepas,* the jobs themselves entail other risks. Members of road crews and forestry projects often complained of being conned into jobs in which either the contractor ran out on them, or the pay was far below what had been agreed upon before they left. For the young girls who work as waitresses and servants, these jobs may turn out to be the entry into, or euphemism for, prostitution, since many would find themselves jobless unless they complied with the sexual advances of their employers and local clients. Although this is difficult to prove, villagers insist that evidence of such work is clear. One need only compare the standard wages for such work (a little over $10/month), with the value of the otherwise inexplicable amounts of gold jewelry, fine clothing, cash, and expensive presents the girls display and lavish on their parents when returning home. Although everyone seems to know who is working in this capacity, this public knowledge does not lead to ostracism from either community or home. Like theft it is just one of the more easily recognized—and better paid—activities attached to living on the edge.

Illicit income-earning pursuits are part and parcel of village life. Among the most important is the theft of estate produce, primarily rubber. One village youth confirmed that "everyone does or has done it, only the stupid ones get caught." Stealing latex is a well-organized operation in which estate foremen, estate clerks, and outside agents are involved. Participation carries virtually no negative social stigma, so little that some young men (usually those who have stopped) proudly recount their latex adventures.

Some do get caught, but this seems to be a relatively ineffective deterrent; if a *dinas* worker, he is demoted but rarely fired. Unemployed youths found stealing tend to get off even more easily. However, for the most part, their information networks are well greased and if a bust is imminent, they simply absent themselves from the village until police inquiries have quieted down. Most thefts are done in small groups at night. The trees are tapped and the latex is sold directly to agents on the spot. In other cases the workers mix the latex with water during working hours, hide the tins in which they have stored their "share," and come back to pick them up when it is dark. Earnings run anywhere from Rp. 1,000 to as much as Rp. 6,000 per night, literally two to twelve times what a man could earn on a roadcrew, as a *dinas* worker, or in some equivalent legitimate job.

Villagers tend to be disquieted by the thefts only when they affect them directly, as when one youth combed the village "borrowing" oil drums (used for collecting rainwater) from his neighbors to store his stolen goods. When the drums were found again they reeked of dried latex and had to be aired for weeks. In another case a father whose son was caught stealing was visited by some young thugs who promised to help him get his son released if he paid them handsomely. The companies, for their part, are usually well aware of the thefts; but since the culprits invariably include their own supervisory personnel such activities are more or less tolerated.

This is not to suggest that everyone in Simpang Lima is a thief, gambler, or prostitute, but enough members of enough households are to make quantitative income questionnaires highly suspect, if not totally unreliable. Remittances from daughters doing such work (which never showed up on family budget questionnaires) went to building several brick houses in the village. Gambling, on the other hand, accounted for forced land sales by several formerly comfortable community members. In this district, household budget figures reflected only a portion of the real earnings and expenditures of some families. Like some of the plantation staff and *pemborong*, many villagers have carved niches for themselves in and around the contemporary contours—and flaws—in the system of estate labor control. By their own account there is nothing particularly illegitimate about doing so. It is their "due" in an economic structure that they can do little to change, and in which they are fully cognizant of their subordinate role.

The dilemma of being at once marginal to, but dominated by, the estates is evident in nearly every facet of community life, affecting the core of community relations and domestic organization. As we shall see below, the household—more specifically the nuclear family of which it is usually comprised—is not necessarily "the stable point of orientation" as it has been described for Java by Hildred Geertz (1961: 5). On Sumatra's rural East Coast, certain critical aspects of Javanese family and social relations have been sharply attenuated while others have continued to be reproduced. Some reasons for this selective change are discussed below.

Domestic Ties and Social Relations in Simpang Lima

I began by describing Simpang Lima as quintessentially Javanese but this is only partially acccurate. Although Javanese ceremonial events are the social practice of everyday life, and the spirit world includes an identifiably Javanese pantheon, both these realms have been requisitioned and transformed by the distinct social reality of living on the plantation periphery.

From the activities described above, we can discern some defining features of Simpang Lima's economic situation. First, it is a community that rests on a relatively meager material base. The soil of its dry land, used for rice crops in the early years of expansion, has been seriously depleted; all this land is now used for root and other dry crop cultivation. In addition the irrigated land is of poor quality, giving low yields, usually of one rice crop per year—if and when there is a harvest. The new high-yielding rice varieties, encouraged and introduced by the government several years ago, were not very successful. In fact, yields tended to be far lower than the 3-ton per hectare average for older varieties. This was already 25% lower than average yields in most of Java and below the average for Indonesia as a whole.[17] High-yielding varieties have proved less resistant to rice pests, which have devastated many harvests since these strands were introduced. In addition they demand ever increasing chemical fertilizer inputs with each successive year of planting. The amounts are far above those provided by the government-subsidized BIMAS (Bimbingan Massal, Mass Guidance) credit program, from which most of Simpang Lima's cultivators have decided to withdraw.

As a productive sphere, Simpang Lima harbors few other employment possibilities. A handful of old people make bamboo and palm-woven products (such as floor coverings, house wall, and hats) but there are no other craft traditions to speak of. Garden produce is an important income source, especially from the regular sale of coconuts, but gardens are singularly un-labor-intensive enterprises and only some households own land planted with such profitable but slow-maturing trees as *rambutan*, cloves, and durian.

Although many of Simpang Lima's members continue to conceive of themselves as *tani*, the fact remains that the community first and foremost is a repository of cheap labor for the regional economy as a whole, that is, for the estates and for smaller capitalist ventures of other ethnic groups. Thus the majority of Simpang Lima's inhabitants earn their livings by seeking employment outside the community, not by intensifying agricultural (or any other) production within. The consequences of this are clearest in the distinct form of production that has developed in and around rice cultivation—particularly when compared to that obtaining in rural Java.

Access to rice land in Java determines a large set of social and economic relationships in which patronage ties play a critical role. For the landless and land-poor members of a rural Javanese village, opportunities to sharecrop and participate in the planting and harvesting of wealthier village landowners' fields is a strategic resource, accounting for a significant percentage of a household's annual income (see Stoler 1977b). In Simpang Lima, sharp differences in *landed* wealth between households have not engendered a similar profusion of community-based asymmetrical social ties. For one, sharecropping arrangements are variable and unfixed, and patronage is not a component of them. These arrangements tend to be pragmatic and ad hoc, and to my knowledge never based on repayment of debt or any other obligation paid off with labor services.

Second, most of the land cultivation is performed by one or two family members rather than by groups of women called into plant and harvest. At the most, two to three members of other households (usually kin) are invited to share in this work. Sometimes young men are employed (for cash wages) for a few days to do the heavy work of hoeing, but these opportunities are few and the arrangements are always on an improvised, temporary basis. Thus access to rice land neither entails strong patronage ties nor confers social power on those who have it.[18] As already suggested, class distinctions are, for the most part, extra village and interethnic, evident in the plantation hierarchy and in the subsidiary sectors that feed off it.

Investment in reaffirming and solidifying community-based social relations, at least on this account, is, consequently, sharply diminished not only among households of unequal wealth but also among those of relatively equal economic status. In rural Java, labor exchanges in rice harvesting among households of similar size holdings are often part of a larger system of reciprocal cooperation (*gotong-royong*) serving to reiterate these wider mutual obligations (Stoler 1977: 681; also see Jay 1969: 254–59). In Simpang Lima, such exchanges—and the reciprocity that they bring about—are far less extensive, suggesting that social practice is geared toward a different emphasis.

This is not to suggest that village land is an unimportant resource; rapidly rising land prices alone attest to its value. But property rights in *agricultural* land are not the fundamental productive relations around which all other relationships now revolve. Unlike the situation in Java, where access to important resources and employment opportunities can still be obtained by currying the favor of wealthier villagers, almost all forms of cash remuneration, including work on the estates, on construction sites, forest and fishing crews, in restaurants, food stalls, factories, and private homes, are essentially outside the social space of the village and accessible only by crossing ethnic lines.

Changing patterns of landownership over the last few years, however, seem to hint at another picture; increased investments in more solidly constructed housing and purchase of residential land by low-level estate staff members who might never have considered retiring there before suggest that in the future villages might become more class and ethnically diverse. Similarly, purchase of village *ladang* (dry fields) by civil servants and merchants from the surrounding district centers, and increasing land speculation are evinced in the rapid turnover of property rights. Nonetheless, what is striking about the land that has passed to outsiders is that it has virtually passed out of the village domain; no longer accessible through labor, rent, or purchase, none of it is cultivated by village inhabitants; all of it is unirrigated, and most of it planted to cloves, which, as noted earlier, need little labor. There is little reason to believe that these better-heeled "retirees" will take up positions as *landed* patrons within the village.

Labor relations in rice cultivation are only one sphere in which the narrow scope of traditional social ties is apparent. In the preparation for *slametan*, for example, neighbors called on to do the bulk of the work are encouraged to help out with more than the incentive of participating in the *gotong-royong* spirit. As in Java, they and their families are provided with numerous meals served throughout the duration of the feast. But many are also paid a cash sum as compensation for their work. More importantly, even among those families who could offer expensive entertainment and food, such large expenditures are rarely made. The *slametan* in Simpang Lima tend to be modest affairs, with relatively small social investments—compared either to corresponding occasions among Javanese in rural Java, or for that matter among Toba Bataks in Sumatra.

The Expressions of Discord

Hildred Geertz once suggested that the concept of *rukun*, meaning "harmony, cooperation, unity of effort, minimization of conflicts," is one of the organizing moral principles of the Javanese family and more generally Javanese society (1961: 47–48). The fact that such standards are rarely attained in practice is of minor import. What is much more important is a pervasive striving for the *appearance* of *rukun*, rather than the actuality of it (ibid. 146, 149). Among rural Javanese in the *cultuurgebied* it is not altogether clear that this is the case. Even the appearance of *rukun* is not kept up. And when attempted it is frequently shattered.

There are some notable examples of this. One is the sneering, divisive, and incessant gossip accompanying the giving of any large-scale feast. Of all those I attended, both men and women criticized the way in which the feast was prepared; they complained loudly that the amount of food was inadequate, that its quality was poor, that the meals smelled "rotten" because they were prepared too early in the day or in a rushed manner too late, that not enough people had been asked to help, that the entertainment was cheap, that the feast givers spent too much—or much too little. Wherever the criticism was directed it was repeated over and over again for weeks after the event, a sustained litany of dissonance, not community "harmony."

This is not to say that the ideal of rukun has entirely disappeared but that far fewer efforts are made to give it moral or practical substance. Whatever "harmonious appearance" there may be is repeatedly destroyed by frequent cases of intravillage thievery. Just before the 1978 Islamic New Year, for example, a series of robberies swept through the community. Bicycles, chickens, goats, coconuts, and rice disappeared from different homes in the space of a few weeks. Each time, a finger was pointed at first one villager, then another.

Malicious gossip does not negate the importance placed on the appearance of rukun, but it goes some way to making it less convincing. And in Simpang Lima such gossip is rampant: Whose daughter is a prostitute in Medan? Who had an illegitimate child by someone else's husband? Whose wife was once a prostitute? Who lives off gambling? Who beats his wife? Who is lazy, miserly, cursed, or impotent? These subjects are obviously the meat of human relations and discourse everywhere, but what is so striking here is that they are not dull undertones in the banter of everyday life but the resounding themes of it.

Nonconfrontation could be construed as one method of keeping up the appearance of rukun, but it too can be charged with hostility. A neighbor's absence from a slametan, a "forgotten" invitation to a rice harvest would not be conceived as nonconfrontation. They are interpreted as open expressions of discord and provoke disparaging commentary. In a world where the subtle nuances of human behavior are so carefully monitored, such "passive-aggressive" slips are as poignant as full-blown quarrels.

Domestic Tensions on the Periphery

The fact of Simpang Lima's absorption into the commoditization process is perhaps most striking not between households—where we do (and expect to) find it—but within them. Here the sharp difference in political and economic experience of the older and younger generations manifests itself in conflicting notions of householding, of who should contribute what to the family fund, and ultimately in different attitudes toward wage labor.

The attenuation of social "harmony" in work and leisure thus permeates the domestic unit itself. In central Java, a rural household tends to operate as a consumption and partial production unit, in which proceeds are pooled among its members. Within this context it is women who dominate the decision-making process and control not only family finances but also the allocation of their children's time and labor (Stoler 1977a: 85). Benjamin White's study and many modeled after it have shown that family labor, including that of small children, is mobilized for a critical set of social and economic activities (1976a).

In Simpang Lima the participation of children in rice cultivation and in most household tasks is minimal. This does not mean that children do not work. As we have seen, many drop out of school by the age of 9 or 10, join estate work gangs, hire themselves out to oil palm harvesters or rubber tappers, or help their fathers or older kin to do the same tasks. But in each case household members are linked largely only to the extent that they have a common employer, the estate. Household labor is not mobilized for agricultural production, domestic production, or village-based activities. When children work in their own right as *buruh lepas* or *tukang brondolan*, they seldom pool their earnings but keep their wages for themselves.

In the village where I lived in central Java, young people needed for rice cultivation, animal and child care, or other tasks did not pick up and leave the village at will. They more often sought a set of income-producing activities, flexible enough to allow them to fulfill their basic responsibilities to the household's productive efforts as well as to meet their own individual needs. In Simpang Lima, households seem to lack this sort of cohesion. In many cases women control neither the labor of their children nor the family purse strings. Women often do not know how much their husbands earn and some parents have no access to their children's earnings. Whether or not children remain part of the household, or even stay in the village, stokes and sustains family tension.

The situation of Simpang Lima's youth is obviously a reflection of the community's dilemma as a whole. Despite those older villagers who like to think of themselves as *tani*, the majority of village members live by working outside the community instead of, as in Java, by combining migration without and intensified production within. Domestic units in Simpang Lima have reproduced themselves, paradoxically, by attenuating their village and internal ties. Young people are chided for not staying at home, for not investing in domestic production, yet it would be an untenable survival strategy if a majority did.

The situation was aptly and bitterly summed up by one old villager who quit estate work in the late 1940s (because as he put it, "I didn't like being ordered about"). He has spent the last 25 years eking out a livelihood, fiercely proud of his independent agricultural life and of having never again done wage labor. Each of his five daughters and sons, on the other hand, one by one has deserted his cause and all are now employed by the estates as *dinas, buruh lepas,* or elsewhere as wageworkers. He sees their choice as a foolhardy one and offers this comment:

The problem with young people today is that they want to sell their labor, they don't want to plant it.

And he is right. Most village youth refuse to work on their parents' holdings, preferring to do the same tasks on the estates for cash wages, which they can spend, sometimes, as their own. Theirs is not an unreasonable evaluation of the situation.

A neighbor who needed her older daughter to help in a trading activity could induce her to quit her job only by offering to pay nearly an equivalent cash wage. Similarly, a father was forced to pay his two sons to work his land because, he said, "they would otherwise do nothing." Rifts between parents and children occur repeatedly over the same issues, the pooling of wages and the allocation of time. The youth want ready cash, the parents want to be *tani.* The conflict again is not under the surface but, in a totally "unJavanese" manner, often open and verbally, if not physically aggressive. One youth who was in constant conflict with his parents over the issue went amok one day, brandishing a kitchen knife in his mother's and father's face, screaming at them, "Kill me, kill me" Whatever psychological problems he may have had, the fact remains that the immediate cause of the outburst was a harsh disagreement as to whether he would get and accept a certain estate job. There are many youths in a similar bind, and a good number simply decide to leave. Some, who successfully find well-paying jobs, send remittances home; others sever their financial ties to the family altogether.

Such efforts as those of the old man above do not negate the fact that Simpang Lima is *not* an agricultural community, and certainly not a self-sustaining one. It is a rural ward, feeding the demands of North Sumatra's estate and regional labor market and "harboring" those workers between their forays into it. But they are maintained not necessarily on the proceeds of agricultural production but on wages earned by other household members in other sectors. What we are looking at then is a mode of consumption, not distinct from capitalism but part of it. The tensions discussed earlier over contributions to the family fund do not mean that these contributions are not made, only that the household as an earning unit has varied and irregular success.

Two things should now be clear: Simpang Lima cannot reproduce the conditions for its own existence and it cannot be considered the locus of an independent, albeit subordinated, mode of production in its own right. Agricultural labor inputs are minimal, often part-time tasks for older villagers, who in turn are supported by other wage-earning members. The commoditization of labor has meant that family labor is difficult to recruit even for the "family" farm. Simpang Lima's mere appearance as an agriculturally based entity and its reality as a rural ward are confirmed by the virtual absence of independent, village-based relations of production, concomitant with attenuated exchange.

Class and Ethnic Identity in Simpang Lima

The picture presented thus far of community and domestic life has admittedly stressed the divisive components of these relations, the economic conditions underlying discord. Still, Simpang Lima is a community, conceived by its members as such, with a set of social and ceremonial exchanges that continually renew and reaffirm these, albeit stormy, ties. Whatever conflicts weaken its core, its members and their children are still what make up the points of reference defining the boundaries of who are "we" and who are "they." Which social groups are designated to either side of this polarity provides one of the markers of Javanese social consciousness and one of the clearest indications of how patterns of exploitation are obscured and identified in rural North Sumatra.

Despite the atomization and breakdown in certain social relations within the community itself, for Simpang Lima's residents the category of *we* always remains Javanese, and more narrowly village bound, while *they* are those outside. Although *we* in its everyday use almost always includes members of the same economic class, the social groups classified as *they* are not defined along class lines. *They* span ethnically defined categories rather than political, economic, or other social classifications. For instance, estate managers, moneylenders, traders, or those who make up the local elite have no especially salient characteristics that apply specifically to these particular combinations of individuals by village standards. On the other hand, ethnic groups are easily classed in the collective plural. *They* are Bataks, Malays (*orang kampung* whispered as though it was a slightly dirty word), or ethnic Chinese. And there is a sharp, pithy, adjectival repertoire to classify them. Bataks are shrewd, coarse, and aggressive, Malays are dirty, Chinese shopkeepers are not to be trusted.

In Simpang Lima it is common to talk about *the* Bataks, much as Bataks talk about *the* Javanese. But there are no glosses to refer to *the* estate elite, or any other group defined purely in economic and political terms. Specific estate managers are singled out as individuals for being especially demanding, aloof, or compassionate, without any generic attributes commonly and consistently applied to them. E. P. Thompson described growing class consciousness in eighteenth-century England as that process in which the working class slowly and collectively began to identify the patterns of exploitation. This happened when the English working class began to see that

"they" denied him political rights. If there was a trade recession, "they" cut his wages. If trade improved, he had to fight "them" and their state to obtain any share in the improvement. If food was plentiful, "they" profited from it. If it was scarce, some of "them" profited more. "They" conspired, not in this or that fact alone, but in the essential exploitive relationship within which all the facts were validated. [1966: 207]

In Simpang Lima there is no singular articulation of an "essential exploitive relationship" as Thompson describes but rather a set of exploitative metaphors that crosscut various spheres of social life and repeatedly affirm that the essential "unjustness" of these relations is outside the victims' control.

Exploitation is not a word that appears often in daily speech, but the notions of oppression, domination, and unjust extractions certainly do. Moreover, the Indonesian word "to dominate" (menjajah), which also means "to colonize," is usually confined to its specific historical context. Only some of the older people who chose to sever ties with the estates use it to impart the distasteful tenor of estate labor relations and its hierarchy as a whole; such as those who quit dinas jobs and explain in Javanese "ora gilem direh" or in Indonesian "saya tidak mau dijajah" ("I didn't want anyone lording over me"). Younger people, on the other hand, who refuse estate employment rarely use this expression. They say they do not want to be terikat, meaning tied and tied down to estate work, and with the new expression the direct hierarchical sense of the relationship drops out. They say one feels "pressed" (dipres) or one is "eaten up" by the work load.

The notion of being "consumed" by a force more powerful than oneself is used to express any number of asymmetrical relationships not confined to work situations—or for that matter to Indonesia alone. Evil spirits, for example, "eat up" and eventually kill those individuals who do not have enough spiritual sustenance to ward them off; a wife can be consumed by a husband who demands more sexual services than she feels she can meet or than she feels are appropriate—it is his excessive appetite that renders her thin and weak. Workers can be "eaten up" by the estates, a metaphor again suggesting that the victim has been subject to an "inappropriate" demand.

The associations evoked by this metaphor are clearly not, in all instances, of the same order. But on the most general level, being *dimakan* (consumed) is a direct or mediated relationship between people. In each case it implies some excessiveness, some degree to which one of the parties has gone beyond the bounds of propriety, justice, and so forth. But more strongly it is a qualitative violation. It is not simply that the worker's labor is used—in which case one would say just that, "She used my labor"—but connotes that the worker her- or himself is destroyed in the process.

The use of *dimakan* as an expression of exploitation implies some finite amount of labor that a worker can expend in any given period of time. Demands over and beyond this amount mean that the person, that is, his ability to maintain and reproduce himself, is consumed as well. Some of the young men who work as oil palm harvesters say they pay dearly for their high bonuses. They say they "burn out" within eight years, that no one can do such work for very long, but they continue to work with this knowledge nonetheless.

At most one can try to limit one's susceptibility and vulnerability to such dangers whether they be spirits, Bataks, or estates. But in the end one cannot control them. The basic relationship is not at issue, merely one's cleverness in operating within a given system with its inherent risks. Between husband and wife, employer and employee, there are appropriate ranges of behavior. Although one is free to change husbands or employers, the basic tenet of the relationship is not questioned.

This subordination to more powerful forces is a leitmotif of the Javanese spirit world in its North Sumatran reincarnation. Clifford Geertz in *The Religion of Java* claims that "the spirit world is the social world symbolically transformed" (1960: 28). Simpang Lima's transfiguration of the Javanese corpus of spiritual personae is a strong affirmation of this. As in Java, the spirit world is invoked as an explanatory presence for almost all anomalous events of daily life: a fainting spell, a windfall profit, an inexplicable black-and-blue, the theft of a coconut, or rain during a feast. It is not Islamic scripture that is called on to account for the timing and causality of such events but the machinations of a spirit world, dense with malign and benevolent personae. Without providing an inventory here, we should note one critical structural feature of this domain.

First and most important, the most dangerous spirits and the strongest black magic are not conceived as Javanese. Invariably they are alien forces, controlled and manipulated by Simalungun Bataks, Toba Bataks, or indigenous Malays. Take for example the spirits called *pulung*. As Geertz defines them for Java, they are "political spirits" possessing only village chiefs and other high-ranking governing persons (ibid. 26). In

North Sumatra the *pulung* have been democratized. Anyone can be possessed by them, and no one can own one. They are dislocated, unbound, and "wild" (*liar*), and therefore highly dangerous. They can rarely be exorcised by a Javanese curer (*dukun*). One needs the more potent *ilmu hitam* (black magic) of either a Malay or more usually a Simalungun. In addition, *pulung* are avaricious spirits; they quickly consume (and kill) their victims unless they are appeased and bought off. Even the most sophisticated of Simpang Lima's residents, one of the schoolteachers, was not above going to four to five different Simalungun healers to locate the "right" spiritual ransom when an elderly relative was paralyzed and possessed.

Within this conceptualization most of the events that are dealt with (sickness, theft, unrequited love) may be mediated only by non-Javanese, but the evil is rarely thought of as caused by them. Curses are almost always perpetrated by neighbors, by living or deceased kin who have drawn on the more potent black magic of other ethnic groups. And thus, the victims cannot use Javanese-based spiritual power in retaliation. As another schoolteacher explained: "Simalungun *dukun* will do anything for money, they are closer to evil and far more adept at dealing with it." Most of the other spirits pale next to the *pulung* variants and can be tamed by less powerful, local Javanese sources.

As in Java, healers tend to have much stronger reputations outside their own native regions. Thus, Javanese *dukun* from distant estates are revered far more than those who live within the community. But in Simpang Lima the principle is taken one step further; it is not only those who occupy a distant geographic space who are "stronger" but *dukun* who occupy a different and distant social space as well. This brief digression into the spirit world provides some additional insight into social consciousness and its limits. At the very least it offers one example of how Javanese on the plantation periphery conceive of their subordination and the mediation necessary for their material (and spiritual) survival.

Labor Control and Social Consciousness

Although Javanese in Simpang Lima are, by their own account, far more hesitant than they were twenty years ago to express their political views and economic grievances, they are neither lacking in knowledge about the system in which they live nor politically unsophisticated about its personal consequence. In fact their understanding of how the system works and perpetuates itself is perhaps too good, in that few of them see any viable way to surmount it.

Simpang Lima's inhabitants are not so much passive as hardened cynics. They are disparaging of the present government-sponsored labor union (FBSI) that supposedly protects their interests. They realize that job security on the estates, even with *dinas* employment, is always tenuous. And those who read the newspapers often make astute political comments about domestic policy—always under their breaths. For several months in 1978 a series of newspaper articles appeared daily, describing the deplorable conditions on many private and government estates, the low wages of estate workers, and the need for more labor protection. Villagers who read the articles were unimpressed, observing that these were the very same conditions that some of them had fought against in the 1950s. As one villager stated it, "If people were imprisoned for [protesting] it then, how is anything possibly going to change now?"

The community is a very different political space than it was twenty years ago, and inhabited by a very different—and an acutely wary—political constituency. The majority of those who were SARBUPRI members, considered agitators or activists, were killed or imprisoned. Those who were classified as *ikut ikutan* (mere followers) have remained in the village under police surveillance, forbidden to travel without permission, and until recently unable to take *dinas* jobs. The district office still maintains files of all former alleged PKI members, their affiliation and other "vital" statistics. Even the village records retain asterisks next to the names of those marked as *orang hitam* (literally "black person"), designating former SARBUPRI members.

These deterrents alone might be enough to dissuade people from any form of outspoken or collective protest. The estates' labor policies make them all the more daunting. As SARBUPRI had predicted in the early 1950s, the use of temporary workers, at a different wage standard and on a different footing from *dinas* employees, would weaken the power of the unions and the bargaining positions of both categories of workers. It has clearly done just that. Over the last decade the companies have cultivated a much smaller core of permanent employees and in some cases have increased the social benefits to them. In contrast, they have taken on a growing number of *buruh lepas*, for whom they admit no responsibility and for whom the government offers little protection. The fact that the workers who belong to both these groups are often from the same household diffuses any possibility of protest all the more. Who would possibly contest *buruh lepas* wages, thereby jeopardizing rice subsidies, health care, and pensions offered in virtue of another family member's employment with *dinas* status?

Working as a *buruh lepas* offers a worker no security, no leverage; in fact it is not conceived as a proper "job" at all. Women say it is convenient; men contend it is only a supplement to their incomes. That Sim-

pang Lima's residents masquerade as Javanese *tani*, ostensibly independent of the vagaries of the labor market, is perhaps their protection
from—and cultural resistance against—an unmitigated subservience to
the estates. The facade, as we have seen, is not always easy to keep up. It
demands recourse to a set of survival strategies that are sometimes risky,
unreliable, or downright illegal. It demands a set of social relations,
distinctively Javanese, but clearly accommodated to a social reality of
ethnic and class domination outside their control.

Older people in Simpang Lima are aware of these contradictions,
though they tend to take the situation in patient stride. They say:

This is the *zaman kemakmuran* [the age of prosperity]. We have jobs, and some
of us are even pretty well paid for them. Look at all the bicycles in the village,
radios and lamps. Whoever saw so many expensive goods years ago? But it's not
the *zaman keadilan* [the age of justice]. It will come soon. And when it does
things will turn upside down. You watch out, because it will touch Jakarta,
Europe and even the United States. No, it will not be confined to North Sumatra
alone.

7
Conclusion: Registers of Resistance

Deli's estate labor history includes most of the ingredients of wide-screen drama: steaming jungle, sexual exploit, extravagant wealth and violence. In fact, Indonesia's relatively modest film industry has already seized upon it, casting its *jeune premier* as the handsome but ruthless Dutch planter and his co-star as the vanquished, violated, but valiant Javanese coolie, sexually abused then cast off with child by the heart-throb of millions of Indonesian adolescents. Fittingly, the film was entitled *Buaja Deli* (literally "the Deli Crocodile," metaphorically "the Don Juan of Deli"), capturing perhaps more succinctly than I did in chapter 2 the combined predation of the colonial beast with the sexual confrontation of white men and Asian women.

Not constrained by the same cinematic necessities as *Buaja Deli*'s producers, I have tried to go beyond the lurid. And to be fair, my story and the film's are not quite the same. *Buaja Deli* is, on some global if not aesthetic level, an account of Deli's colonial history: a history of place, specific peoples, a pioneer venture, and nationalism. It is the story of colony and plantation, and for a Western audience at least, it brings back home the First World's plunder of the other side—it is *our* cars, after all, running on *their* rubber.

While these subplots have been included within our narrative, the history here has been one of a different subject, focusing on the "sensational" only in an effort to see more clearly its context, in order to discern the less spectacular but persistent relationships of domination and resistance that labor control implies. In this sense, this has not been so much a history of who controlled whom—hardly a surprise anyway—but the history of the idea of labor control and its implementation as it structured and recreated the tenor and purport of Deli's laboring life.

202

In plotting these contours I have traced over an uneven terrain, varying in source, scope, and subject. I have told and retold the same story, first from one side, then from another, viewing the estate structure and its internal hierarchies in both temporal and spatial perspective. At other moments, I have panned a view of far wider breadth, stretching from Jakarta to Amsterdam and back again to East Sumatra's coolie barracks. Here too, in relating the machinations of corporate capital to the intimate intrigues of estate relations, I have frequently appealed to anthropological concepts in reading the historical record, and to historical explanations in dealing with the "anthropological" domains of everyday life.

Thus, analytically I have sliced out segments of both disciplines, risking the hazards such a venture entails. One of these, noted by the Genoveses several years ago, is social history's "current fad of anthropology," in which a vague repertoire of putatively ethnological concepts ranging from *culture* to *race* has dislodged class confrontations— power and control—as the focus of historical analysis (Fox-Genovese and Genovese 1976:205–20).

In the account offered here of Deli's history an attempt has been made to avoid the inherent reductionism of the one approach and the imprudent glosses of the other. In focusing on both the structure and experience of labor relations, I have tried to attend to the class determinants of social action as they were manifest but more often obscured by the ethnic, racial, and gender relations of everyday life. This concern, in turn, is part of a more general aim: providing additional empirical content to the claim that people are "both the authors and actors of their own drama" (Marx 1973:115). Or, in other words, I try to view the course of capitalist development as a process activated through, not simply imposed on, class relations.

In this effort certain analytic devices have allowed me to sift through the historical record and set the parameters of inquiry. These have been the double-edged concepts of labor control and corporate hegemony, both requiring attention to the changing spheres of domination and resistance within and without the labor process itself. As it turned out, discerning the historical events that both expressed and inspired "labor resistance"—let alone divining its structural consequences—was not as straightforward a venture as one might at first have imagined. Every perceptible change in labor policy, and every subtle shift in the bargaining position of management and labor were potential candidates and each one occurred in the presence of a convergence of factors external and internal to estate labor relations.

In order to render this range of contingencies manageable—that is, to *analyze* what happened—we have had to appeal to some standard against which we could "measure" these innumerable, and analytically slippery, shifts and alterations. In short, some events were clearly more salient than others, more likely to provoke systemic transformation. The first task has been to isolate these crucial transformations, and the second to demonstrate that they were neither inevitable nor accidental in themselves but invariably patterned by a particular disposition of power, continually and successfully reproduced, despite the challenges to it.

In chapters 2 and 3, for example, we saw that from the estate industry's inception through World War II corporate labor policies in Deli were divided by what appeared to be two distinct strategies. The earlier policies were characterized by outright coercion, legally enforced through a penal sanction on indentured labor contracts. By the late 1920s the predominance of these particular forms of social violence was on the wane; the first tentative steps were taken to abolish indenture (totally phased out only in 1941) and new priorities were given to establishing a resident labor reserve, local reproduction of the work force through family recruitment, and permanent labor settlements offering the semblance of village life.

Concomitant with this shift were dramatic changes in the technical and organizational factors of production, allowing the companies to realize profits more through increased labor productivity than through a higher intensity of, and increased, laboring hours. Paralleling this tendency was a rapid decline in the frequency and vigor of violent encounter between white managers and Asian workers, fewer assaults on company property, and lower incidence of collective labor protest.

Several alternative interpretations could plausibly be invoked to account for this interlude of social and economic reform. For example, this rationalization of the industry could be interpreted as an outcome of international market pressures, the most obvious being the depression, which forced industries worldwide to substantially reduce their labor costs or fold completely. Management in North Sumatra's estate industry availed itself of essentially this rationale when it summarily dismissed and repatriated 50% of its work force, more than 160,000 persons.

Alternately, the change from indentured to "free" labor could possibly be explained as part of the determined course of capitalist development in its progression from extraeconomic forms of coercion to those embedded within the labor process itself, or as a fulfillment of capital's tendency toward higher levels of labor productivity and decreased total labor time in periods of crisis. Or finally one might argue that the abolition of indenture was a direct result of the workers' conscious and presumably successful campaign against the unjust labor policies of the

industry, a thesis supported by the sharp diminution in the number of
murders and assaults on whites that followed the lifting of the penal
sanction.

While each of these interpretations is plausible in terms of some
economic and social constraints on estate labor relations, none of them
alone accounts for why things happened as they did in Deli. Focusing on
the changing and contested terrain of labor control kaleidscopes the
pattern of these events into a richer configuration. We found, first of all,
that the shift from indenture to "free" labor was in name only, signaling
not a curtailment of coercion but a displacement of the spheres in which
it operated. Second, we have seen that the depression did not prescribe
the course of the industry's rationalization or the kind of restructuring it
would entail. The companies did not simply dismiss 160,000 workers
arbitrarily. They attended their choices with care; those fired were invariably suspected of being "dangerous," "extremist," and "undesirable"
elements, whereas those retained were chosen for their loyalty, industry—and docility. Whether the latter were anywhere near "dangerous"
is beside the point; by hit and miss such criteria were assured of encom-
passing most of those workers who had ever displayed the smallest
modicum of defiance—on an individual or a collective basis. The companies repatriated first unmarried (read: troublesome) males and fired
but did not repatriate married women, forcing those married men who
were graced with estate jobs to toe the line under rigorous new rules of
labor discipline.

Sumatra was hardly, as already noted, the only place in the world
where the depression meant large wage cuts and severe unemployment,
but the *scale* on which this occurred in Deli was far greater than any
"objective" measure of economic necessity dictated. In neighboring Malaysia, for example, rationalization of the rubber industry was accompanied by a much smaller reduction in the work force; in fact there is
some evidence to suggest that estate recruitment increased there for the
same period (Jain 1970:224).

In Deli, the dismissal and, most importantly, *repatriation* to Java of a
large portion of the estate population were seen as political as well as
economic imperatives. And, as usual, the planters' analyses of the situation was not far off the mark; in South Vietnam, where immigrant estate
workers from the north were simply fired (without being repatriated to
their home regions), the plantation proletariat were active participants
in the labor actions that accelerated during the depression years (see,
e.g., Hémery 1975 and Vien 1974). In North Sumatra in the 1930s, on the
other hand, estate-based protest, widespread during the 1920s, was virtually brought to a dead halt.

Thus the strategies of labor recruitment and control, not surprisingly, were as much a response to the presumed potential for insurgency as they were to the strict accounting of estate profits. This is clearly borne out by the otherwise inexplicable eclipse of estate labor protest in the succeeding years—when real wages continued to fall—unless the national context of political repression is kept in mind. Taking these events as part of some predetermined course of capitalism, or alternately as the inevitable outcome of politically conscious protest, is to miss the paradoxical development of labor control and the forms of resistance chosen.

The institution of family housing, protection from physical and verbal abuse, and more even sex ratios had an equivocal effect; while on the one hand, these changes alleviated some of the more palpable forms of oppression, immediately experienced by workers as unjust, excessive, and warranting violent retaliation, on the other hand, these were the very same concessions that allowed the basic structure of labor relations to remain unaltered and exploitation to intensify in modified form. From another perspective we have seen that the act of "reconstituting" as a peasantry on the plantation periphery in both the prewar and postindependence periods was a register of resistance that also served to enforce the subordination of this mostly Javanese population living on the edge.

The predepression incidents of labor protest thus brought about a modicum of restraint in terms of the more abusive practices of management, but these incidents, and the fear they engendered, were instrumental in molding the course that retrenchment took, ultimately weakening the basis for overt and sustained political activism. Coupled with an increasingly greater show of force on the part of the Dutch colonial state, the Deli labor force, more so than other groups in the Indies, was kept quiescent for most of the 1930s—a quiescence sharply contrasting with rebellions and revolts of the peasantry and urban poor that reverberated throughout the Dutch, British, French, and American colonial empires of Southeast Asia during the same period.[1]

In the colonial chapters of Deli's estate history there is a repeated prescience of issues of confrontation and control that largely emerged in substantive form only during the postindependence years. For example, the estate population's ambiguous political positioning—at once both central and marginal—was hardly the recent product of independent politicization, but flowed from the corporate policies of labor control designed decades earlier to avert politicization at nearly any cost. The importance of the Javanese population in North Sumatra for the Dutch colonial and later national economy meant that even the smallest ripples of political awareness and defiance were perceptible to and reacted against by those in power. In this sense their potential ability to disrupt the social order was more significant than the actual havoc wreaked by other indigenous groups less vital to and dependent on the foreign estates. In addition some of the estate conditions that could facilitate collective action and common interests (concentrated residential complexes of workers living in similar circumstances) were the same conditions that allowed easy surveillance and repression of actions based on even relatively innocuous demands.

Perhaps the most basic paradox affecting politicization, however, was to be the disparity between the apparent and real conditions of the labor force's proletarian versus peasant expectations, interests, and status. As I have argued, this disparity grew out of the very process of commoditization and was an integral component of the strategies behind incentives for immigration, the policies of labor recruitment and control. The industry's attempts to establish a "normal" labor market similar to that prevailing in Java was at the heart of the various labor settlement schemes proposed throughout the prewar period. These programs, as we have seen, were based on allocating a *less* than minimum agricultural subsistence base for the laboring population, one adequate to provide for their reproduction when push came to shove but far below what would allow workers to become independent of estate employment.

During the Japanese occupation these carefully planned schemes seemed to be turned to the serious disadvantage of their authors. Taking off from a temporary land allocation program initiated by the planters before World War II, and expanded by the Japanese during the occupation, a massive squatter movement emerged, driven by the—for once combined—impetus of economic necessity and political resolve. During these years many estate workers did secure the rudiments for an independent subsistence base and spent the next decade struggling to maintain and extend their holdings, encroaching farther onto estate lands and causing a severe labor shortage in the process (although that "shortage" too had its ambiguities, as we saw).

In this atmosphere, where militant labor actions joined with audacious land seizures, the workers' voice was at its most strident and resonant pitch. These organized labor and squatter movements presented an unprecedented challenge to the omnipotence of corporate authority, not only by contesting the conditions of estate work but, more importantly, by withholding labor power from the estate labor market—as thousands of workers temporarily moved out from under the companies' shadow. Paradoxically, this very withdrawal ultimately not so much undermined the companies' control as eroded the strength of the estate labor movement itself as squatters cum estate workers wavered in their allegiance to proletarian versus peasant interests and actions. Although the composition of the power elite was drastically altered, the disposition of power remained virtually unchanged.

In chapter 6 we saw how the appearance of this bifurcation between peasant and proletarian status has continued to feed a myth of two distinct production systems—one that serves the interests of the contemporary estate industry equally well. Although many members of the peripheral estate communities have been marginalized from one sector of the capitalist labor market—that of the estates—this has not disencumbered them of dependence on it. It has simply forced them to participate in a more diverse range of wage-earning pursuits in North Sumatra's wider regional economy.

Clearly the most striking feature of North Sumatra's estate labor history is the fact that despite a war, revolution, independence, strong labor unionism within the estates, and an aggressive squatter movement without, Simpang Lima and communities like it bear a remarkable resemblance to the ideal labor colonies envisioned by the companies more than fifty years ago. This is not to argue for the totally willful construction of history, or to suggest that the planters single-handedly "decided" capital and labor's course—two points I have repeatedly made—but to understand the convergence of conditions that has advanced the commoditization process and left Simpang Lima as a peasantry manqué, with only a poor approximation of peasant life.

Looking at North Sumatra's plantation periphery in terms of a "reconstituted peasantry" and a resistant response to the estate industry with "its externally imposed regimen" has helped us see what this process of apparent peasantization or deproletarianization has been partially about (Mintz 1974:132). In North Sumatra we have evidence indicating that these communities represented such a resistant stance: in the clandestine Javanese settlements that grew up around the estate peripheries at the turn of the century; in the thousands of ex-estate workers— deserters and those with contracts expired—who were willing to accept stringent sharecropping agreements, pay high land rents, or simply live as *numpang* (passengers or lodgers) on borrowed land in order to get some access to a small plot for subsistence farming—and this before the real squatter movement had even begun; in the literally tens of thousands of Javanese plantation workers and indigenous Sumatran land poor who, without legal guarantee, seized more and more estate area after independence and spent the next decades tenaciously clinging to it; and finally in some of Simpang Lima's inhabitants today, who still believe that they can lives as *tani* despite overwhelming evidence to the contrary. We have also seen, however, that this seemingly reemergent peasantry has had only dubious results, manifest in the fact that the interests of capital have been served by the selfsame phenomenon with far more consistent success.

What I have tried to show by looking to North Sumatra's contemporary social realities and to the historical formation of them is the critical role played by this conceptual separation for *both* capital's domination and labor's resistance throughout the industry's erratic expansion. As should be clear by now, *this "reconstituting peasantry" of Javanese contract coolies and their descendants was by design, never really reconstituted at all.* Even the spontaneous labor settlements ostensibly outside the purview of capitalist relations were, in time, brought within the vortex of capitalist control. By landscaping the *cultuurgebied's* social and economic space the industry was able to provide the "atmosphere" of village life without the material basis for it; with subsistence farming both an expression of resistance and a long-standing goal, it was all the more easily subsumed within a finely tuned system of labor control.

Thus the commoditization process in its present phase has not been marked by a further alienation of workers from the means of production but by their limited and continued access to it. By living in such places as Simpang LIma, its inhabitants must sell their *tenaga* (labor power), bear some of the costs of its reproduction, and accept that they must sell it cheap. Access to land—even minimal amounts—blurs the realities of estate work. And village life—even without land—allows people to contend—as many do—they they work only as *buruh lepas* when they choose. The commoditization process thus remains partially obscured by the industry's historical constructions of social space and by the workers' contemporary accommodations to it.

The attention placed here on corporate policies of labor control and on the contradictory modes of control and resistance prompts some observations about the nature of subsumption to capitalism in the Third World in general. We have seen, first of all, that "extra-economic" forms of coercion have remained as essential to the development of contemporary capitalism as they did to its earlier stages. In this respect we have also seen that the state has played, and continues to play, an essential role as a direct and an indirect agent of labor control. The conflation of legitimate economic demands with political insurgency and criminality has expedited the repression of labor movements throughout the First and Third Worlds—and Indonesia is certainly no exception.

When we consider the idioms of racial, sexual, and ethnic antagonisms that have permeated the experience of labor relations on the East Coast, it is clearer why open class confrontation has never marked Deli's estate history and why exploitation has appeared in muted and fragmented form. This does not weaken the case for analytic emphasis on class structure but, on the contrary, provides the very reason for it, in that it was through reference to class-based conflicts that these other arenas of contest have been found to be structured and hence more coherently explained.

Furthermore, I have shown that the manipulation of gender hierarchies was a primary instrument of labor control called upon by corporate and state authorities alike. North Sumatran agribusiness, in large part, pivoted on the marginalization of women at critical economic junctures. Men have not always benefited from these policies, and the companies have not always correctly gauged the social consequences of their actions. What is evident is that estate policies have not only compounded the subordination of women but have ensured the political and economic vulnerability of the work force as a whole.

As Charles Tilly did in another context, I have taken violent events as "tracers of a much wider, more elusive set of politically significant encounters" (1975:248). Conversely, we have also seen that the silences of (apparent) submission have not always signaled acquiescence but marked alternate routes of adaptation and protest. Admittedly and necessarily our vision of laboring life has been distorted by the lens of corporate management, but this distortion has not always been to our disadvantage. Through the planters' discourse we have learned which forms of social practice were conceived as a threat to their hegemony, and which structural features of the industry were implacable, brittle, least elastic, and therefore most vulnerable to assault.

In viewing the major political events of North Sumatra's history from the somewhat unconventional perspective of the coolie barracks—that is, from the perspective of those who were neither the primary agents of social change nor its passive victims—we are better able to evaluate the socioeconomic conflicts that underscored these "political" maneuvers and to appreciate their consequences for at least a segment of the laboring poor.

Notes

Chapter 1

1. See Rodney 1981:652–54, where he notes that after emancipation ex-slaves did not flee from plantation work but from the "niggeryards" to residential compounds outside the estates as an act of assertion and resistance, in an attempt to strengthen their bargaining position vis-à-vis the planters.

2. These include Cunningham 1958, Liddle 1970, Oudemans 1973, and Penney 1964.

   Two recent dissertations on the prewar period also include substantial discussions of the plantation economy and Javanese community: O'Malley 1977, and van Langenberg 1976. While many of these studies provide useful information concerning the Javanese estate laboring population, for the most part their labor history is tangential to the above analyses. Even Karl Pelzer, whose firsthand knowledge of the estate industry spanned several decades, confined his research in *Planter and Peasant* 1978 and *Planter against Peasant* 1982 primarily to agrarian not labor history, leaving aside the crucial relationship between them.

3. The fact that the Javanese estate workers were sometimes a pawn in these larger power struggles has meant that they have been relegated to a marginal role probably more often than they deserve. In Anthony Reid's otherwise fine-grained treatment of class and ethnic conflict and collaboration, *The Blood of the People* (1979), only minimal reference is made to the Javanese laboring poor. To some extent this is not ill-founded; not only did colonial and estate officials as well as indigenous Sumatrans often share this view, but much of Reid's study focuses on Aceh to the north of the *cultuurgebied* proper.

4. See Stedman-Jones 1978 for a similar criticism of "social control."

5. See Brenner 1978 for a well argued reproof of Wallerstein's invocation of different systems of labor control to explain peripheral articulation in the world capitalist system.

6. Wright 1978:67 makes a similar point in his analysis of class structure and the labor process.
7. An attenuated list of otherwise illuminating studies that have not dealt with this question include those in Julian Steward's classic *The People of Puerto Rico* (1956); Rubin, *Plantation Systems of the New World* (1959); Jain, *South Indians on the Plantation Frontier in Malava* (1970); Mandle, *The Plantation Economy* (1973); Hutchinson, *Village and Plantation Life in Northeastern Brazil* (1957) and Thompson, *Plantation Societies, Race Relations, and the South* (1975). Also striking is George Beckford's *Persistent Poverty* (1972), which provides an overview of underdevelopment in plantation economies of the Third World with no reference to labor protest. Notable exceptions are Cooper, *From Slaves to Squatters* (1980), Taussig, *The Devil and Commodity Fetishism in South America* (1980), Genovese, *Roll, Jordan, Roll* (1976), and *From Rebellion to Revolution* (1981), including an extensive bibliographical essay on slave revolts.
8. This latter approach is, of course, the one taken by Genovese, and to a far more limited extent by Mintz (1974).
9. Thus, for example, in Kumari Jayawardena's otherwise excellent study, *The Rise of the Labor Movement in Ceylon* (1972):232, the nature of plantation labor relations is understood in terms of the "feudal features" of employer–worker ties. She argues that these were obstructions to political or trade-union organization.
10. This does not mean that plantation and industrial labor relations are parallel but that the latter can offer useful referents for analysis. See, for example, Mintz 1979:173–97.
11. Piven and Cloward 1979:xxii, 98; also see Braverman 1974, Aronowitz 1973, Edwards 1979, and articles in the collections of Gutkind et al. 1978, and Nichols 1980.

Chapter 2

1. The complex agrarian legislation that applied to "directly ruled" vs. "indirectly ruled" territories is discussed at length in other sources, too far afield to outline here. See Pelzer 1978, especially chap. 6, for an informed and detailed discussion of the peculiarities of the system of land appropriation by foreign companies—and its consequences—in Deli.
2. Oil Palm's success as an industrial crop followed from the recent technological advances in the processing of cooking fats, confections, and cosmetics, for which it could now be used as a basic ingredient. See Courtenay 1969:71. As an industrial raw material it provides the grease for tin-plating and is used as a softening and finishing agent in cotton textile manufacture. See Sayuti 1962:21.

   Just as its production demands technologically sophisticated processing and storage procedures, its cultivation requires a carefully monitored organization of labor for crop maintenance and harvesting since the ultimate market value and industrial use of the fruit and oil extract are largely dependent on precise timing between field and factory. The replacement of more expensive raw materials by palm oil, and thus the rapid increase in its annual consumption worldwide, reflects this "successful" union of scientific expertise and an exacting system of labor control. Note, however, that in Malaysia, now the largest palm oil producer in the world, various land development schemes have been in effect since the 1960s to bring smallholders into palm production (Thoburn 1977:131–162).

3. This section is drawn primarily from Anthony Reid's *The Blood of the People* (1–5).

4. Ibid. 3. See Pelzer 1978:69–70, who also notes that this system of land appropriation did not go uncontested. The sultan of Deli not infrequently leased land to the companies that were not under his control, notably in the area of Karo Batak chiefs, who, being treated as "vassals," had been gypped of their "fair share" of the booty. Pelzer writes: "These chiefs attacked the sources of the sultan's newfound income by burning the planters's tobacco drying sheds . . . [in an effort] to convince the planters of the necessity of negotiating contracts for land in the Karo Batak territories with the respective chiefs rather than with the sultans."

5. For details on how the East Coast was legally and in practice sliced up see Pelzer 1978:66–85, and Bool 1903, which is the foremost source on these land contracts, and from which most of Pelzer's discussion derives.

6. Pelzer notes that local Malay and Batak inhabitants viewed this "waste" land in a somewhat different light since it "served as hunting ground and was also used for gathering of forest products such as building materials, firewood, resins, foodstuffs, raw materials for the making of tools, and many other products. But above all it was potential swidden land" (1978:71).

7. Deli tobacco, at this time, was planted on an eight-year rotation basis.

8. See Bool 1903, esp. 48–50, and passing references to these squatter settlements throughout his work.

9. For an early discussion of how the estate companies were quickly put at the mercy of these coolie brokers see Stibber 1912.

10. According to Professor Willem Wertheim the "argument" behind the penal sanction was that the situation (of coolies not working) on the Deli estates could be compared to mutiny on a sailing ship!

11. Dutch language sources on the history of the coolie ordinances and the penal sanction are too numerous to list but for a sampling see Heijting 1925, and in English, Laskar 1950 and Thompson 1947.

12. See in particular M. H. Székely-Lulofs's novels, *De Andere Wereld* (1946) and *Rubber* (1932); also Ladislao Székely's *Tropic Fever: The Adventure of a Planter in Sumatra* (1979) [1937], which pales next to his wife's much richer and more realistic account. See Kleian 1936 and Brandt 1948.

13. Van den Brand 1904:66–70, in the section entitled "Hoe Verdient Eene Javaansche Vrouw Haar Sarong? [How does a Javanese women pay for her clothes?]; see also Middendorp 1924:51, who mentioned the increase in prostitution. On female wages see BZ: MR 585x/20; Tideman 1919:137 also refers to the "women who abandon themselves" to prostitution.

14. Two exceptions are Wertheim 1959:252, and Said 1977, where van Kol is quoted extensively.

15. Afd. II, Archive of the Nederlandsche Rubber Maatschappij, Mar. 1914.

16. Ibid., 29 Nov. 1918; Van Kol 1903:98 also comments on the sale of coolie children by their mothers but attributes the cause to *economic*, not moral, deprivation.

17. See Middendorp 1924:51, and van den Brand 1904, who also allude to such practices.

18. These children were referred to as *kebun kinderen*, a Dutch-Malay linguistic composite literally meaning "estate children" but used as a pejorative for illegitimate offspring.

19. KvA 1919:22. At least one estate manager in 1913 "ordered" his workers to bear no more children—how this was enforced, by induced abortion or by dismissing pregnant workers, it not known. (See KvA 1913.)

20. See KvA 1913:90; van Kol 1903, Said 1977, van den Brand 1904 and Middendorp 1924 for numerous references to such practices.

21. See, for example, van Blommestein 1910, who estimated that the mortality figures dropped from 60 to 15 per 1,000 workers in an article that is primarily concerned with substantiating the virtues of the penal sanction. Also see Schuffner and Keunen 1910, who claimed that the mortality rate among workers on these estates dropped from 60 to 9.5 per 1,000 workers in the 10-year period. In this study only workers between the ages of 20 and 50 were included, which for obvious reasons should lower the mortality rate considerably.

22. Blink 1918:117. Some workers were urged by the companies to return to their home villages to recruit others (for which they were given an extra bonus) but these were only a fraction of the thousands that annually chose repatriation. See Vierhout 1921:21.

23. Deli Planters Vereeniging 1932:15 reads in full: "If it should be the case that the number of settlers increases as a result of having many children, gradually the land granted them will be inadequate to provide their subsistence—in other words, if a sort of overpopulation and poverty develops, then the surplus will have to seek work on the estates and thus the desideratum will be achieved—a local labor pool."

24. Ibid.; see also Heijting 1925:109. The question of agricultural colonization and labor settlements is discussed in nearly every *Arbeidsinspectie* report issued by the Kantoor van Arbeid for the years concerned; this section draws heavily on this source.

25. AR, Afd. II, RCMA, 13 Aug. 1914.

26. Ibid., 26 Mar. 1912.

27. MR no. 585x/20.

28. This new company concern was reflected in more studies on the relationship between the productive and reproductive activities of estate women. One such inquiry showed that married women working as contract coolies bore fewer children than those women who were not under labor contracts. On the Deli Maatschappij estates 93% of the births in the period 1923–27 were among women *not* under contract (see Straub 1928:28). The

implication was clear: to encourage population increase the firms would have to encourage the recruitment of married women who were not engaged as contract workers. Whether the companies were fully cognizant of this report is a moot point; the labor policies implemented after the depression appeared directly responsive to these priorities.

29. The timely end to the penal sanction, concomitant with a drastically diminished demand for labor, has often been attributed to political lobbying in the United States against the importation of crops cultivated by indentured workers. In fact, this Blaine amendment was a crafty piece of legislation applied only to those crops in competition with agricultural production of the *same* crops (such as tobacco) grown in the United States; thus such essential items as rubber were never included.

    The amendment was, after all, designed to protect U.S. tobacco growers and merchants, not Javanese coolies. Attempts to causally relate the rapid demise of the penal sanction to such external pressures underestimates the internal tensions within the estate industry, manifest in various registers of labor resistance discussed in the following chapter; here, it is important to recognize how these objections were used to restructure the political and social composition of the estate population. (See Gould 1961:29.)

30. The emphasis on a permanent and stable family-based estate population was quickly reflected in the changing sex composition of the workers and in the respective wage levels for men and women. From 1925 (a boom year for the industry) to 1940, female wages decreased from 80% to 56% of male wages, with the sharpest reduction coming during and continuing after the depression. The number of women participating in the estate labor force, on the other hand, showed an upward trend; during the first decade of the 1900s only 10% were women, during the next two decades 20% to 26%, and by 1938 37% of estate workers—the highest percentage in the prewar period.

Chapter 3

1. Obviously this cultural baggage alone did not *cause* submission, but was part and parcel of a wider set of colonial policies that helped to enforce it.

2. "Little person" or "common citizen" is the literal translation of *wong cilik* but here it connotes "nonentity;" Dixon 1913:30.

3. The best sources on the exacting hierarchy within which these company staff members lived and labored are the novels written about and by them. See first and foremost Székely-Lulofs, *Rubber* (1932); also *De Andere Wereld* (1946) by the same author; Brandt, *De Aarde van Deli* (1948); Petersen, *Tropical Adventure* (1948); Székely, *Tropic Fever* (1979) [1937]; and Kleian, *Deli-Planter* (1936) for a wide range of nostalgic and bitter accounts from this period. Also see Clerkx, *Mensen in Deli: een maatschappijbeeld uit de belletrie* (ca. 1960), who provides a sociological analysis of Deli's colonial society based on these and other novels.

4. In much the same way Foucault has described another subject: "We must not imagine a world of discourse divided between accepted discourse and excluded discourse; or between the dominant discourse and the dominated one; but as a multiplicity of discursive elements that can come into play in various strategies. It is this distribution that we must reconstruct, with the things said and those concealed, the enunciations required and those forbidden . . . and with the shifts and reutilization of identical formulas for contrary objectives that it also includes" (1980:100–101).

5. Figures collected from the Kantoor van Arbeid's annual *Arbeidsinspectie* reports for the years concerned.

6. Thompson 1947:150. For a discussion of the early formation and features of the nationalist and communist movement on Java see McVey 1965: esp. 7–47 and Blumberger 1935:1–8; for the emergence of labor unions on Java, see Blumberger 1931:129–63.

7. See O'Malley 1977:286, nn. 4, 5. Iwa Kusumasumantri's political work among estate drivers was described to me by a former estate labor union leader in a series of interviews in Paris and Amsterdam.

8. An exception is the material cited by O'Malley 1977, which draws on Iwa Kusumasumantri's autobiography and police interrogations carried out in 1930.

9. Afd. II, Archive of the Nederlandsche Rubber Maatschapij, 16 May 1913.

10. OvSI 1917:35. These chronicles were usually published annually (sometimes every few years) with vital—if not always accurate—statistics on estate production, export earnings, shipping and transport facilities, and demographics of the estate laboring population. More interesting for the purposes of this analysis are the sections on labor problems and political activities on the estates, especially after the mid-1920s, when concern over these issues increased enormously. Although the quantitative material may not be altogether reliable, the *Kronieken* are an invaluable source concerning the white community's perspective on its own power position vis-à-vis native political organizations and labor unrest.

11. Van Lier 1919:297. This government report appeared in the *Encyclopedisch Bureau* but was written by the head of the Arbeidsinspectie.

12. *Arbeidsinspectie 1920*. p. 36.

13. The following section draws on several sources already cited: these include Blumberger 1935:169–209, McVey 1965, V. Thompson 1947, and Kahin 1952.

14. Article 161 *bis* reads: "He who, with the intent of disturbing the public peace or disrupting the economic life of the community, or knowing or being in a position to know that such disturbance of the public peace or disruption of the economic life of the community would be the result, causes or abets that several persons abandon or in spite of lawfully given order refuse to carry out work for which they have contracted or to which they are bound by virtue of their employment, will be punished with imprisonment of up to five years or a fine of not more than 10,000 guilders" (quoted in translation in McVey 1965:151).

15. See Said 1977:176–216, where *Benih Timor's* record of the trial is reproduced.
16. OvSi 1927:36. Increased security measures on the East Coast were also related to events closer by in West Sumatra, where a communist action had been thwarted in early January 1927. Although there was certainly a strong flow of communication and people between Sumatra's West and East Coast left-wing movements, there is no evidence cited in government reports or in studies of the communist movement during these years that Deli was included in plans for an action in 1926–27. On the other hand many of the key figures in the West Coast PKI had spent time in, passed through, or were imprisoned in Medan. (See Anonymous 1928:24). According to this report changes in the political climate on the East Coast between 1925 and 1926 were in part a function of the spread of communism from the West Coast (ibid. 25).
17. Based on interviews cited in n. 7.
18. See *Pewarta Deli* of 29, 30 Mar. and 1 Apr. 1929 for the transcript of the trial and for the caustic commentary of the editors on the court proceedings.
19. KvA n.d. *Veertiende*:92; also see *Memorie van Overgave* van Sandick:18. The latter is one of many such reports written by government officials when they vacated their positions. Sometimes, as in van Sandick's case, the information concerning labor conditions is culled from local level reports and those supplied by the Arbeidsinspectie, rendering this high official summary somewhat superficial.
20. As quoted to me in English by a Dutch former estate manager, who in turn was told this pithy maxim by his own father—a planter.
21. As part of a continuing debate in *History Workshop* on class consciousness and social change Simon Clarke makes a similar point in another context when he writes: "People do not experience oppression and exploitation immediately as class oppression and exploitation, they experience it in a series of fragmented and differentiated forms; as exploitation and oppression imposed by specific individuals and through specific institutions. The unity of the exploitation and oppression of one class by another cannot be discovered immediately in experience nor *a fortiori* in the consciousness that develops on the basis of that experience" (1979:152).

Chapter 4

1. See for example Michael van Langenberg's *National Revolution in North Sumatra: Sumatera Timur, and Tapanuli 1942–1950* (1976) and Anthony Reid's *The Blood of the People: Revolution and the End of Traditional Rule in Northern Sumatra* (1979) as well as the secondary and archival sources cited therein. Both accounts make valuable but brief reference to the particular history of the Javanese estate laboring community in the nationalist movement and later independence struggle.
2. This brief synopsis of independence politics obviously does injustice to the

complexities of these arrangements, which have been discussed in detail and with far more expertise by others elsewhere. See, e.g., Kahin 1952 and Reid 1974. This chapter is not a study of the nationalist movement or independence struggle in North Sumatra, much less in Indonesia. The former task has been done by van Langenberg, on whose meticulous archival work I have frequently drawn. The task here is more modest, i.e., to reexamine the course of the revolution as it affected, and was affected by, the political and economic practice of the Javanese estate laboring population on the East Coast.

3. The organization of estates under the Japanese is described in Dootjes 1948:13–23, and by van de Weerd in an unpublished and undated report prepared when he was one of the foreign estate consultants to the Japanese military command, entitled "Rapport Werkzaamheden Estates Advisory Board." Also see AR, Afd, box #220, May 1946. The following section is drawn from these sources.

4. Based on interviews in 1977–79 with estate workers and other residents from the Asahan district of North Sumatra.

5. Kahin 1952:108 notes that many *romusha* on Java were used to work the plantations but in North Sumatra [according to local informants], where it seems that estate workers were under closer supervision, these workers themselves, instead of outside *romusha*, were simply moved from closed estates to more strategic ones. Also see Dootjes 1948:23 and Pelzer 1978:127.

6. See reports in AR (Afd. II, box #220), and Pelzer 1978:127.

7. AR, Afd. II, box #220.

8. Anderson readily acknowledges this elitism but maintains that for Java at least it was largely overcome.

9. In fact there was a plantation board (Dewan Perkebunan) established in December 1945 to which estate clerks were responsible, but it exerted little influence on the local administration of the estates. See Reid, 1979:220.

10. Afd. II, box #220, Aug. 1946.

11. Afd. II, box #220, July 1946.

12. Afd. II, box #220, Aug. 1946.

13. Afd. II, box #220, Aug. 1946.

14. Afd. II, box #220, Oct. 1946.

15. Afd. II, box #220, May 1946.

16. This view was supported by workers employed on estates throughout the district, despite the fact that there seems to have been large variation in the amounts of produce extracted by the Japanese on different estates.

17. Afd. II, box #220, July 1946.

18. GG4/963/46.

19. NEFIS, 22 Mar. 1946.

20. GG4/963/46.

21. Afd. II, box #220, May 1946.

22. E50, July 1946.

23. For detailed accounts of the outbreak of the social revolution see Said 1973, Langenberg 1976, and Reid 1979:218–51.

24. While relations between the local aristocracy and the Javanese plantation populace were not benign, it should not be forgotten that many ex-estate workers were able to escape their coolie contracts in virtue of land rights granted them by local Malay rulers eager for additional income. In short many Javanese on the plantation periphery might have felt more beholden than hostile to the Malay elite.

25. One of a series of interviews made in the Netherlands in 1979 with former staff employees of several Dutch-owned plantation companies operating on the East Coast. In respect to those individuals who were kind enough to talk to me for many hours and to welcome me into their homes, their names are not included here. The interviews were carried out in English, thus the slight awkwardness of some of the quotations.

26. Interview II.

27. Interview II.

28. Interview III.

29. Actually there were several earlier strikes before the Dutch returned in the summer of 1946. One of the largest was at the Bunut factory of the HAPM (now Uniroyal) estate in August 1946, when field personnel and factory workers staged a collective walkout (and then tied up the Batak estate manager) in protest against the fact that he had reneged on a promise to provide them with a package of in-kind wages (including dried fish, cooking oil, and salt) by that payday. The only reference to these strikes appears in the intelligence reports on file at the AR, Afd. II, box #220. For the Dutch who had not yet returned, the 1948 strike was indeed the first one directed specifically against them.

30. E53, May 1948.

31. MR, 92/x/48; BZ, E53; AR,
    Afd. II, Political Reports, Feb.–Aug. 1948.

32. MR, 325/x/48.

33. MR, 900/x/49; BZ, E53, July 1949; OvSI 1949:121.

34. These appear in the BZ, MR 838/49, and in related papers referenced therein.

35. Some companies investigated the possibilities of applying more advanced technology and introducing more mechanization of the production process as a means to counter the labor shortage. But these improvements offered little alleviation of the problem and were never adopted on a large scale. See BZ, E53, Nov. 1949.

36. MR 794/x/49.

37. MR 900/x/49.

38. E50, Dec. 1948.

39. For a history of the political machinations preceding the emergence of SOBSI see Tejasukmama 1958, U.S. Dept. of Labor 1951, and Sayuti 1968.

40. Medan, 11 Aug. 1950.

41. There is some disagreement among those who were present during the later revolutionary and early postindependence years (1946–52) in different parts of the *cultuurgebied* about when SARBUPRI was formed and whether it was the first organization among the plantation workers. SARBUPRI was

nominally established in North Sumatra quite soon after it appeared in Java (around 1946), although it initially served more in Sumatra as an arm of the anti-Dutch Republican forces than as a labor union. Thus although the Sarekat Buruh Perkebunan (SBP) was created after SARBUPRI, it probably should be considered the first real estate-based labor organization because it functioned as a union with a plantation workers' constituency and was primarily concerned with their demands. Conflicting accounts of which was the first union to appear may additionally reflect the fact that SARBUPRI seems to have been confined in this early period only to the Republican-held areas.

Former members of the SBP maintain that it was a nonpartisan union with no specific political persuasion until after its merger with SARBUPRI in late 1950–early 1951. At that time it became increasingly dominated by the more radical politics and policies of SARBUPRI, which was rapidly growing in membership and strength. While some former SBP followers maintained an independent organization under that name, a larger number either joined SARBUPRI or PERBUPRI (Persatuan Buruh Perkebunan Republik Indonesia) which was to become the major counterforce to SARBUPRI's influence. The new SBP/SARBUPRI represented the most radical segment of the North Sumatran labor movement. According to one former SBP member, SARBUPRI's aim was to challenge both the state and the companies, which they initially did with great success. Other unions took a much more conservative position supportive of the government, and therefore indirectly of the foreign firms.

42. The virtual absence of women from accounts of North Sumatra's independence struggle constrasts sharply with their relatively high profile in written and visual sources from Java for the same period. From oral histories it is evident that women provided crucial labor power as food producers throughout much of 1945–49 but were rarely active members of the *laskyar* units. The fact that gender roles went unchallenged may be one important indication of just how completely the social hierarchy remained intact.

Chapter 5

1. See Hasibuan Sayuti's discussion of this issue in "Political Unionism in Economic Development in Indonesia: Case Study, North Sumatra" (1968:265–83). Also, company reports filed with AVROS contain detailed accounts of disputes concerning what workers viewed as overbearing foremen.

2. These examples are drawn from *Warta Sarbupri*, the newsletter published by SARBUPRI in the 1950s, AVROS reports, and interviews with former managers resident on the East Coast during these years.

3. The first figure is derived from the AVROS compilation of union members collected from every estate within the association, supplemented with letter no. 45/B1, 8 Mar. 1956, Overzicht Vakverenigingen Ondernemingsarbeiders in Oost-Sumatra. The second figure is from Wolf 1948:69. These

figures should not be taken as an accurate estimate of SARBUPRI's membership. *All* informed scholars of, and participants in, the labor movement
agree that *angka-angka buatan* (made-up statistics) were the norm, not the
exception since each new labor minister and every political party with
union affiliation had a vested interest in distorting these numbers to suit
their own immediate political objectives at the time. The SARBUPRI figures collected by AVROS are slightly more reliable simply because they
were so assiduously recorded every year from each estate, and more importantly, the numbers seem to accord with the vast number of workers who
took part in the SARBUPRI-led labor actions.

4. Mintz 1965:110. Note that in Mintz's Rand-financed study of Indonesian
    communism this description was no accolade, but part of what the author
    deemed was SOBSI's willingness "to counsel tactics of violence without
    regard to the effect on the economy or stability of the country" (ibid.).

5. The following examples are taken from AVROS reports filed in Medan, and
    from the archive of the Federation of Upland Estates, AR, Afd. II, The
    Hague. Although North Sumatra was not included in this federation,
    AVROS frequently sent summary reports to the Java-based planters
    associations.

6. These figures are taken from the monthly and annual lists compiled by
    AVROS of total land under squatter cultivation by district and crop. See
    GAPPERSU, *Angka-Angka Statistik*, table xiii.

7. From "Memorandum over de invloed van partiele zowel als algemeen
    stakingen op de productie der ondernemingscultures gedurende 1950 en
    over de eerste weken van 1951, "24 Jan. 1951, Federation of Upland Estates,
    AR, Afd. II.

8. From "Beschouwingen over het vraagstuk der arbeidsproductiviteit,"
    AVROS, 10 Oct. 1951, Medan; see also Federation of Upland Estates, AR,
    Afd. II.

9. This statement by Raden Achmad Natakusuma from the Batavia office of
    Labor Union Contact in the Department of Social Affairs was not well
    received by other participants. See summary report of this meeting on labor
    unions held on 20 October 1949, filed with AVROS.

10. Stated by Heer Keulemans, head of the Department of Cultural Affairs in
    East Sumatra; see n. 7.

11. AVROS report, 6 July 1950.

12. Between 1950 and 1953 SARBUPRI was supported by both the PKI and the
    PNI (nationalist) parties. AVROS during these years harbored strong hopes
    that the PKI faction would assume diminishing control but this was not the
    case. See AVROS report on labor union activities by Wittebol, Medan, 14
    Nov. 1952, for more on this issue. I am indebted to Jacques LeClerc for
    arduous hours he spent in discussing with me the intricacies and politics of
    labor union fissions and mergers. He, of course, is in no way responsible for
    any misrepresentations herein. See fig. 5.1 for one version of how these
    fissions developed in North Sumatra.

13. See n. 2. Two other estate unions drew workers away from SARBUPRI
    during the late 1950s; the PNI-affiliated KBKI (Konsentrasi Buruh Ke-

rakyatan Indonesia: Indonesian Peoples' Labor Federation) union and the Islamic party-affiliated SBI (Sarekat Buruh Islam Indonesia: Indonesian Islamic Labor Union) union, whose memberships in 1956 were, respectively, 6.5% and 5% of all North Sumatran estate workers.

14. For a brief discussion of this strike see the end of chap. 4.

15. AVROS, n.a., "De arbeidsbeweging in Indonesie," 24 Aug. 1951, p. 16.

16. Both Sayuti (1968) and Tejasukmama (1958) contend that this was the primary purpose of left-wing trade unionism. Mortimer (1974) and Feith (1962) seem to agree that it was a two-way street. That is, the unions made good use of the political leverage offered by party support, and Jacques LeClerc (personal communication) suggests that it was the unions which used the parties rather than the other way around.

17. Afd. II, Archive of the Federation of Upland Estates, 24 Jan. 1951.

18. In addition, in those areas beset with both labor unrest and attacks by armed bands, estate divisions were sublet on a "production sharing" basis to contractors, who were totally responsible for all the work involved. One such arrangement is described in the Anglo-Sumatran Company's shareholder report for 1951 as follows: "In order to curb the activities of illicit tappers, who were not only stealing the latex, but doing considerable damage to the trees by reckless wounding [sic], an arrangement was made in March of this year to sublet the outlying division of Bandar Maria [an estate in Deli Serdang] which was very difficult to supervise to a contractor for a limited period. In return for this permission he had undertaken to deliver 35% of all rubber harvested by him with a minimum of 5,000 kilos per month. This arrangement which is under the supervision of the Company's manager has so far proved fairly satisfactory, but recent advisers indicate that the contractor also has been confronted with the lawless conditions prevailing."

19. SKU (Syarat Karyawan Umum) refers to the general working regulations for all estate laborers adopted by the Central Dispute Committee (P4P) in 1956, which stipulated social security, in-kind payments, family support, pensions, and so forth. The informant was using the term here, not in reference to this specific resolution, but as a generic term for social benefits accruing to permanent estate employees.

20. Based on interviews with several former Dutch supervisory personnel.

21. AVROS, SARBUPRI file, 15 Dec. 1953.

22. AVROS, SARBUPRI file, 26 Mar. 1954.

23. AVROS, Rep. on the 4th SARBUPRI Cong. July 1954.

24. AVROS, trans. of Pendorong, 5 Dec. 1956.

25. Afd. II, RCMA 1950 Shareholders Rep., 24 Jan. 1951.

26. AR, Afd. II, Fed. of Upland Estates, 16 May 1957.

27. Pendorong, 5–6 Dec. 1956.

28. See RCMA annual shareholders reports, 1945–66, AR, Afd. II.

29. "Vital" industries included all railway, public motor, air and sea navigation, harbor, gas and electric, mining, and banking enterprises. Services listed as "vital" included post, telegraph, telephone, radio, water, and harbor services. Also included were government printing shops, service

stations for gasoline, pharmacies, the Salt Revenue service, the Netherlands Trade Company, and sections of printing offices for the state. See U.S. Dept. of Labor 1951:136.

30. From interviews in North Sumatra with individuals who were direct participants in the labor movement at the time.

31. See AVROS circulaire no. 54, 14 Dec. 1957.

32. Based on interviews with former union activists, in particular a former SARBUPRI labor leader. Also see Mortimer 1974. The latter is a carefully documented analysis dealing in part with the inverse relationship between the PKI's ascendancy to power and its effectiveness in promoting the interests of the urban and rural poor.

33. Again see Mortimer's analysis of this process (1974), and Feith 1963:309–409.

34. NASAKOM is an acronym coined in 1961 from NAS (nationalist), A (agama, religious), and KOM (communist) and refers specifically to the PKI's participation in government.

35. See Mortimer 1974:276–328 and Helmi 1981 for different perspectives on the aksi sepihak (unilateral action) movement.

36. With the exception of the violent confrontation between squatters and police at the Bandar Betsy estate in 1964.

37. Figure 5.2 was drawn up from AVROS's monthly and annual calculations of work stoppages and other labor actions in North Sumatra. As absolute figures they are probably not very reliable. For instance, it seems that for a work stoppage that lasted three days, each of the days was counted as a separate action. Nonetheless, since the relative values for each year are more important, from this perspective the overall pattern over the decade 1952–62 is absolutely clear.

38. This refers to the SKU conditions described in n. 19.

39. Interviews carried out in Amsterdam and Paris, Fall 1979, Spring 1980.

40. Also see Thomas and Glassburner 1965:169.

41. Attributed to the head of the Department of Labor in Sayuti 1968:32.

42. Hawkins 1966:269. See also Blake 1962:113, which is based on a somewhat different method of calculation.

43. Documents concerning assaults on workers and management were taken from estate reports filed with AVROS, Medan, and AVROS's (at this time called GAPPERSU) own recapitulations for 1958, 1959, and 1960 of "security disturbances" on all member estates.

44. The following account is based on Feith 1962:527–31 and Smail 1968:128–87.

45. Among the estates most frequently subject to attack was Goodyear's Wingfoot plantation. Because of its size (nearly 14,000 ha, the largest estate complex in Southeast Asia) and location (in the rebel's stronghold of Labuhan Batu) it was particularly difficult to protect and its managers repeatedly complained via AVROS to central government military authorities that they were under siege. This is somewhat curious because the United States gave moral and armed support to the rebels rather than to Sukarno, whose communist sympathies were seen as a major threat by many U.S.

politicians. U.S. Secretary of State Dulles, for one, Feith writes in *The Decline* (1962:586), "had implied a degree of sympathy with the Padang [PRRI] group . . . and PRRI army commanders were receiving very modern American arms, which could not have been bought without some measure of approval from the U.S. government." In August 1958, after a particularly serious attack on Wingfoot, its acting manager talked with the (procentral government) commander of the 2d Infantry, Manaf Lubis, who suggested to him that Simbolon was intent on threatening American property so as to force U.S. intervention to protect its citizens. In the end, the United States did not directly intervene; as the political tide shifted in Sukarno's favor, the United States made conciliatory gestures to show its support for him (AVROS files and Feith 1962:590).

46. Wingfoot estate report filed with AVROS, Aug. 1958.
47. All these incidents and those mentioned below are taken from the AVROS files on "security" for the years concerned.
48. Pelzer 1957:153. Statements in the following section are based on estate reports on squatter actions filed with AVROS in the years concerned.
49. Based on interviews, 1977–79 in North Sumatra, especially Asahan, with former squatters, managers, and others, who observed and/or participated in these actions.
50. Panitia Agraria T & T/Bukit Barisan, 20 July 1957, filed at AVROS.
51. Based on interviews, Paris 1980. Also see Liddle 1970:83.
52. Hawkins 1963:270, and interviews. The SARBUPRI informant said there were as many as 900 arrests; Hawkins simply states that there were many. I have seen no material in AVROS files to corroborate the exact number.
53. From AVROS list of labor actions and their causes for 1962.
54. See Hasibuan Sayuti's analysis of why SOKSI enjoys the support of the rising managerial elite (1962:106–153).
55. This point is made briefly by Sayuti 1968:127–28, but is much better explicated by Jacques LeClerc, who analyzes the etymology of these terms and the political implications of their use (1973:407–28).

Chapter 6

1. See, for example, Wertheim 1966; van der Kroef 1970–71, less for its analysis than its extensive bibliography; and more recently Wertheim 1979.
2. Different estimates on the number killed are reported in the references cited in n. 1, and in the bibliographical references of the articles therein.
3. Labor force statistics for the North Sumatran estates were collected from the North Sumatran Plantation Association, formerly AVROS, now BKSPPS (Badan Kerja Sama Perusahaan Perkebunan Sumatera).
4. Ibid.
5. This information is based on World Bank reports issued during these years; see, for example, Report no. 2033 (20 Apr. 1978), pp. 9–11, on the North Sumatran estates project.
6. See figures cited in Departemen Pertanian 1979 and compare *Sensus Per-*

kebunan, vol. II (1963) with *Sensus Pertanian 1973, Perkebunan Besar,* vol. IV.

7. Most of these changes were reported by estate personnel during interviews in 1977–79. For information on the technological changes in rubber specifically, see Montgomery 1978.

8. Obviously this is relative since all these are labor intensive compared to U.S. and Western European factories and agribusiness.

9. Based on statistics collected for the period 1968–78 from 6 major estate units (foreign and government run) in North Sumatra. Some private national estates not included in this sample have an even higher percentage of temporary workers; in fact several use no permanent workers at all.

10. Pasaribu and Sitorus 1976:35 also allude to this purported "labor shortage."

11. See World Bank Report no. 2033, p. 12.

12. Calculated from BKSPPS labor statistics.

13. For a detailed description of the various factions that make up this political-bureaucratic elite see Robison 1978.

14. Note that transfers were common before the war as well, but because workers lived in estate dwellings, the moves were not complicated by ownership of homes, land, and other property.

15. These observations derive from a combined employment-pregnancy history survey carried out among all married and ever-married women in Simpang Lima.

16. In addition, rapid replanting schedules mean that villagers are no longer given permission to plant crops in the felled areas as fallow periods are now shorter. The supply of firewood has also been a problem in recent years. It had previously been provided by collecting dead branches from the underbrush surrounding the rubber trees. Villagers now complain that the expansion of palm cultivation has limited their easy access to firewood because the palms are not mature enough to provide wood and even the mature trees are less suitable than rubber wood for burning.

17. Based on Agro-Economic Survey statistics for 1974 (Benjamin White, personal communication).

18. Obviously land is, and has been, a critical social resource throughout the entire history of the estate industry's expansion, as evidenced in all the preceding chapters. It is furthermore a critical point of conflict in villages that are ethnically mixed. Here I am referring to it only within the context of social relations between Javanese.

Chapter 7

1. See references cited in Jain 1970. See also Scott 1976:114–56 and Brocheux 1981:247–76.

Bibliography

A Note on Sources

In addition to published and ethnographic sources, this study frequently refers to archival, limited edition, and narrowly distributed materials. From the Dutch colonial archives, use was made of those from the Ministry of Interior Affairs (Ministerie van Binnenlandse Zaken, referred to in the notes as BZ), the Ministry of Defense (Ministerie van Defensie, MD), and the Algemeen Rijksarchief (AR), all located in The Hague. For a detailed account of how these archives are organized and what they contain see O'Malley 1977:382–83. The Algemeen Rijksarchief, in particular, has shareholder reports, and internal company correspondence of Deli estates dating from the turn of the century. The files of the former Sumatran Planters' Association (AVROS, now BKSPPS) has important documents for the postindependence period, some of which are also available at the AR.

For readers interested in consulting these sources, my citations list first the appropriate archive (for example, AR for the *Algemeen Rijksarchief*). AR is followed by a division number (for example, Afdeling II), a specific archive name (for example that of the RCMA company), a box number, and a date. In the case of documents from the Ministries of Defense and Interior I provide the codes and formats used in the ministries themselves.

Among those Malay- and Dutch-language newspapers and other publications consulted were *Pewarta Deli*, *Deli Courant*, *De Planter*, *Waspada*, *Warta Sarbupri*, and various articles included in AVROS's collection of newspaper clippings. Miscellaneous unpublished sources include World Bank Reports, company statistics, and transcriptions of personal histories collected from former estate managers, estate labor union leaders, and workers.

In the published sources below frequent reference is made to materials found at the Koninlijk Instituut voor de Tropen and the Koninlijk Instituut voor Taal-, Land-, en Volkenkunde. These include the Annual Chronicle of the East Coast of Sumatra Institute (*Kroniek*), summary reports of the Labor Inspectorate (*Arbeidsinspectie*), and pamphlets put out by the AVROS and DPV planters' 227 associations. The Tropen also stores some *Memorie van Overgave* (Dutch Assistant Resident reports completed at the end of an appointment), which are cited in the text.

Published Sources

Alatas, Syed Hussein
  1977 *The Myth of the Lazy Native.* London: Frank Cass.
Allen, G. C., And A. C. Donnithorne
  1962 *Western Enterprise in Indonesia and Malaysia: A Study in Economic Development.* London: Allen & Unwin.
Anderson, Benedict R. O'G
  1972 *Java in a Time of Revolution: Occupation and Resistance, 1944–1946.* Ithaca: Cornell University Press.
Anonymous
  1925 *Deli-Batavia Maatschappij 1875–1925.* Amsterdam: Deli-Batavia Maat.
  1928 *Rapport van de commissie van onderzoek ingesteld bij het gouvernementsbesluit van 13 Februari 1927 No. 1a. Deel I.* Weltevreden: Landsdrukkerij.
  1935 *Volkstelling 1930.* Batavia: Landscdrukkerij.
  1947 "The Recovery of Sumatra's East Coast Province." *Economic Review of Indonesia* 1, no. 12 (Dec.).
  1952 *Deli-Data 1938–1951.* Mede. 36. Amsterdam: Oostkust van Sumatra.
  1954 *Warta Sarbupri.* Jakarta: D. P. P. Sarbupri.
Aronowitz, Stanley
  1973 *False Promises: The Shape of American Working-class Consciousness.* New York: McGraw-Hill.
Aziz, M. A.
  1955 *Japan's Colonisation and Indonesia.* The Hague: Nijhoff.
Beckford, George
  1972 *Persistent Poverty: Underdevelopment in Plantation Economies of the Third World.* New York: Oxford University Press.
Beiguelman, Paula
  1978 "The Destruction of Modern Slavery: A Theoretical Issue." *Review* 2, no. 1 (Summer): 71–80.
Biro Pusat Statistik
  1966 *Sensus Perkebunan: Sektor Perkebunan 1963.* Vol. II.
  1976 *Sensus Pertanian 1973: Perkebunan Besar.* Vol. IV.
  n.d. *Statistical Pocketbook of Indonesia: 1957.* Jakarta: BPS.
  n.d. *Statistical Pocketbook of Indonesia: 1958.* Jakarta: BPS.
  n.d. *Statistical Pocketbook of Indonesia: 1959.* Jakarta: BPS.
  n.d. *Statistical Pocketbook of Indonesia: 1960.* Jakarta: BPS.
  n.d. *Statistical Pocketbook of Indonesia: 1961.* Jakarta: BPS.
Blake, Donald J.
  1962 "Labour Shortage and Unemployment in Northeast Sumatra." *Malayan Economic Review* 7, no. 2 (October): 106–18.

1963   "The Estates and Economic Development in Northeast Sumatra."
        Malayan Economic Review 8, no. 2: 98–109.

Blink, H.
1918   "Sumatra's Oostkust in hare Opkomst en Ontwikkeling als Econo-
        misch Gewest." *Tijdschrift voor Economische Geographie.*

Blommestein, van
1910   *Hygienische en Geneeskundige voorwaarden, waaronder de in con-
        tract werkende arbeiders in Deli.* Medan: N. V. "De Deli Courant."

Blumberger, J. Th. Petrus
1931   *De Nationalistische Beweging in Nederlandsch-Indie.* Haarlem:
        Tjeenk Willink.
1935   *De Communistische Beweging in Nederlandsch-Indie.* Haarlem:
        Tjeenk Willink.

Boeke, J.
1953   *Economics and Economic Policy of Dual Societies.* Haarlem: Tjeenk
        Williams.

Bool, H. J.
1903   *De Landbouw concessie in de Residentie Oostkust van Sumatra.*
        Utrecht: Oostkust van Sumatra Instituut.

Bool, H. J., and R. Fruin
1927   *Handboekje voor den Deli-Planter.* [n. ed.].

Brand, J. van den
1902   *De Millionen uit Deli.* Amsterdam: Hoveker & Wormser.
1904   *Nog eens: De Millionen uit Deli.* Amsterdam: Hoveker & Wormser.
n.d.   *Slavenordonnantie en koelieordonnantie.* Amsterdam: Hoveker &
        Wormser.

Brand, W.
1979   *1879 HVA 1979: Its History, Development and Future.* Amsterdam:
        HVA.

Brandt, W.
1948   *De Aarde van Deli.* The Hague: van Hoeve.

Braudel, Fernand
1972   *The Mediterranean and the Mediterranean World in the Age of Phil-
        ip II.* New York: Harper & Row.

Braverman, Harry
1974   *Labor and Monopoly Capital.* New York: Monthly Review Press.

Brenner, Robert
1978   "The Origins of Capitalist Development: A Critique of Neo-Smithian
        Marxism." *New Left Review* 104: 25–92.

Brocheux, Pierre
1981   Les communistes et les paysans dans la révolution vietnamienne.
        Histoire de l'asie du sud-est: révoltes, réformes, révolutions. Ed. P.
        Brocheux. Lille: Presses Universitaires de Lille. Pp. 247–76.

Broersma, R.
1919   *Oostkust van Sumatra, Eerste Deel: De Ontluiking van Deli.* Batavia.
1921   *Oostkust van Sumatra: De Ontwikkeling van het Gewest.* Deventer.

Bruin, A. G. de

    1918 *De Chineezen ter Oostkust van Sumatra,* Mede. No. 1. Leiden: Oostkust van Sumatra Instituut.

Clarke, Simon

    1979 "Socialist Humanism and the Critique of Economism." *History Workshop.* No. 8.

Clerkx, Lily

    1960 *Mensen in Deli: een maatschappijbeeld uit de belletrie.* Amsterdam: AZOA, Universiteit van Amsterdam.

Cooper, Frederic

    1980 *From Slaves to Squatters: Plantation Labor and Agriculture in Zanzibar and Coastal Kenya, 1890–1925.* New Haven: Yale University Press.

Courtenay, P. P.

    1969 *Plantation Agriculture.* London: Bell & Sons.

Cunningham, Clark

    1958 *The Postwar Migration of the Toba-Bataks to East Sumatra.* New Haven: Yale University. Cultural Report Series No. 5.

De Javasche Bank

    1952 *Verslag over het boekjaar 1951–1952.* Jakarta: G. Kolff.

Debray, Régis

    1970 "Notes de prison—'Temps et Politque.'" *Les Temps Modernes.* No. 287 (June 1970).

Deli Planters Vereeniging

    1932 *Een en Ander over Javanenkolonies en Arbeiders-vestigingen.* Medan: AVROS.

Departemen Pertanian

    1979 *10th Departemen Pertanian 1968–1978.* Dept. Pertanian: Jakarta.

Dinger, J. Th.

    1929 *Het Verbroken Evenwicht.* [n. p. ed.].

Dixon, C. J.

    1913 *De Assistent in Deli.* Amsterdam: J. H. de Bussy.

Dootjes, F. J. J.

    1938/39 "Deli, The Land of Agricultural Enterprises." *Bulletin of Colonial Institute of Amsterdam,* vol. 2.

    1948 *Kroniek 1941–1946, Mededeling No. 32.* Amsterdam: Oostkust van Sumatra Instituut.

    1950 *Kroniek 1948–1949.* Amsterdam: Oostkust van Sumatra Instituut.

Drooglever, P. J.

    1980 *De Vaderlandsche Club 1929–1942: Totoks en de Indische Politiek.* Amsterdam: Franeker.

Edwards, Richard

    1979 *Contested Terrain.* New York: Basic Books.

Feith, Herbert

    1958 "The Wilopo Cabinet, 1952–1953: A Turning Point in Post-Revolutionary Indonesia." *Modern Indonesia Project.* Ithaca: Cornell University Press.

1962 *The Decline of Constitutional Democracy in Indonesia.* Ithaca: Cornell University Press.

1963 "Dynamics of Guided Democracy." *Indonesia.* Ed. Ruth McVey. New Haven: Yale University Press. Pp. 309–409.

Foucault, Michel
1980 *The History of Sexuality, Vol. I: An Introduction.* New York: Vintage.

Fox-Genovese, Elizabeth, and Eugene D. Genovese
1976 "The Political Crisis of Social History." *Journal of Social History* 10, no. 2.

Fryer, D. W.
1965 *World Economic Development.* New York.

GAPPERSU (Gabingan Persatuan Perkebunan Sumatera Utara)
1960 *Angka-Angka Statistik.* Medan.

Gautama, Sudargo, and Budi Harsono
1972 *Survey of Indonesian Economic Law.* Bandung: Lembaga Penelitian Hukum dar Kriminologi.

Geertz, Clifford
1960 *The Religion of Java.* London: The Free Press of Glencoe.

1968 *Agricultural Involution: The Process of Ecological Change in Indonesia.* Berkeley: University of California Press.

Geertz, Hildred
1961 *The Javanese Family: A Study of Kinship and Socialization.* London: The Free Press of Glencoe.

Genovese, Eugene
1976 *Roll, Jordan, Roll: The World the Slaves Made.* New York: Vintage.

1981 *From Rebellion to Revolution.* New York: Vintage Books.

Ginting, Meneth, and Ruth Daroesman
1982 An Economic Survey of North Sumatra. *Bulletin of Indonesian Economic Studies* 18, no. 3: 52–83.

Gould, James W.
1961 *Americans in Sumatra.* The Hague: Martinus Nijhoff.

Gutkind, Peter, R. Cohen, and J. Copans (Eds.)
1978 *African Labor History.* Beverly Hills: Sage.

Guyot, George
1910 *Le problème de la main-d'oeuvre dans les colonies d'exploitation.* Paris: Pedone.

Hanegraaff, A.
1910 *Hoe het thans staat met den Assistenten en de Veiligheid aan de Oostkust van Sumatra.* The Hague: Van der Beek.

Hawkins, Everett D.
1959 "Labor problems in a newly independent country: The case of Indonesia." Mimeo.

1963 "Labor in Transition." *Indonesia.* Ed. R. McVey. New Haven: Yale University Press.

1966 "Job Inflation in Indonesia." *Asian Survey* 6, no. 5.

Heijting, Herman G.
1925   De Koelie-Wetgeving voor de Buitengewesten van Nederlandsche-Indie. The Hague: W. P. Stockum.
Helmi
1981   Di tengah pergolakan. Limburg: Yayasan Langer.
Hémery, Daniel
1975   Révolutionnaires vietnamiens et pouvoir colonial en Indochine. Paris: Maspero.
Hindley, Donald
1964   The Communist Party of Indonesia. Berkeley: University of California Press.
Hotchkiss, H. Stuart
1924   "Operations of an American Rubber Company in Sumatra and the Malay Peninsula." Annals of the American Academy of Political and Social Sciences. March.
Hughes, John
1967   Indonesian Upheaval. New York: McKay.
Hutchinson, H.
1957   Village and Plantation Life in Northeastern Brazil. Seattle: University of Washington Press.
International Bank for Reconstruction and Development
1969   "North Sumatra Estates Project—Indonesia" (Report no. PA-19, June 2).
1978   "Project Performance Audit Report: Indonesia—First and Second North Sumatra Estates Projects." (Credit 155-IND and Credit 194-IND Report no. 2033).
International Labour Office
1966   Plantation Workers. Geneva: ILO.
Jain, R. K.
1970   South Indians on the Plantation Frontier in Malaya. New Haven: Yale University Press.
Jay, Robert
1969   Javanese Villagers: Social Relations in Rural Modjokuto. Cambridge: MIT Press.
Jayawardena, Kumari
1972   The Rise of the Labor Movement in Ceylon. Durham: Duke University Press.
Kahin, George McT.
1952   Nationalism and Revolution in Indonesia. Ithaca: Cornell Univeristy Press.
Kahn, Joel
1980   Minangkabau Social Formations: Indonesian Peasants and the World Economy. Cambridge: Cambridge University Press.
Kantoor van Arbeid (KvA)
1913   Arbeidsinspectie en Koeliewerving. Batavia.
1919   Verslag van den dienst der Arbeidsinspectie in Nederlandsche-Indie, 1917–1918. Weltevreden.

1920   *Verslag ven den dienst der Arbeidsinspectie in Nederlandsche-Indie, over het jaar 1919.* Weltevreden.

1923   *Verslag van den dienst der arbeidsinspectie in Nederlandsche-Indie. Over de jaren 1921 en 1922.* Weltevreden.

1926   *Tiende verslag van de arbeidsinspectie voor de Buitengewesten 1925.* Weltevreden.

1927   *Elfde verslag van de arbeidsinspectie voor de Buitengewesten, 1926.* Weltevreden.

1937   *Arbeidsinspectie 1933, 1934, 1935, 1936.* Batavia.

1939   *Arbeidsinspectie 1937–1938.* Batavia.

n.d.   *Verslag van den dienst der arbeidsinspectie in Nederlandsche-Indie. Over het jaar 1920.* Weltevreden.

n.d.   *Twaalfde verslag van de arbeidsinspectie voor de Buitengewesten, 1927.* Weltevreden.

n.d.   *Dertiende verslag van de arbeidsinspectie voor de Buitengewesten, 1928.* Weltevreden.

n.d.   *Veertiende verslag van de arbeidsinspectie voor de Buitengewesten, 1929.* Weltevreden.

n.d.   *Vijftiende verslag van de arbeidsinspectie 1930, 1931, 1932.*

Kleian, J.
1936   *Deli-Planter.* The Hague: van Hoeve.

Kol, van H.
1903   *Uit onze kolonien.* Leiden: A. W. Sijthoff.

Langenberg, Michael van
1976   "National Revolution in North Sumatra, Sumatera Timur and Tapanuli, 1942–1950." Ph.D. dissertation, University of Sydney.

Langenveld, H. G.
1978   "Arbeidstoestanden op de ondernemingen ter Oostkust van Sumatra tussen 1920 en 1940 in het licht van het verdwijnen van de Poenale Sanctie op de arbeidscontracten." *Economische en Sociale Historisch Jaarboek.* The Hague: Martinus Nijhoff.

Laskar, Bruno
1950   *Human Bondage in Southeast Asia.* Chapel Hill: University of North Carolina Press.

LeClerc, Jacques
1973   "Vocabulaire social et répression politque: un exemple Indonésien. *Temps Présent et Histoire* no. 2.: 407–28.

Liddle, R. William
1970   *Ethnicity, Party and National Integration: An Indonesian case study.* New Haven: Yale University Press.

Lier, E. J. van
1919   "Het Arbeidersvraagstuk." *Mededeelingen van het Bureau voor de Bestuurszaken der Buitenbezittingen. De Buitenbezittingen-De Oostkust van Sumatra,* vol. 11, pt. 3.

Lulofs, C.
1920   *Verslag nopens de overwogen plannen en maatregelen betreffende de Kolonisatie van Javaansche Werklieden op de Cultuuronder-*

nemingen ter Oostkust van Sumatra in verband met de voorgenomen afschaffing van de z.n.g. poenale sanctie in de koelieordonnantie. Medan: AVROS.

Maas, J. G.
1948 "The Recovery of the Perennial Export Crops in East Sumatra." *Economic Review of Indonesia* 2, no. 1.

Mackie, J. A. C.
1962 "Indonesia's Government Estates and Their Masters." *Pacific Affairs* 34, no. 4, pp. 337–60.

Mandle, Jay
1973 *The Plantation Economy: Population and Economic Change in Guyana, 1838–1960.* Philadelphia: Temple University Press.

Mansyur, P.
1978 *Gerilya di Asahan-Labuhan Batu 1947–49.* Medan: Department of Information.

Marx, Karl
1973 *The Poverty of Philosophy.* New York: International Publishers.

McNicoll, Geoffrey
1968 "Internal Migration in Indonesia: Descriptive Notes." *Indonesia* no. 5.

McVey, Ruth
1965 *The Rise of Indonesian Communism.* Ithaca: Cornell University Press.

Memmi, Albert
1973 *Portrait du colonisé: précédé du portrait du colonisateur.* Paris: Payot.

Middendorp, W.
1924 *De Poenale Sanctie.* Haarlem: Tjeenk Willink.

Mintz, Jeanne
1965 *Mohammed, Marx and Marhaen: The Roots of Indonesian Socialism.* London: Pall Mall Press.

Mintz, Sidney
1959 "The Plantation as a Socio-cultural Type." In Vera Rubin, ed., *Plantation Systems of the New World.*
1974 *Caribbean Transformations.* Chicago: Aldine.
1978 "Was the Plantation Slave a Proletarian?" *Review* 2, no. 1 (1978): 81–98.
1979 "The rural proletariat and the problem of rural proletarian consciousness." *Peasants and Proletarians: The Struggles of Third World workers.* Ed. Robin Cohen, Peter Gutkind, and Phyllis Brazier. London: Hutchinson.

Mintz, Sidney, and Richard Price
1973 "An Anthropological Approach to the Study of Afro-American History." New Haven: Yale University, mimeo.

Montgomery, Roger
1978 "The 1973 Large Estate Census of Plantation Rubber. *Bulletin of Indonesian Economic Studies* 14, no. 3 (1978): 63–85.

Mortimer, Rex
    1974   *Indonesian Communism under Sukarno: Ideology and Politics,*
           1959–1965. Ithaca: Cornell University Press.
Mulier, W. J. H.
    1903   *Arbeids-toestanden op de Oostkust van Sumatra.* Amsterdam.
Nichols, T., ed.
    1980   *Capital and Labour: A Marxist Primer.* London: Fontana.
Nieuwenhuys, R.
    1978   *Oost-Indische Spiegel.* Amsterdam: Querido.
Nitisastro, Widjojo
    1970   *Population Trends in Indonesia.* Ithaca: Cornell University Press.
O'Malley, William
    1977   "Indonesia in the Great Depression: A Study of East Sumatra and
           Jogjakarta in the 1930s." Ph.D. dissertation, Cornell University.
Oostkust van Sumatra Instituut (OvSI)
    1917   *Kroniek 1916.* Amsterdam: J. H. de Bussy.
    1918   *Kroniek 1917.* Amsterdam: J. H. de Bussy.
    1926   *Kroniek 1925.* Amsterdam: J. H. de Bussy.
    1927   *Kroniek 1926.* Amsterdam: J. H. de Bussy.
    1928   *Kroniek 1927.* Amsterdam: J. H. de Bussy.
    1929   *Kroniek 1928.* Amsterdam: J. H. de Bussy.
    1930   *Kroniek 1929.* Amsterdam: J. H. de Bussy.
    1931   *Kroniek 1930.* Amsterdam: J. H. de Bussy.
    1949   *Kroniek 1948.* Amsterdam: J. H. de Bussy.
Oudemans, Robert
    1973   Simalungun Agriculture: Some Ethnogeographic Aspects of Dualism
           in North Sumatran Development." Ph.D. dissertation, University of
           Maryland.
Paauw, Douglas S.
    1978   "The Labor-Intensity of Indonesian exports." *Ekonomi dan Keu-*
           angan Indonesia 26, no. 4: 447–56.
Pasaribu, Amudi, and Bistok Sitorus
    1976   "An Economic Survey of North Sumatra." *Bulletin of Indonesian*
           Economic Studies 5, no. 1: 90–105.
Pelzer, Karl
    1945   *Pioneer Settlements in the Asiatic Tropics.* New York: Pacific
           Institute.
    1957   "The Agrarian Conflict in East Sumatra." *Pacific Affairs* 30 (June):
           151–59.
    1961   "Western Impact on East Sumatra and North Tapanuli: The Roles of
           the Planter and the Missionary." *Journal of Southeast Asian History*
           2, 2.
    1978   *Planter and Peasant: Colonial Policy and the Agrarian Struggle in*
           East Sumatra, 1863–1947. The Hague: Martinus Nijhoff.
    1982   *Planter against Peasant: The Agrarian Struggle in East Sumatra,*
           1947–1958. The Hague: Martinus Nijhoff.

Penny, David
   1964   "The Transition from Subsistence to Commercial Family Farming in North Sumatra." Ph.D. dissertation, Cornell University, Ithaca.
Petersen, H. Tscherming
   1948   *Tropical Adventure.* London: Rolls.
Piven, Frances Fox, and Richard A. Cloward
   1979   *Poor People's Movements: Why They Succeed, How They Fail.* New York: Vintage.
Pluvier, J. M.
   1953   *Overzicht van de Ontwikkeling der Nationalistische Beweging in Indonesie in de Jaren 1930 tot 1942.* The Hague: Van Hoeve.
Price, Richard, ed.
   1979   *Maroon Societies: Rebel Slave Communities in the Americas.* Baltimore: Johns Hopkins University Press.
Prillwitz, P. M.
   1947   "The Estates in the East Coast Province of Sumatra." *Economic Review of Indonesia* 1, no. 9.
Pringgodigdo, A. K.
   1950   *Sejarah Pergerakan Rakyat Indonesia.* Jakarta.
Reid, Anthony
   1970   "Early Chinese Migration into North Sumatra." In *Studies in the Social History of China and Southeast Asia.* Ed. J. Ch'en and N. Tarling. Cambridge University Press.
   1971   "The Birth of the Republic in Sumatra." *Indonesia* 12.
   1974   *Indonesian National Revolution 1945–1950.* Melbourne: Longman.
   1979   *The Blood of the People: Revolution and the End of Traditional Rule in Northern Sumatra.* Kuala Lumpur: Oxford University Press.
Ridder, J. de
   1935   *De invloed van de Westersche Cultures op de Autochtone Bevolking ter Oostkust van Sumatra.* Wageningen: Veeman and Zonen.
Robison, Richard
   1978   "Toward a Class Analysis of the Indonesian Military Bureaucratic State." *Indonesia* 25: 17–39.
Rodney, Walter
   1981   Plantation Society in Guyana. *Review* 4, no. 4: 643–66.
Rubin, Vera, ed.
   1959   *Plantation systems of the New World.* Washington, D.C.: Pan American Union.
Said, Mohammad
   1973   "What was the 'Social Revolution of 1946' in East Sumatra?" *Indonesia* 15.
   1976   *Sejarah Pers di Sumatera Utara.* Medan:Waspada.
   1977   *Koeli Kontrak Tempoe Doeloe.* Medan: Waspada.
Sandra
   1961   *Sedjarah Pergerakan Buruh Indonesia.* Jakarta.
Sartre, Jean Paul
   1976   *Critique of Dialectical Reason.* London: New Left Books. [first published Paris: Gallimard, 1960].

Sayuti, Hasibuan
 1962   "The Palm-Oil Industry on the East Coast of Sumatra." *Prospects for East Sumatran Plantation Industries: A Symposium.* Ed. Douglas Paauw. New Haven: Yale University Press.
 1968   "Political Unionism and Economic Development in Indonesia: Case Study, North Sumatra" Ph.D. thesis, University of California, Berkeley.

Schadee, W. H. M.
 1919   *Geschiedenis van Sumatra's Oostkust.* Amsterdam: Oostkust van Sumatra.
 1923   *Kroniek 1923.* Amsterdam: J. H. de Bussy.

Schuffner, W., and W. A. Keunen
 1910   *De Gezondheidstoestand van de Arbeiders verbonden aan de Senembah-Maatschappij op Sumatra gedurende de jaren 1897 tot 1907.* Amsterdam: J. H. de Bussy.

Scott, James C.
 1976   *The Moral Economy of the Peasant.* New Haven: Yale University Press.

Shirasishi, Aiko
 1977   *Lahirnya Tentera Pembela Tanah Air.* Jakarta: Lembaga Ekonomi dan Kemasyarakatan Nasional.

Smail, John R. W.
 1968   "The Military Policies of North Sumatra: December 1956–October 1957." *Indonesia* 6.

Stedman-Jones, G.
 1978   "Class expression vs. Social Control." *History Workshop* no. 4.

Steward, Julian, ed.
 1956   *The People of Puerto Rico.* Urbana: University of Illinois Press.

Stibber, D. G.
 1912   "Werving van contract-koelies op Java." *Verslag der vergadering van de Nederlandsche Afd. der Nederlandsche-Indische Maatschappij van Nijverheid en Landbouw.* Amsterdam: J. H. de Bussy.

Stoler, Ann L.
 1977a "Class Structure and Female Autonomy in Rural Java." *Signs* 3, no. 1 (1977): 74–89.
 1977b "Rice Harvesting in Kali Loro: A Study of Class and Labor Relations in Rural Java." *American Ethnologist* 4, no. 4: 678–98.
 1978   "Garden Use and Household Economy in Rural Java." *Bulletin of Indonesian Economic Studies* 14, no. 2: 85–101.
 n.d.   "The Company's Women: Labor Control in Sumatran Agribusiness." *Serving Two Masters: Third World Women in the Development Process.* Ed. Kate Young. London: Routledge, Kegan & Paul. In press.
 n.d.   "North Sumatran Transitions: Transformations in Plantation Labor and Peasant Life." Ed. Maurice Godelier. *Questions of Transition.* Forthcoming.

Straub, M.
  1928   *Kindersterfte ter Oostkust van Sumatra.* Amsterdam: Koninklijke
         Vereeniging Koloniaal Instituut.
Sutter, John O.
  1959   "Indonesianisasi: Politics in a Changing Economy, 1940–1955."
         Ph.D. thesis, Cornell University, Ithaca.
Székely, Ladislao
  1937   *Tropic Fever: The Adventures of a Planter in Sumatra.* Kuala Lum-
         pur: Oxford University Press, 1979.
Székely-Lulofs, M. H.
  1932   *Koelie.* Amsterdam:Elsevier.
  1932   *Rubber.* Amsterdam: Elsevier.
  1946   *De Andere Wereld.* Amsterdam: Elsevier.
Tan Malaka
  n.d.   *Dari penjara ke penjara* (part I). Jakarta: Widjaya.
Taussig, Michael
  1980   *The Devil and Commodity Fetishism in South America.* Chapel Hill:
         North Carolina University Press.
Tejasukmama, Iskandar
  1958   "The Political Character of the Indonesian Trade Union Movement."
         Ithaca: Modern Indonesia Project.
Thalib, Dahlan
  1962   "The Estate Rubber Industry of East Sumatra." *Prospects for East
         Sumatran Plantation Industries: A Symposium.* Ed. Douglas Paauw,
         50–66. New Haven: Yale University Press.
Thee, Kian-Wie
  1977   *Plantation Agriculture and Export Growth: An Economic History of
         East Sumatra, 1863–1942.* Jakarta: LEKNAS-LIPI.
Thoburn, John
  1977   *Primary Commodity Exports and Economic Development.* New
         York: John Wiley.
Thomas, Kenneth D., and Bruce Glassburner
  1965   "Abrogation, Take-over and Nationalization: The Elimination of
         Dutch Economic Dominance from the Republic of Indonesia." *Aus-
         tralian Outlook* 19, no. 2.
Thompson, E. P.
  1966   *The Making of the English Working Class.* New York: Vintage.
Thompson, E. T.
  1975   *Plantation Societies, Race Relations, and the South: The Regimenta-
         tion of Populations.* Durham: Duke University Press.
Thompson, Graeme, and Richard C. Manning
  1974   "The World Bank in Indonesia." *Bulletin of Indonesian Economic
         Studies* 10, no. 2. 56–82.
Thompson, Virginia
  1947   *Labor Problems in Southeast Asia.* New Haven: Yale University
         Press.

Tideman, J.
  1919   "De Huisvesting der Contractkoelies ter Oostkust van Sumatra."
         Koloniale Studien.
Tilly, Charles
  1975   *The Rebellious Century.* Cambridge: Harvard University Press.
Treub
  1929   "Onveligheid op de Indische Cultuurondernemingen." *Vragen en*
         Tijds. September.
U.S. Department of Labor
  1951   *Labor Conditions in Indonesia.* Washington, D.C.: Department of
         Labor.
Van der Kroef, Justus M.
  1965   *The Communist Party of Indonesia.* Vancouver: Vancouver Publica-
         tions Center, University of British Columbia.
  1970–71 "Interpretations of the 1965 Indonesian Coup." *Pacific Affairs* 43,
         no. 4 (1970–71).
Versluys, J.
  1938   *Vormen en soorten van loon in den Indische landbouw.* Leiden.
Vien, Nguyen Khac
  1974   *Histoire du Vietnam.* Paris: Editions Sociales.
Vierhout, M.
  1921   *Het Arbeidsvraagstuk in verband met de Noodzakelijke Ontwikkel-*
         ing der Buitengewesten. Weltevreden: Albracht.
Volker, T.
  1928   *Van Oerbosch tot Cultuurgebied.* Medan: Deli Planters Vereeningen.
Waal, R. van de
  1959   *Richtlijnen voor een ontwikkelingsplan voor de Oostkust van*
         Sumatra. Ph.D. dissertation, Agricultural University of Wageningen,
         Wageningen.
Waard, J. de
  1934   "De Oostkust van Sumatra." *Tijdschrift voor Economische Geo-*
         graphie no. 7.
Wallerstein, Immanuel
  1980   *The Capitalist World Economy.* London: Cambridge University
         Press.
Weerd, van de
  n.d.   "Rapport Werkzaamheden Estates Advisory Board."
Wertheim, W. F.
  1959   *Indonesian Society in Transition.* The Hague: van Hoeve.
  1966   "Indonesia before and after the Untung Coup." *Pacific Affairs* 39
         (Spring–Summer 1966).
  1979   "Whose Plot?—New Light on the 1965 Events." *Journal of Contem-*
         porary Asia 9, no. 2: 197–215.
White, Benjamin N. F.
  1976a "Production and Reproduction in a Javanese Village." Ph.D. disser-
         tation, Columbia University, New York.

1976b "Population, Involution and Employment in Rural Java." *Development and Change* 7: 267–90.

Wijnmalen, H. J.
1951 "Aantekeningen betreffende het onstaan, de ontwikkeling en het optreden van de vakbeweging in Indonesie na de onafhankelijkheidsverklaring van 17 Aug 1945." *Indonesie* 5: 434, 461.

Williams, Raymond
1977 *Marxism and Literature.* London: Oxford University Press.

1980 *Key Words: A Vocabulary of Culture and Society.* Glasgow: Fontana.

Withington, William A.
1964 "Changes and Trends in Patterns of North Sumatra's Estate Agriculture, 1938–1959." *Tijdschrift voor Economische en Sociale Geografie* 55, no. 1.

Wolf, Charles Jr.
1948 *The Indonesian Story.* New York.

Wolf, Eric
1959 Specific Aspects of Plantations Systems in the New World: Community Sub-Cultures and Social Classes." *Plantation Systems of the New World.* Ed. Vera Rubin. Washington, D.C.: Pan American Union.

World Bank
1972 "1972 Agricultural Sector Survey, Annexe 3." *Development Issues for Indonesia.* 5 vols. East Asia and Pacific Department. Washington, D.C.: World Bank.

Wright, Erik Olin
1978 *Class, Crisis and the State.* London: Verso.

Index